Edges of Reality
Mind vs. Computer

Edges of Reality
Mind vs. Computer

WILLIAM D. MAY, Ph. D.

 **INSIGHT BOOKS**

PLENUM PRESS • NEW YORK AND LONDON

Library of Congress Cataloging-in-Publication Data

On file

QA
76.9
.C66
M39
1996

ISBN 0-306-45272-3

© 1996 William D. May
Insight Books is a Division of Plenum Publishing Corporation
233 Spring Street, New York, N.Y. 10013-1578

An Insight Book

10 9 8 7 6 5 4 3 2 1

To my wife and my mother

101

Preface

10101010101010101010101010101010101010101

Computers fascinate me. The possibilities offered by artificial intelligence, virtual reality, and robots seem boundless. Still, although computers calculate so quickly and seemingly offer so much computational power, they are sorely limited in what they can ultimately do. I believe that our world is much more complex than many people believe and that computers will never be as powerful as most people think.

Limits intrigue me. Logical limits are those that say there are problems that neither computers nor humans will ever solve. They may be easy-to-state problems and they may have simple solution procedures, but still they can never be solved. Physical or space–time limits are another; these are the quantum and cosmological boundaries that border the large and the small objects of the universe and the beginning and the end of time. This book is not aimed entirely at a final theory of the universe — I find such a goal interesting, but ultimately frustrating. Four of the last five chapters (about 15% of the total) of the book cover that issue. Mostly, the book considers theories and situations that we face today or will face someday.

There is something deeply satisfying about understanding a problem that can never be solved or comprehending why some action can never be done. I have always found myself asking: Why can't I go there, why can't I do that, why can't I solve that problem? Often there is no answer, but sometimes there is a good reason. To understand a limit that makes a task impossible requires a complete understanding. This understanding must be so thorough, so complete, that you can clearly see that no process can ever solve the problem or perform the action. You can clearly see the edge, the limit to how far you can go. Knowing the limits, seeing the edges, has always impressed me; it seems a unique form of knowledge, and it conveys a special sense of understanding. That understanding, that feeling of deep satisfaction, is what I hope to pass on with this book.

These edges of reality, these limits, are all based upon scientific theories. The complexity of these theories varies from moderate to extremely difficult if you state them in terms of equations, formulas, and mathematical theorems. There is another way. By relying on nonmathematical explanations, analogies, and a range of examples, you can accurately explain these ideas. For years I have been using a similar approach in teaching; the longer I teach about computers, the fewer mathematical theorems I use, and the more analogies and simple examples I give. This is my goal for the book.

The book covers several topics that are popular these days: upper limits on thought and computers by Turing and Gödel, consciousness — whether or not computers can have it, infinity, cosmology, and free will. These are deep topics, but the book deals with them in an understandable way. Real-world examples are given to explain these theories: our laws, the stock market, resource allocation, and many more. It emphasizes that these limits don't just affect the far future. They limit us today; no future technology can ever hope to solve some problems that face us every day.

Many of today's problems are provably unsolvable — you'd be amazed at how many — and will remain so forever. I have taught computer algorithms for years, and I am still surprised at new problems that would save us time, money, and resources if we could solve them, but we can prove that we never will.

Computer concepts show up in life itself. Another theme of the book is comparing and contrasting computers and life: virtual reality, how computerlike the origin of life was, can computers ever be conscious, and what could free will be that no computer can ever emulate.

101

Acknowledgments

1010101010101010101010101010101010101010101010101

I would like to thank my wife Rhonda for putting up with all the hours I spent in the den. I am grateful to Insight editor Frank Darmstadt for seeing the potential in the work and making several suggestions that really improved it; one in particular turned into the best example in the book. Finally, the views expressed in this work are my own and do not necessarily reflect the views of either the United States Government or Virginia Tech.

101

Contents

1010101010101010101010101010101010101010101

Edges of Reality
Mind vs. Computer

1010101010101010101010101010101010101010101

Chapter I

Scientific Thought — a Quick History

> *If I have been able to see farther than others,*
> *it was because I stood on the shoulders of*
> *giants.*
>
> SIR ISAAC NEWTON[1]

1010101010101010101010101010101010101010101

What is a limit or boundary or edge of our reality? It is a problem we can never solve, a thought we can never think, a place we can never go, a complexity too large or too small to ever explore, and a time we can never visit. And "never" really means never. No future technological breakthroughs, no great scientific discoveries will ever change these limits, these edges of reality. The main theme of this book is that people are limited by boundaries; these are logical and physical limits that bound us: the edges of our reality. A secondary theme is a comparison between computers and people, the main issue being whether the human mind has some ability that computers don't have and never will have.

Many of the book's topics are complex and controversial; some require preliminary discussions before the main points can be entertained. However, the discussions aim at a few key related issues; it is possible to summarize them now before we start, which will give us an overview for much of the rest of the book. Our logical limits and the computers versus humans issue can be codified in a simple form, for an overview. First, we know that computers think faster than humans and always will. It is an advantage; it does not constitute superior mental ability, however. This is an important distinction: Faster-calculation ability means being able to solve problems faster. Yes, this is an undeniable advantage that computers have. But there is more to superior reasoning than just speed; some types of reasoning are provably beyond a computer's ability, and, in addition, some human reasoning is believed to be beyond a computer's ability. A good deal of this book looks at two different issues concerning computers and humans: (1) problems that computers cannot solve and (2) evidence that there are problems that humans can solve and computers cannot.

There are known classes of problems that computers cannot solve, and there exist types of reasoning that computers cannot do. We categorize these classes by certain theories that describe them — to generally denote these theories, we use the term *limit*. A limit on computers (or humans) is an entire class of problems that they cannot solve or a type of reasoning that they cannot do. A Gödel limit denotes the fact that there are certain types of reasoning (to be defined later) that are impossible, therefore putting an upper limit on our reasoning. A Halting limit means that certain procedures (to be defined later) are impossible to ever complete, therefore limiting us in an absolute sense. A computationally intractable limit denotes the fact that certain computational problems (we will see many examples later) require far too many calculations to ever do, and therefore this is a practical upper limit on computers. We will eventually discuss the following limits: Don't worry about the properties of the limits now, they will become clear later.

- Gödel limits are upper limits on computers and humans.
- Halting (or Turing) limits are upper limits on computers and humans.
- Computationally intractable is an upper limit on computers.
- Humans and computers can solve all algorithms (Church's thesis).
- It is impossible to do 100! operations; hence this is an upper limit on computers.

These statements mean that computers can't solve computationally intractable problems and that the Gödel and Halting logical limits affect both humans and computers (examples of each type will be presented, some as concrete as procedures to check the validity of government tax laws). (Kurt Gödel, Alonzo Church, and Alan Turing were the most prominent mathematical logicians during the breakthrough years in the 1930s. We will be hearing more about them later.) No computer, no matter how big it is or how fast it is or how long it runs, can ever do 100! computations — it is impossible ($100! = 100 \cdot 99 \cdot 98 \cdots 2 \cdot 1$). The laws of physics and the size of the universe prohibit this many operations. Therefore, any problem that requires this many operations to solve is impossible. There are many practical problems that run into this limit.

The computers versus humans issue has two possible outcomes, namely,

1. Humans can solve as many problems as computers.

or the final big conjecture,

2. Humans can solve more problems than computers.

All but the last conjecture will be discussed in the middle sections of the book after a series of developmental chapters — these develop some facts and theory about computer processing. These are not just theoretical results either — they apply to real life. A pair of chapters show occurrences of Gödel, Halting, and other logical limits in everyday concerns such as tax laws, assault and battery laws, and free speech.

Later chapters discuss the last conjecture — can people solve any problem or think any thought that computers can't, now or ever? There are two threads to the argument, one pro, one con. Con first: Life is very computerlike; a series of chapters makes this point. Life's machinery, DNA and RNA, operates like computers do; there is a vast amount of genetic blueprint information stored in DNA, and it must be read like computer data and then acted upon. This analogy would strengthen the logical equality of humans and computers. On the pro side, quantum experiments show an unexplainable dependence on observation: The results are different when observed than otherwise. Many scientists attribute this to human observers. This would strengthen the case for humans having abilities that computers can never have.

How we think, how much we can know, what controls our actions, how it all began — these are the questions that have been around since humans could talk and reason. Before the present, there could only be speculation. Now the maturing of several theories is showing the way to the answers even if the answers are still beyond view. This book explains these theories and how they converge with each other to strengthen each other. Many of the theories are fairly new: Provable upper limits on human thought and computers date from the 1930s (the previously mentioned Gödel, Church, and Turing); virtual reality is from the 1970s and 1980s; the convergence of biological ideas about evolution and their analogs in computers started in the 1970s; chaos and its effects date from the 1970s (Mandelbrot was a pioneer here); and many cosmological ideas appeared in the 1980s (Stephen Hawking, Roger Penrose, and many more). It is the convergence and interplay of these ideas that shape this book.

To get where we are going, it would be helpful to recall what those before us have done and why. To be sure, Aristotle, Newton, Maxwell, Darwin, Einstein, Bohr, and others weren't trying to find upper limits on human endeavor; like all scientists, they were trying to discover what nature was really about, how it worked, and how to model it. They weren't looking for limits — limits were all around them. They were looking for answers, and the answers that they found have a profound impact on how we view our future today. Aristotle found answers about logic that are used in today's computers; Newton's models of motion are still quite accurate today; Einstein's theory of relativity is perhaps the most accurate model that we can measure even today. We don't need all of their discoveries or theories for our purposes, just a few. We do need to understand how these theories arose before we expand upon them. For these reasons, we will review some history of scientific thought in order to understand why the great minds of the past chose the paths that they did and how their contributions help us understand our limits, today.

QUICK HISTORY

Our reasoning abilities were slowly developed over hundreds of thousands of years. Humans faced the need to hunt and gather food, find shelter, outwit predators, and maintain increasingly more complex social structures. The continuing need to solve these problems helped evolve human thinking abilities. The first use of strict logic as we know it was a mathematical proof in about 600 B.C. by the Greek thinker Thales.

The Greeks invented logic. You have heard it often enough, and it is true in a broad sense. Aristotle and his band of student followers posed riddles like *This sentence is false* and spent years codifying methods to explain and avoid these paradoxes. Picture a group of rich young men walking around in togas and sandals and spouting off complicated theories and musing over the contradiction (if the sentence is false, then the sentence as stated is true, which can't be). Probably at the time it seemed philosophical and rather useless to their families (picture a father of a student: an earthy type who made a fortune by hard work, a father who had to pay Aristotle to tutor his son and then had to listen to this abstract discussion at the supper table). But these methods, which Aristotle and his students developed to avoid logical problems, put the entire branch of knowledge on a solid foundation.

Logic has been widely used before and after the Greeks; people think and (usually) reason logically. The Greeks codified the study of logic, which gave it a sturdy foundation for the ensuing centuries; they defined terms like hypothesis and conclusion, and they identified the correct structure of deduction. It wasn't until the nineteenth century that others made major improvements in the formal logic of the Greeks; several European mathematicians finally ran into problems for which Greek logic was insufficient, so they had to change and improve it. One major logical theme in several later chapters will be that of a contradiction, similar to the riddle, which is a troublesome area in law and politics in addition to being a main ingredient in the Gödel and Halting limits.

Isaac Newton has been gone for over two centuries now, yet his views represent a set of theories that we are still coming to terms with. Although the idea of a computer was unknown in his day, computers behave according to his theories — they are deterministic. Newton, the inventor of the Newtonian theory of physics and calculus, was the mental giant of his age. He used the calculus and a special type of equation, a differential equation, to formulate extremely accurate models of physics. Today, physics is mainly the study of differential equations: differential equations of motion for particles, differential equations of quantum state, differential equations of matter. Newton's law relating the velocity of moving objects and gravity was the first of the kind. A differential is a rate of change of another variable (acceleration is the differential of velocity), which is the basic concept of calculus. Calculus was unknown before Newton; in effect, Newton had to develop his tool — calculus — at the same time that he was developing his theories of motion. His models were so accurate, so concise, and so elegant that they influenced the way scientists came to see the world; scientists started actively looking for mathematical descriptions of nature.

The deeds and personalities of many famous deceased scientists have mellowed in each successive retelling of their accomplishments. This is not so with Newton — he was a super genius and he was a fighter. He argued with many academics and scientists of his own country and many politicians too (one particularly bitter battle was with the Astronomer Royal, John Flamsteed). Toward the end of his lifetime (he died in 1727), he argued with supporters of the German mathematician Leibniz about who had really invented calculus. Leibniz independently invented some of the same calculus concepts as Newton but at a slightly later time (Newton made several breakthroughs about 1666); he had a more workable notation, which was more widely used than Newton's.

However, Newton, alone, was the father of the classical school of physics: a group that once thought that all motion and all reactions could be eventually explained by a set of basic principles or equations from which all else followed. In other words, once set in motion, the universe and all inside it would move along according to (and only according to) a set of universal laws — determinism. This seems to make the universe a purposeless machine. At the time, this placed some classicists in conflict with the Church; indeed, Newton on his deathbed pointedly refused to take last rites. The universe didn't seem to need a guiding hand, a god. Of course, this theory didn't have a good answer to the universe-creation problem, but then again neither did anyone else at the time. The classical school reigned supreme for several hundred years; other theories extended it, and one large contribution (by James Clerk Maxwell, a Scottish mathematician during the time of the American Civil War) extended the classical approach to the new arena of electromagnetic phenomena. This supremacy of the classical school lasted up until the 1920s; then classicism hit a stone wall — quantum physics with its underlying randomness.

Determinism is the antithesis of free will; computers are deterministic, people may be or may not be. Newton's theories are the embodiment of determinism; we will look at his theories to see exactly what extra qualities humans need to surpass computers.

The 1920s and 1930s are remembered as the peaceful time between the two world wars punctuated by the depression. What we don't often remember is that these decades were also a period of explosive growth in logic and physics. These two modern fields of knowledge both play a large role in resolving the final issues.

Early in the 1900s, a young Swiss patent office worker published a series of three papers that pushed physics from the classical world toward the modern world of the quantum. Albert Einstein's accomplishments back in 1905 were breathtaking in their scope and depth, even from the often jaded perspective of the present. No historical revisionist will ever diminish the significance of these breakthroughs. Books have been written about Einstein, the man and the deeds; we don't need to repeat it all. For the main themes, two of Einstein's theories are all that we need. First, his theory of relativity limits our eventual exploration of the universe and prevents (probably) time travel. Second, his long-running debate with Niels Bohr and other leading proponents of quantum theory helped shape and sharpen the quantum theory that we have today. As we saw before, Newtonian classicism maintained a foothold until the late 1920s. Then a series of several quantum experiments and the discovery of several new quantum theory models and equations led to an irrevocable break with classicism.

Between 1926 and 1928, many basic principles of quantum mechanics were formulated (e.g., the Schrödinger equation and the Heisenberg uncertainty principle); they were simple enough to state, had a wealth of experimental verification, and caused this irrevocable break with classical physics. This breakaway from the old and familiar classicism was threatening enough for the scientists of the time. In particular, in response to quantum randomness, Einstein made his famous remark "Does God play dice with the universe?" Even more threatening were the various interpretations of what the experiments really meant. The bright lights in the physics world during the 1920s and 1930s, including Bohr, Schrödinger, Dirac, and others, tried explaining the strange experimental results in a larger framework, and so they came up with various interpretations.

Later we will take a hard look at these experiments, these interpretations, and Einstein's problems with them. Quantum theory is hard, but central. The quantum is a basic building block of physics, like the photon, which makes up light. At this quantum micro level, nature doesn't work in the same way as at the macro level of everyday life. A special theory describes events at this micro level, quantum theory. We can't discuss possible differences between humans and computers nor can we really understand the beginning and the end of the universe without the quantum. The quantum is not a limit, maybe not even an answer, but most physicists believe that many answers lie close by the quantum.

There is hope in the quantum. Experiments in quantum theory appear to show an unexplainable relationship between matter and consciousness. Humans are conscious; computers are not. This relationship may give humans an advantage over computers.

Logic also went through traumatic times in the 1930s. Logic as codified by the Greeks and extended by others is useful for law, politics, theology, and other areas. It has severe limitations in mathematics, computer science, and other areas of science, however. For several centuries, scientists simply put up with these limitations; however, in the late nineteenth and early twentieth centuries the limitations were causing paradoxes — the issues had to be faced. At this time, the English mathematician, logician, philosopher, and social critic Bertrand Russell, his co-worker Alfred North Whitehead, and others were responsible for putting mathematical logic on firm foundations. Without their work, Gödel never could have made his discoveries; in a later chapter we will look over the Russell–Whitehead logic contributions. The best minds of the age had looked for the ultimate set of logical axioms from which all mathematical knowledge follows. Gödel forcefully proved that the search was for naught. It was now and forever impossible. Other logicians like American Alonzo Church and Englishman Alan Turing proved mathematical theorems that showed that digital computers had absolute upper limits on what they could do. Gödel's theory on incompleteness is one hard inescapable limit all by itself; it was originally proven only for a narrowly defined mathematical system, but its implications are far broader.

By the 1930s, the concept of a computer was well established in the scientific community, and mathematical logic was on firm foundations. Church and Turing used these two concepts to prove results that later led to an understanding of the procedures that computers could accomplish — the so-called Church–Turing thesis. Called algorithms, these procedures are the foundation of computer processes (people can do them too) and as such form a lower limit on human capabilities. Our question will be: Can humans do any nonalgorithmic processes? If so, it would immediately set us above computers, which can't.

Life — what it is, how it started, where it goes from here — is a separate issue. Darwin's theory of evolution was the first great revolution in thought about life. However, the twentieth century has seen almost as great an upheaval in how life is considered. Again computers have given us a great insight. Life based on DNA is very similar to a computer procedure called recursion. Indeed, we can design computer structures that form evolutionary chains of "computer life," all within the confines of a computer. Furthermore, the new field of neural networks has given us a great deal of insight about how the human brain works and how it learns from experience. Both fields of study have demystified the human brain and human thought process. Throughout the book, the human thought process is compared and contrasted with the computer's. Ultimately, human minds and computers merge in virtual reality. Virtual reality of the far future promises many exciting yet frightening possibilities: conscious computers with emotions and motives and the possibilities of human minds being stored within computers.

Darwin, during his voyage on the *Beagle,* discovered evolution as a science. Evolution doesn't limit us in any way, but twentieth-century discoveries about features of DNA and RNA have changed the way we think about humans. If we are the end product of billions of years of evolutionary development guided by the computerlike RNA and DNA, then perhaps our capabilities do not exceed those of computers.

The basic structure of DNA was discovered in 1953 by Nobel Prize winners Watson and Crick. After their work became widely known, people started drawing parallels between DNA functions and computer operations. During the 1970s and 1980s, computer knowledge was common and people were starting to talk and think in computer terms. DNA's structure and functions had been known well for 30 years by then; what was new was looking at the reproductive process in computer terms. Computer-biology started almost as gaming. Today, there are several software packages that display biological-type reproduction, evolution, and mutation of "computer creatures" (e.g., the PC game *Simlife*). These computer creatures are not living of course, and at any given time they are simply magnetic storage in the memory of computer systems. Much simpler than any real living creature, they depend on mathematical functions to decide when they evolve, split to raise offspring, or die. They are a long way from amounting to anything significant. Still, they give pause for thought.

During the same period, the discipline of virtual reality started. Still in its infancy, the field holds the promise of changing the world someday, maybe soon. Contrary to computer creatures, virtual reality appears close to being very significant. As with computer biology, virtual reality first appeared in gaming, and the improvement in realism has been explosive. Today's virtual reality games allow the player to interact with role-playing, speaking actors in a drama in which the player chooses his own path through complicated plots. These games will only get better; the games in 10 years will be very realistic, and after that we may see direct brain–computer links that increase the realism exponentially.

Computer creatures and virtual reality are two aspects of the life–computer relationship that we must explore. If humans are inherently more capable than computers, if humans really have some extra capability that lets us solve problems that computers never can, if we really don't have anything to fear from computers in the end, then it might show here — either computer creatures will never grow to become conscious creatures or virtual reality will always fall short of *real* reality.

Then there is the limit that bounds us absolutely and inescapably, a limit on our very existence and consciousness: the end of the universe. Before the twentieth century this wasn't a big issue because everyone thought that the universe would last forever. Until the twentieth century and the great cosmological revolution, the universe was thought to be static and eternal. The universe wasn't going to end; people might die, but religion held out hope that consciousness would be eternal, at least for the righteous. Advances in astronomy and telescopes caused large increases in the estimated size of the universe during the early 1900s. Then, starting in 1926, Edwin Hubble analyzed astronomical data and came out with his famous observation that the universe was red-shifted from us — moving away in all directions at once. The universe wasn't static, it was expanding.

Obviously, this expansion had not been going on forever. Now the theorists of the 1940s and 1950s faced an enigma: how to explain this situation. Conjectures about a universe that expanded from an initial, small, superdense object were put forward by several scientists. These conjectures were reformulated and merged to become known as the Big Bang theory. One of the earliest proponents was a priest and physicist, Georges Lemaitre of Belgium, which is fitting since the theory had obvious religious overtones. The Big Bang seemed to explain everything, and as more observations matched the logical consequences of the Big Bang model, it became widely accepted and pushed the static universe model out of the picture. It didn't cause many problems with religion either because it fit in quite well with the biblical account of Genesis.

There was only one small problem: The theory said how the universe started, but it didn't say how it would end. Creatures, like us humans, with finite life spans are always more interested in the end than the beginning. We accept birth and beginnings; we defy death and endings. Everyone would like to live forever in the future; no one cares that they haven't lived all eternity in the past. Therefore, we will look at the various theories surrounding the end of the universe.

Theories of both the beginning and the end revolve around some small-scale physics objects and forces. During the 1970s and continuing in to the 1990s, various theories have come out about how the universe could have arisen in the first place. Saying that the Big Bang took place is one thing; explaining how something that big could start is quite another thing. Some widely accepted ideas have come from the minds of Stephen Hawking, his coworker Roger Penrose, Americans Kip Thorne and Steven Weinberg, and others. Their research into black holes, quantum physics, and space–time singularities has led to some mathematically plausible models about how the Big Bang could have come about and what it was like. Notice the phrase "mathematically plausible": there is a dearth of hard data here and likely always will be — it has been 15 billion years since the Big Bang.

OVERVIEW OF THE BOOK

An underlying theme of this book is thought: the mechanics of the thought process for both humans and computers and the upper limits on the thought process. Limits on reason and thought come from several factors: unknown origins or initial conditions, infinite complexity, upper limits on logic and computation, chaos, and the quantum randomness of the universe. These factors all limit us; they are all hazy curtains that limit our view of the world in different directions — they are the edges of our reality.

The book is divided into four sections, and it follows a progression. In the first section, we look briefly at a concept that will come up repeatedly: models of our physical surroundings, how we view the cause–effect nature of our surroundings. Later, we consider the limits on reality and people caused by endless, infinite numbers and space and then touch on the limits caused by our inability to predict because of chaos. The second section focuses on computers and computers versus humans. A series of three chapters builds toward demonstrations of the upper limits on computers and human thought. Practical problems with scientific and social significance are shown in a pair of chapters to be essentially impossible to solve. A chapter discusses artificial intelligence (AI) and virtual reality. One chapter makes the transition from computers to life, humans, and human consciousness; it discusses how lifelike computers can be and how the question of the origin of life on Earth is related to computer recursion. In the third section of the book, the conscious mind and reality are considered. Four chapters concentrate on the uniquely human aspects of thought. The free will question, the mysteries of the conscious mind, and the effect that consciousness has on quantum reality are all explored. The three chapters in the fourth and final section come back to physical reality and revisit the big questions in the context of the previous chapters.

For a detailed overview, let's look at a chapter-by-chapter breakdown of the book. The book starts with a tour of numbers, both large and small, featuring a problem that can't ever be solved by a computer. This is followed by a chapter on modeling reality. Next, infinity is explored from both the mathematical and physical points of view. An important concept related to infinity, countable numbers, is discussed since it will be used later to prove that computer thought does *not* have infinite capabilities. Infinity in the context of time, space, and the Big Bang will finish this chapter. The next chapter is about chaos; it shows that even with almost perfect cause–effect knowledge (model) of a situation, the situation may not be predictable.

Computers, their capabilities and limits, are considered in the next few chapters. First, a number of issues are discussed in an introductory chapter: what is and what is not a computer program, a comparison and contrasting of computer programs with human thought, and the deterministic nature of a computer program. Finally, the chapter ends by showing how a computer program can be represented as a number — a very large number. This numerical representation will be used later with the concept (countable numbers) from the chapter on infinity to prove that there is an *absolute upper limit* on computer thought. Next are chapters that explore other limits on computers and the human brain. One chapter focuses on practical engineering problems that require so much calculation that a universe filled with computers running for billions of years couldn't solve them — computationally intractable problems, a practical upper limit on thought and calculation. Upper limits on reasoning are considered in a chapter on logic. Both human thought and computer algorithms require the field of logic, and, in the past century, the ancient field of logic has been put on a strict mathematical basis. The chapter focuses on the basics of logic and some far-reaching developments in the twentieth century such as Gödel's incompleteness theorem and logical paradoxes.

By this point, we have established three separate upper limits on thought: Gödel incompleteness, the Halting problem of computer programming, and computationally intractable problems. Theory is fine; however, the next two chapters really make the point that our current world is constrained by these limits. We explore what these theoretical limits really mean in the real world. Examples are given from mathematics, logic, computer programming, ethics, politics, and law. At this point, we are ready to discuss specifically how a computer can think like a human. AI bridges the gap between the computer logic and humanlike intelligence. Two widely used techniques are discussed in the chapter on AI: evaluation and rule-based systems. Concluding this chapter is a section on the virtual reality of today, the near future, and speculations about the far future.

The next chapter considers various topics related to computers imitating life. Machines are everywhere around us, but most of us don't think of ourselves or the cells that make us up to be machines. However, DNA is a vastly more complex machine than humankind can make for itself; it is based on a method of self-replication that involves a computer-related concept of recursion. RNA has a computerlike quality to it also; it reads patterns and acts based on what it reads. We look at this analogy between life's component molecules and computers, then follow by speculating about molecule-sized machines and computers, futuristic medicine, and how they might combine to extend human life to infinity. Another speculative notion that has caught people's attention recently is the possibility of future advanced computers actually being conscious like humans — virtual life. The last topic of this chapter is how computer-related ideas play a role in finding the origin of life on Earth or ascertaining whether life really did originate on Earth. We need to know how computerlike we are; the answer affects our computers versus humans issue.

The third section of the book deals with the deeper aspects of human thought: free will, the role of the conscious mind in reality, and quantum mysteries. Free will versus determinism is an age-old topic that has taken a new turn since the arrival of quantum theory in the 1920s. We consider exactly what determinism is and what free will could be, what it could arise from, and how it might work. This leads into a discussion of the conscious human mind and what special significance consciousness might have. This special significance is studied further in a chapter on quantum mysteries, in which the enigmatic quantum measurement act is discussed and we consider what role humans play in this enigma. Finally, after considering both the pros and cons of the computers versus humans issue, we consider what role the quantum plays in free will or nonalgorithmic thought. Quantum randomness is the pivotal issue here; apparently, human minds are associated with it and computers are not. It represents the best chance of settling the issue in favor of humans; it is also among the deepest topics in science today.

Physical limits and the beginning and the end of the universe are the subjects of the rest of the book. First, we consider the small (particles and forces) of the universe and then go on to the large (galaxies, clusters of galaxies, superclusters, and great attractors). Objects of both extremes are layered in size, and we speculate about what might lie beyond our current observation powers.

Ultimately, we get to the universe that we live in and why is it that we do live here. In the last 20 years speculations have abounded about anthropic principles. There are many speculations about the universe and its origin that relate to computers and humans. The anthropic principle has many forms that see humans (or conscious beings) as essential to the universe; in this view the universe exists only because it is being observed. Other views of the universe see it as order arising from an underlying randomness or chaos. Still others speculate that the universe is actually inside a computer; perhaps we all are virtual beings. Many such speculations have hinged on the topics that we will have covered by then: computer thought versus human thought, free will, Gödel's incompleteness theorem, logic, chaos, cellular automatons, and artificial intelligence.

Based on what we have seen in the preceding chapters, we will speculate on answers to several "big questions" that philosophers, cosmologists, and theologians dwell on: Is there free will? Will computers ever think and feel just like people? How did life originate? Is eternal life possible? Finally, we close with what might lie beyond it all. What is the nature of the universe and the nature of God? We will examine all these questions and more as we look at modern physics and cosmology.

Although we will consider theories in this book, there is a practical flavor: Many applications to the real world and examples from everyday life will also be presented. An ancient Greek called Thales was famous in his own time for predicting an eclipse of the sun. That eclipse happened on exactly the day (May 28, 585 B.C., from computer simulations of lunar orbits) of a battle between the Lydians and the Medies; it obscured the sun so completely that it stopped the battle. In that time if you predicted something like that, your fame was assured; so many events of Thales' life are known. One small incident is one of my favorite stories about scientists (and definitely my wife's favorite). Thales was walking along with a female companion one evening and was so intent on studying the stars in the sky that he didn't see a ditch and fell into it. The woman asked him: "How can you tell what's going on in the heavens, when you can't see what lies at your own feet?"[2] Some abstraction, some theory is absolutely necessary; however, completely ignoring the real world and its problems is something that I have tried to avoid in this book.

Chapter 2

Numbers — Large and Small

> ... of all the sciences known as yet, Arithmetic
> and Geometry alone are free from any
> taint of falsity or uncertainty.
>
> RENE DESCARTES (1596–1650)
> *Rules for the Direction
> of the Mind* (1629)

1010101010101010101010101010101010101010101

Large numbers are one of the most fascinating areas of mathematics; here imaginations can run wild at the sheer immensity of the numbers. The problem with some of the numbers that we see in science is that we don't have any firsthand experience with numbers this size. Nothing in our everyday experience is of the same magnitude as the age of the earth (4 billion years) or the federal budget (1 trillion dollars). Most people can't envision the differences in large numbers; these numbers are way beyond our everyday experience and we can't associate them with anything tangible. John Allen Paulos, author of the best-seller *Innumeracy*, pointed out how many people feel about large numbers and the amount of misunderstanding that exists when he paraphrased many people's view: "A million dollars, a billion, a trillion, whatever. It doesn't matter as long as we do something about the problem."[1] There is a social ill, they want it resolved; however, for a social problem a million is cheap, a billion is moderate, a trillion is the entire federal budget. So how badly do they want the problem solved? Numbers that end in ". . . illion" tend to blur together.

It is not just budgets or populations or interstellar distances that we need large numbers for. This book aims at showing limitations of computers and human minds; often we will see a mental process that seems simple, but to complete it we must go through an impossible amount of combinations. Professor Paulos recalls the French poet Raymond Queneau, who once published a 10-page book. Each page had 14 lines of a sonnet on it, and the pages were cut to allow a sonnet to be formed by any combination of the 10 first lines with the 10 second lines with the 10 third lines and so on.[2] The reader could create 10^{14} different sonnets. The poet Queneau claimed that all of the sonnets made sense, but it would take any person essentially forever to check out this claim. Just reading every possible sonnet, all words of which are written on 10 pages, is an impossible task for a human.

A SENSE OF SIZE

Scientific notation is a compact notation for representing large numbers, but powers-of-10 notation can lull us into underestimating the overwhelming size of these numbers. A book is an easy-to-grasp idea; it comprises many pages, with several hundred words and a few thousand letters on each page. Consider Table 1, in which several large numbers are represented by the number of characters (letters) in books based on the following approximations: 2500 characters = 1 page; 400 pages =

Table 1
Large Numbers and Their Representation by the Number of Characters in Books

10^3	Number of characters on two-fifths of a page of a book
2×10^3	Years since Christ walked the Earth
5×10^3	Years since the "iceman" died and was buried beneath the snow in the Alps
7×10^3	Years since the beginning of recorded history
10^6 (1 million)	Number of characters on 400 pages
7×10^6	Population of New York City
3×10^6	Number of operations per second of a good PC
60×10^6	Years since dinosaurs walked the Earth
10^9 (1 billion)	Number of characters in 80 feet of books
10^9	Operations per second of a supercomputer
2×10^9	Number of bits of information in a single DNA molecule in human being
5×10^9	Population of the Earth; also the estimated age of the Earth in years
15×10^9	Age of the universe in years
10^{12} (1 trillion)	Number of characters in a stack of books one city block long and 80 feet high (city block ~ 1/10 mile ≅ 528 feet, room for 1056 6"-wide books)
10^{12}	Annual budget of the United States government in dollars

1 inch (thickness); 1 inch of pages of a book = 1,000,000 characters; books measure 6" × 9". Thus, the number of years in an average lifetime equals the number of characters on *one line of text*; Columbus discovered the New World *eight lines of text* ago; recorded history started *three pages of text* ago; early man walked the earth *200 pages of text* ago; and the Earth was formed *4000 books* ago. It is hard to get a good perspective for really large numbers. Even visualizing a mammoth stack of books and imagining the numbers of characters found in them doesn't suffice for larger powers of 10. One sextillion is 10^{18}; picture it if you can. A number called the "googol" is a one followed by a hundred zeros; there is nothing physical that requires this large a number to count it.

Small numbers in scientific notation are usually greater than zero but not by much. Most of our use of numbers is to measure; normally we don't measure large negative numbers (even the national debt isn't that much in the red). Instead, there is a need to quantify very close to the value of zero. For instance, an electron has a resting mass of about 9×10^{-31} kilograms.

The range or ratio of sizes that we will encounter in the universe can be captured in a range of 10^{100}. Time is thought not to be measurable in intervals shorter than 10^{-43} seconds (from quantum mechanics); the upper limit on time in the universe might be about 100 billion billion years or 10^{20} years. All of this is easily within the 10^{100} range. Scientific notation is a useful, compact form of expressing long strings of digits, but don't be lulled into underestimating the size that these numbers represent.

An ancient myth tells of a temple on a mountain where priests spend their days patiently moving a set of 64 golden rings from one stake to another. The rings are of different sizes and originally were stacked largest (on the bottom) to smallest. There are three stakes, and the priests' job is to move the original stack from one stake to another; they can use the third stake as a temporary place to move some rings in preparation for another move. The rules that they must obey are simple: Move one ring at a time and never put a larger ring on top of a smaller ring. The myth says that when the priests finish with their task, the stars will fall, the skies will blacken, and time will end.

We need not worry; the sequence of moves requires 2^{64} moves to complete; at one move per second, that is about 6×10^{11} years or about 40 times the present age of the universe. This problem is typical of many problems: easy to state, easy to do each step, incredibly lengthy to complete. A large computer could do these steps much faster than a person and could finish this problem, although it might take a few centuries. However, there is a simple demonstration of a problem that no computer can ever solve.

NO COMPUTER CAN DO THIS PROBLEM

Now we consider an example of a large number that is vital to the rest of the book. Computers are a main topic, specifically limits on computers — problems that computers can never do. Most of these limits are rather deep and will take some preliminary development; however, one computational limit can be shown now.

We ask the following question: What are the most computer operations that can ever be done? This means that we want to find a number that is larger than the total number of all the computer operations (e.g., multiplications, additions, printing a word, moving a data point, etc.) that can be done by all past, present, and future computers in the entire universe. At first glance, this looks crazy and impossible. Since we don't know how many computers there will be in the future or how fast they will be, how can we compute such a number? We can by using numbers that are upper bounds on three quantities: the maximum number of operations per second of any computer, the maximum number of computers possible, and the lifetime of the universe. Surprisingly, there are estimates for all three.

A digital computer operates on data stored in bits that are made of a material that can have two different measurable states, designated 1 and 0. Digital computers have these general characteristics: One computer operation can change the value of the bit; bits, being material objects, can never be smaller than a single proton; computers signal bits to change value at the speed of light using electricity. An upper limit on computer operation speed happens when the time interval becomes so small that light can't traverse the diameter of an atomic nucleus (roughly 10^{-15} cm at 3×10^{10} cm/sec; anyhow it takes more than, say, 10^{-30} seconds to traverse this diameter). Clearly, two different operations could not be performed on that bit in that small a time. An even smaller number and firm upper limit no matter what the technology, hence a more conservative limit, is 10^{-43} seconds for a single operation. By quantum theory, time intervals less than about 10^{-43} seconds will no longer relate to continuous time as we know it. In a certain sense, this is the shortest possible time interval; nothing can happen faster than this. Therefore, for certain, the processing speed of the most advanced possible digital computer would be less than 10^{43} operations per second.[3]

Computer speed is measured in operations per second, and cosmological time is measured in years. Let's relate the two so we can look at upper limits on computer operations when we theoretically run them for times like the age of the universe. The number of seconds in a year (60 sec/min × 60 min/hr × 24 hr/day × 365 days/year = 31,536,000 sec/year) is about 3×10^7 or 30 million as an approximation; for an upper bound, we can use 10^8. For the lifetime of the universe, we rely on current estimates which say 10^{20} years; by this time it is estimated that all stars will have burned out and come loose from their galaxies, and all matter will be very cold and just floating around.[4] The number of protons and neutrons has been estimated at 10^{80}, so we will use that as an estimate of the number of matter particles within the universe.[5,6]

Computers can run more operations in three ways: (1) run for a longer time, (2) run faster, and (3) run operations on more computers (in parallel). For our most-possible-computer-operations calculation, we maximize all three at once. First, let it run from the beginning until the end of the universe (say, 10^{20} years or 10^{28} seconds); second, let each computer run as fast as allowed by physics (10^{43} operations per second) and third, there can't be more computers than particles of matter, so an upper limit on individual computers (or parallel processors) must be the number of particles in the universe (say 10^{80}). So we hypothetically allow our 10^{80} computers to run at 10^{43} operations per second for 10^{28} seconds, which gives an absolute upper bound of operations that can be done at $10^{80+43+28}$, which is 10^{151}. Any process requiring more computer operations than that is computationally impossible.

You can't beat this limit. You can't build bigger computers or more computers — there isn't any more material in the universe. You can't build a faster computer — the laws of physics say no. You can't run your computer any longer than this — the universe will end on you too.

Consider the task of listing all the possible routes that you can take when visiting a set of cities when you visit each city only once. For example, designate Chicago, Detroit, and Miami by C, D, and M respectively. There are 2 possible routes for the set of 2 cities, Chicago and Detroit, namely, CD (visit Chicago first, then Detroit) and DC. For the 3 cities there are these 6 routes: MCD, CMD, CDM, MDC, DMC, and DCM. The formula that computes how many paths there are for N cities is $N!$ (e.g., 2 routes are 2!, 6 routes are 3!).

Listing all possible routes of visiting 100 cities in the United States is an easy-to-state problem that requires more operations than this upper limit. If you wanted to have a computer list *all* possible routes that visit each of the cities, the number of routes would be 100! or 10^{158}. This is an impossible calculation because listing one route would take several computer operations apiece so the total would be more than our limit. Therefore, this is an impossible problem for *any* computer, past, present, or future. No future technology can create such a computer to do this problem, no space-faring race of aliens can have such a digital computer that could do it — it is simply too many calculations.

This example focused on the 100! limit on computations; but another impossibility was the actual list: It must be more than 100! words long and there isn't enough material (10^{80}) in the universe to print the list on. Now there are types of computers other than digital ones (analog and quantum computers are the most prominent) and these two types both can do some special calculations in one computer operation that would take a digital computer many operations. Still, none of these can do this problem either.

In the scheme of things, Earth is a small place in the universe; 100 is not an astronomical-sized number — it represents everyday sets of objects. Yet, one of our problems using our scale size for numbers leads to a completely impossible problem. Our world is more complex than you might believe, and computers will never be as powerful as you might think.

Chapter 3

Modeling Reality

*The whole of science is nothing more than a
refinement of every day thinking.*

ALBERT EINSTEIN[1]

Scientific models are our way of describing complex cause–effect
relationships in a compact form (all sciences use them extensively to predict the effects of various inputs or causes: Physics
predicts the motion of the planets; meteorology predicts the
weather). Modeling has two areas that interest us: First is the
type of data or number that represents observations of causes
or effects, and the second is the functional form of the model.
We need to consider differences in models for two purposes: (1)
in order to start the computers versus humans debate, a description of the data that each processes is needed, and (2) modeling
sets the stage for our later discussions of chaos, physics, free
will, and theories of everything (TOEs). Cause–effect relation-

ships are usually described by models in a mathematical form, with cause being represented by the independent variable and effect by the dependent variable. In the simplest form, a model would look like a simple mathematical formula or equation: $f(x) = y$ or $f(cause) = effect$, where $f = the\ model$. More complex models are common in which the cause and effect are several variables and the model function can include almost any mathematical construct known. In the next section we consider the distinction between types of models of physical processes.

This reliance on mathematics is not accidental; our world seems to correspond to mathematical formulas and equations in a way that some have found too coincidental. Many have used the phrase "the unreasonable effectiveness of mathematics" in describing physical effects. Others have attributed philosophical or religious significance to this mathematical nature of reality. The famous quantum pioneer, Paul Dirac, once said: "God used beautiful mathematics in creating the world." Mathematics is known as the "queen of the sciences" for just this reason, and mathematicians have done research in many of the sciences because of this mathematical nature of reality. The only thing that they can't do with mathematics is to win a Nobel Prize in mathematics. In case you have ever wondered, there isn't any Nobel Prize offered in mathematics and never has been. The story is that Alfred Nobel, the inventor of dynamite, who used part of his considerable fortune to establish the Nobel Prize fund, stipulated that there not be a Nobel Prize awarded for mathematical accomplishment. According to the story, Nobel's wife's lover, Mittag-Leffler, was a prominent mathematician of the time, and Nobel didn't want to risk him winning the award.

TYPES OF MODELS

Models predict or estimate. Prediction doesn't have to be a future prediction or estimate; it could be a prediction for a different place, or for a different mixture of chemicals, or for a different set of stock purchases. Nor does model prediction have to be exact; different precision is required for different applications.

There are three modeling situations: discrete models, continuous models, and situations that cannot be modeled. Newton's law (extended example of this later) relates velocity to acceleration by the formula *velocity = acceleration × time + initial velocity*. Since the independent variable time is a continuous quantity, this is a continuous model. Continuous models usually use the real numbers as their number base because of the infinitely divisible nature of the real numbers. A simple discrete model is assigning grades for a school exam. Any grade between 95 and 100 receives an A, or any between 90 and 94 a B. Exams are graded on an integer scale, which is a discrete scale; therefore, classify the model as a discrete model. Model classification is that simple. Another discrete model would be a model of the stock market. Most stock market data (some exceptions) are daily data; Dow Jones averages, S&P 500, volume on the New York Stock Exchange, advancing and declining stocks, and many more are computed each day, and investors use the daily data to predict future trends. Usually, there aren't any data recorded like the exact number of advancing stocks at 2:37 P.M. each day.

A situation that cannot be modeled is predicting what the next decimal digit will be in a random string of numbers. For example, if the random decimal number .360455918362241 . . . is given to you, then you can't reliably predict the next digit; it is not possible to come up with a formula that predicts the next digit (at least not any better than 1 chance in 10). No mathematical function will take the first *N* digits of a truly random number and determine the next one. "Determine" is the key word here; if you could determine the next digit, by definition the string of numbers would not be random. This situation is not restricted to just mathematics either; there is a strong belief that underlying all physical processes is a quantum randomness that cannot be predicted just as the next digit in a random number cannot be predicted.

INFORMATION

Most physical processes can be modeled with the real numbers (or complex numbers, which are simply pairs of real numbers). Consider the real number π, which equals 3.1415926 . . . the decimal expansion never stops. That means that the representation for π has an infinite number of digits after the decimal point. A key point is that there is never a *last* digit in the expansion; real numbers cannot have an infinite number of digits and have a last digit — there must always be more digits. For example, .0000000 . . . 01 is *not a real number* if the ellipses represent an infinite number of digits. This means that there cannot be a smallest positive real number; there must always be positive real numbers smaller than any given positive real number. If the above number was truly a positive real number, then it would have to be the smallest possible, but that is impossible. This property of the real numbers is called "infinite divisibility" — any distance can be divided into still smaller parts. Computers use discrete approximations to continuous variables to calculate with; for example, the infinite decimal expansion .0037914472688 . . . would be approximated by .0037914472 in a computer, with more decimal places available if the user increased the computer's effective word length for a particular application. This means that computers aren't limited if a finite approximation to a number is good enough.

Real numbers also have *information content,* to use the language of modern theoretical computer science. This is a technical concept that touches on some of the most perplexing problems in philosophy and the ultimate nature of the universe — problems such as determinism and free will. The discussion of the next two numbers will describe the concept of information content in its most basic form. A repeating decimal like .66666666 . . . = 2/3 has *finite* information content because an alternate form (2/3) is finite in information content. A random number like .016732549643810820 . . . has *infinite* information content because no finite formula or method can describe it exactly.[2]

Real numbers, like integers and rationals, represent only a finite amount of information content in the sense that only a finite amount of computer storage is necessary to represent them. To understand this, look at the two equivalent forms of the repeating decimal .66666 . . . and $\frac{2}{3}$; the latter form is the most economical. Clearly, a computer with only a finite amount of storage cannot store an infinite number of 6's for the decimal representation, but it could store the fraction $\frac{2}{3}$. A similar argument holds for π: all the decimal expansion can't be stored in a finite amount of space, but the infinite series can be exactly described in a finite number of words. This series description could be computed to any number of significant digits if needed. A random series of digits is different. No finite formula can be written down and used to compute all the digits; the most economical possible description is necessarily infinite. If the most economical description of a number is infinite, then we say that the number has an infinite information content.

A computer might handle four- or eight-byte-long numbers; it may have the capacity to increase the number length; but it can never handle an infinite length number all at once. In normal life this is not a problem; computers can be programmed to handle numbers to any desired accuracy, so the output is always accurate enough. In some high-powered scientific calculations, this is not so; we will see this in the chapter on chaos. The biggest problem is knowing beforehand how accurate the input numbers must be.

Analog computation instead of digital computation allows some operations with infinite precession numbers. Consider two weights (not masses, which could be discrete) of infinite-divisibility numbers: Computers can't calculate the sum exactly, but putting both on the same scale gives an exact analog solution. (This works also for voltage or heights and other physical phenomena.) The problem is the measurement act; for example: No scale has infinite precision. Therefore, even if we know that the scale has the exact analog solution, we can't read it off exactly. This is more than a small point since people are analog in nature, and it might be that computers cannot exactly simulate human behavior because of this digital–analog difference. The consequence of infinite information is that it can't ever be computed by any computer. In a sense, computers can't ever really *know* the number or its information content. These numbers are forever beyond a computer's complete understanding in this sense. If the only information that they can never understand is limited to some numbers, then there isn't any problem. However, many physicists think that this infinite-information-content problem is mirrored in physical reality.

Models hold major implications for our exploration of limits and the computers versus humans issues. Digital computers compute with discrete models; humans compute with continuous models. This may or may not be an important distinction. Known limits on computer calculations (Halting limits and computationally intractable limits) are based on a discrete model assumption for computer calculation. We don't have any analogous theories about limits on continuous computation (sometimes called analog computation).

Humans are analog or continuous because their component parts exist in a three-dimensional continuous space and because their functioning depends on nondivisible (analog) time. We move through a three-dimensional space that is real-valued; this means that lengths, volumes, and other physical dimensions can take on values that are irrational real numbers. We move in a time dimension that is continuous, real-valued and nondivisible, which is to say that time can be an irrational real value, also. Computers, on the other hand, work only at discrete times, and they store only rational numbers. They are discrete.

Infinite information is stored in most real numbers. In this narrow sense, humans store an infinite amount of information; however, it's very hard to see an advantage in possessing the information stored in the last infinite number of digits of some number, when 10 or 20 or 200 digits are all that you ever need. Infinite information storage usually means storing the *significant* part of an infinite number of data, not storing the infinite *in-*

significant part of a finite number of data. A similar objection occurs when comparing discrete models with continuous models. If humans have an edge on this point, then it will be very difficult to find.

If analog or continuous computation can solve problems that discrete computation cannot, then humans can probably solve problems that digital computers can't. Wouldn't that resolve our computers versus humans issue in favor of humans? This is a hard question with no answer — maybe or maybe not. The problem is that there are analog computers. If there are problems that discrete methods cannot solve, if continuous methods can solve these problems, and if human consciousness is not required to solve them, then maybe a special analog computer could solve the problems too. It is not much consolation to determine that humans are definitely mentally superior to digital computers but then turn around and admit that *analog* computers are our mental equals. We would like consciousness to play a role.

There is one last thing to consider: The universe might be discrete! This is not widely believed, but some theorists consider it a possibility. We will discuss the implications more in later sections on cellular automatons and the small-scale structure (elementary particles and forces) of nature. Should this by some chance be true, then the analog versus discrete argument is irrelevant, and the computers versus humans issue hinges solely on consciousness.

MODELS AND TOES

Discussions about models and their characteristics appear often in the rest of the book, since models are a compact representation of our knowledge. Some models will be practical ones, the kind that we use to make everyday decisions with and which are developed from scientific experimentation, economic data analysis, or data collection from a host of activities. They are accurate to different degrees; some are rough approximations (such as the time it takes to make a car trip) and some are much more accurate (such as Newton's law). None of the physical models of large-scale systems are completely exact — meaning accurate down to every last decimal point. Some models, such as mathematical equations that don't describe any physical situation, are exact, but we won't be discussing them. However, for some discussions we need the theoretical concept of an *exact* physical model: absolutely, perfectly, down-to-the-last-decimal exact.

Assume that you must make a 20-mile trip in an automobile and that you intend to travel at 60 mph. Your *model* of the situation is a mathematical relationship: *distance = speed × time;* therefore, you figure that it will take you 20 minutes to make the trip. In scientific jargon, the 20-minutes figure is the output of your model; it can also be called many other things: a prediction, an estimate, or the dependent variable. Notice that some might interpret this equation as calculating the average time that it would take you to drive the distance. An average would allow for many unexpected happenings and still be close enough for everyday purposes. However, let's consider it as an attempt at an *exact* estimate. "Close" is not good enough, and those "unexpected happenings" need to be parameterized and included in a better equation or model. Now we have a far, far more difficult problem.

You realize that your model and your estimate are not exact; many small variations in the car's speed, an error in the measured distance, or traffic stoppage situations could cause your model to miss the actual time. Could you fix the model—add more terms like an *acceleration* term or a smaller-effect term like *change in acceleration*? (Recall from calculus that acceleration would be the first derivative of speed and that change in acceleration would be the second derivative.) Well, you could add terms like these and make the model somewhat more accurate — but not exact. More difficult would be the inclusion of terms that could accurately predict the influence of outside forces, like wind or rain, on your car's speed. For example, *distance* = [*speed* − (3 mph × *rainfall in inches per hour*)] × *time* is a fictitious formula that compensates for you driving more slowly if the rainfall is heavier. Clearly, a compensation of this type would not be exact but would itself depend on other more basic factors. Still, this mathematical relationship would represent a more accurate model of the situation. Nearly impossible would be the inclusion of terms that could accurately predict traffic-stoppage situations since these depend on human factors that are driven by other extraordinarily complex models or by random or free will factors.

By now the point is clear: The more exactness we demand of our predictions, the more complicated our modeling process will be. For our everyday concerns, when an error of plus or minus five minutes in travel time is acceptable, then an approximate formula works fine. But for scientists who may require an accuracy of 10^{-12} mph, a vastly more complicated model might be required. And it is probably impossible, given the near impossibility of predicting human factors such as traffic stoppage. Even worse is the theoretical situation where we ask if any set of equations can be exact (down to every last decimal place).

This is the scientist's dilemma! Everything, literally everything, is affected by outside influences. *Exact* prediction requires a closed model that includes all possible outside influences. If you think that the car-trip model has a lot of potential outside influences, think about the meteorologist's problems with modeling the weather or the economist's difficulty with modeling and predicting the stock market or the medical researcher's problems with modeling the chemical reactions within the human body. It seems that a model of any possible situation would have to include as submodels a multitude of other models — endless sets of mathematical equations hopelessly intertwined. That may be deceiving, however.

Variations in car speed, wind velocity, low-pressure centers, the S&P 500 index, highs and lows on the New York Stock Exchange, inflation rates, rates of phosphorus diffusion in the bloodstream, bioelectrical connectivity in the brain — all these factors are derived or dependent variables. They depend on other lower-level variables, which in turn depend on other variables that are still more basic. Maybe the chain stops.

If we could isolate the set of all rock-bottom basic variables and formulate a complete set of equations related to them, then we might have a complete closed model or final theory in hand. Quantum theory gives some hope that this ambitious plan might be possible. We will cover the peculiarities of quantum theory in Chapter 15. For now, it suffices to say that current quantum theory depends on a few basic assumptions and several mathematical formulas that can determine the motion of the fundamental particles and their related forces. Then combine these equations to determine the resultant motion for (theoretically) any number of elementary particles. This could serve as a model for a car trip, the weather, or a human brain activity (all theoretically of course). Quantum theory is not yet complete — meaning that all known forces cannot be explained within its scope; however, many physicists hope to complete the theory into a TOE at some future point. Physicist Leon Lederman put it succinctly: "We hope to explain the entire universe in a single, simple formula that you can wear on your T-shirt."[3]

To see this point, let's consider another example from basic physics: the velocity that a falling object attains. The problem dates back to Newton sleeping under an apple tree; the solution helped start calculus. Newton's law relates the acceleration of a falling object to the forces upon it (mostly gravity, with some air friction resistance) and the mass of the object. In words, the basic equation reads *acceleration = force/mass*. Recalling calculus (for those readers who have forgotten calculus, just accept that the next part is right), the velocity of the object at any time is found by integrating the above equation and getting *velocity after t seconds = acceleration × t + initial velocity*. Notice that the velocity at a time *t* depends both on the acceleration and the initial velocity, which must be treated as a given. (Initial velocity is an example of a special factor in physics: initial conditions.)

Hundreds of years of testing have verified that the above is one accurate equation. Comparatively, it is far more accurate than the analogous equation for the car's velocity — but not exact. The acceleration is due to gravity, which is almost constant but not quite. We could improve the model by determining a more accurate estimate of gravity based on the object's initial height (gravity's force on an object goes down the further away the object is from the center of the Earth), and also we could try to determine the reverse force due to air resistance as the object rushes through the atmosphere. Still more improvement is possible by evaluating the shape of the object as an airfoil (more aerodynamic shapes have less resistance and fall faster). Even further improvement can be make by adding in factors like air density (at higher altitudes or colder temperatures, air is less dense and therefore causes less resistance). For extreme accuracy, we could consider the object not as one object, but as a mass of smaller objects (molecules) bound together and passing through a medium of other molecules (the atmosphere).

In addition, we could model secondary forces that have only very small contributions: the moon's gravitational force and its contribution to the total force on the falling object, the same contribution for Mars, Venus, Jupiter's smallest moon, Saturn's fourth ring, the debris orbiting Alpha Centauri, all the stars in the Andromeda galaxy, and all the galaxies in the nearest great attractor, or the force from every single last atom in the universe. Overkill? Sure it is for any practical problem. However, we are talking about theoretical results.

Finally, we have the ultimate model of this falling object: It involves every particle in the universe; in order to model this falling object exactly, we have to consider everything. We can't do this in practice, of course — we are talking theoretically. However, let's look at the situation. At this stage we have more objects but similar objects (elementary particles), and these particles all obey the same models, the fundamental laws of quantum theory and relativity. What this means is that we have changed the original problem of modeling large-scale bodies with varying air resistance and gravity to one of modeling many small bodies colliding with many other small bodies. We now have fewer types of equations, but many, many more of them. And we can go on. Molecules are made of atoms, which are composed of smaller entities: electrons, protons, and neutrons. Below that level, we go further until we reach the final level of detail — quarks and fundamental forces like the electroweak and the strong. We think that we know the equations (or at least the general theory) that model the interactions between single particles. The problem then becomes only one of computing the interactions between a universe full of these identical particles, which are governed by identical equations. What is left is computation (a completely impossible amount of it), not modeling.

Consider what would have happened if we had tried a similar exacting approach to developing a final model without breaking the original object and atmosphere into individual particles. Consider the following small effects that must be taken into account: minor rotation effects on the irregular object due to aerodynamic forces, the object's deformation due to opposing gravitational forces from Venus and Jupiter's largest moon, the heating of the atmosphere at the object's altitude due to the moon's reflection, the gravitational gradient on the object due to a solar-sized object traveling at near relativistic speeds in Andromeda, and so on. We don't have exact sets of equations to describe these phenomena. Developing models takes time and experimentation. No one is now interested in some of those effects nor are they likely to be in the future. We are stuck; exactness is beyond us.

The concept of modeling is crucial to the determinism issue: Are all future actions predetermined? Is the universe simply playing out a predestined drama? A discussion of this revolves around the concept of modeling. There seem to be three possible general forms for models of the universe, and the final answer on determinism hinges on which form is true. Possible forms can be categorized as: (1) the model is finite, with a finite number of basic variables and no unmodeled or random outside variables; (2) the model is finite as in case 1 but with random quantum outside influences; and (3) the model is infinitely complex or unknowable in some sense. Case 1 is classical determinism, somewhat discredited today; case 3 covers the other possibilities when truth is infinitely deep and complex or forever unknowable for one of many reasons. What would be a *final theory* then? This would be an instance of case 2: a finite model or set of equations from which all variables could be accounted for. (Note: this does *not* imply determinism. Randomness throws future predictions off.) Currently, physicists do not have a final theory; instead, they have a *standard model*, which might some day grow and change into a final theory. Presently, the standard model is quite a ways off; it still contains 18 numerical parameters whose values need to be determined by experiment, not theory; beyond that, it contains several arbitrary features, and it does not have the concise, elegant form that the famous and powerful theories possess.[4]

Physical theories, especially quantum theory, are so accurate that a hot topic among cosmologists and physicists these days is whether a final theory is just around the corner. This final theory would be the complete set of fundamental equations (a greatly improved standard model) that describe the fundamental particles, the fundamental forces, and all their interactions. In theory, such a set of equations together with the initial conditions of the universe (probably forever unknown to us of course, but this is theory) would suffice to explain all activity in the universe at later times. A top candidate for the honors is a theory called superstrings. This theory envisions several extra dimensions besides our normal four (three space, one time), with some of these dimensions acting like forces. Created originally in the 1960s and extended by John Schwarz of Caltech and Michael Green of Queen Mary College in London, this mathematical theory has caught on with converts like Ed Witten, one of the most brilliant physicists and one of the best mathematical minds around today. Note that a TOE does not say that we can predict all activity at all later times; a final theory's equations probably would have to allow for random quantum effects, which would make exact prediction impossible. Certainly, this is one interesting question, but there is considerable debate about whether current findings are leading toward such a theory or away from it. We will not discuss this until much later, after we have discussed quantum theory and the theory of particles and forces.

Chapter 4

Off the Edge to Infinity

The atoms are in continual motion through all eternity. Moreover, there is an infinite number of worlds, some like this world, others unlike it.

EPICURUS (341–270 B.C.)
Letter to Herodotus

The eternal silence of these infinite spaces terrifies me.

BLAISE PASCAL[1]

Infinity — the mention of the word brings up allusions to other words like eternal, interminable, endless, boring, and unmeasurable. Visions of a choir of angels endlessly repeating every known hymn or of a spaceship traveling through endless space come to mind. While eternal life seems ideal, the thought of heaven as a limitless white landscape with hymnal music constantly filling the air leaves the hope that there be more to life eternal. While the universe seems hopelessly vast, should it be infinite we would seem to be lesser players in its (and our) final destiny. People have thought about infinity for centuries, but in some sense it is still as undefinable, as illusive, as mysterious as ever. Infinity is not a single concept, not a single number, and not a single amount; it needs to be described, and related ideas need to be carefully defined. Infinity describes numbers, the spatial dimensions of the universe, and that concept of final truth — whatever it may be. Infinity is certainly an upper limit, a curtain that we can't hope to see beyond. In this chapter, we will look at two edges of reality: origins and infinite complexity.

Two different infinities will be shown; one, the infinity of the counting numbers, is the infinity of computers in a sense; the other, the infinity of the real numbers, is the infinity of the real world. It is important to see that the infinity of the real world is *larger* than the infinity of computers. This leads later to a proof that digital computers are in a sense computationally limited and cannot exactly determine the real world because of this difference.

The universe is thought to be about 15 billion years old, and the Earth about 4 billion years old, there are about 5 billion people alive today, and an estimated 100 to 500 billion people have lived in the past. As large as these numbers are, they represent no more than an instance in infinity. An average person lives about 70 years; this is about 1/60,000,000th the age of the earth. The iceman frozen in the Alps for 5300 years has lain in his icy tomb for all of recorded history, but only 1/800,000th of the life of the Earth. The age of the universe is about 10^{10} years. The number termed a "googol" is defined as 10^{100}, a totally inconceivable number; a "googolplex," defined as $10^{(googol)}$, goes way past the realm of conceivable numbers into the fathomless void of sets beyond human conception. However, a googolplex is essentially zero when compared to infinity. Symbolically, infinity has been described by ∞ since the seventeenth century; the symbol denotes an endless path looping back upon itself. Tarot cards show infinity as the Juggler or the Magus. Whatever its name or symbol, infinity represents an upper bound, a limit, or an unreachable goal. In this chapter, we start with infinity as it relates to numbers, then go on to infinity as a spatial and time concept.

COUNTABLE SETS

> *There are as many squares as there are numbers because they are just as numerous as their roots.*
>
> GALILEO GALILEI (1632)[2]

Infinity is not a number; you can't add or multiply with it, and as such it difficult to deal with in logical discussions. Nor is infinity a concept that we need for everyday measures or counting. However, our demonstrations of logical limits on computers will make use of infinity by showing problems that require an infinitely long time to compute, and therefore are impossible, and therefore are absolute upper limits on computer thought. Therefore, we need to handle infinity in the way that mathematicians do. The most natural concept of infinity is as an upper bound on the natural numbers (1 2 3 4 . . .). (The way mathematicians view infinity is equivalent; they define infinity as the number of elements in the set of natural numbers.) This definition is easier since there are several "sizes" of infinity, and they are most naturally described in terms of cardinality (size) of sets. Mathematicians have developed the idea of a set being "countable" if it has a one-to-one correspondence with the natural numbers. Most people think of a set as countable if you can count it, presumably in a finite amount of time. This would imply that countable means finite, but mathematicians distinguish between "finite" and "countable" by allowing infinite sets to be countable if they have a one-to-one correspondence with the "counting" numbers — the natural numbers. A one-to-one correspondence means that every element in the set corresponds to some unique positive integer (counting numbers) and, furthermore, that every positive integer corresponds to some element in the set. In other words, every element in the set corresponds to one and only one positive integer.

Infinite sets have properties that seem counterintuitive. The most important property is that an infinite set has subsets that can be put into one-to-one correspondence with themselves. This seems like a contradiction: How can a set that is "larger" than another set have a one-to-one correspondence? Don't you eventually run out of elements in the smaller set and have none left to correspond to the remaining elements in the larger set? The answer is no. Being infinite means never having to run out. This counterintuitive property of infinite sets is the reason that mathematicians have had to develop alternative methods of sizing sets and have had to develop different sizes of infinity. Consider the integers, a set containing all non-negative integers (the counting numbers) and also all of the *negative* numbers. This set seems twice as big as the set of counting numbers, but it can be paired off one-to-one with the counting numbers by the pairing of 0 to 0, then 1 to 1, then 2 to –1, then 3 to 2, then 4 to –2, then 5 to 3, and so on and so forth. Eventually, every positive and negative integer will be paired off with a unique counting number. Mathematicians would say that this proves that the integers are countable.

This property of natural numbers seems strange upon first study. Most of us are familiar with finite sets and their properties; two finite sets — one of which is a proper subset of the other — can never have this property. A one-to-one correspondence is impossible. An infinite set has this additional property that you never run out of numbers if you are pairing up one at a time, and therefore unusual results like this are possible.

Even more pointed is the fact that the rational numbers are countable. For each counting number n, there are two integers: n and $-n$; the fact that we could form a one-to-one pairing between the two sets was interesting but not startling. Between each pair of natural numbers n and $n + 1$ there is an infinite number of rational numbers, and there doesn't seem to be any way that a one-to-one correspondence is possible between sets as disparate as these, but there is.

The hierarchy of numbers is usually the following: natural numbers, integers, rationals, real numbers and then complex numbers. Real numbers combine all integers, rational numbers, and irrational numbers into one set. This set has several interesting properties of its own, but its main application is as the number system of science.

INFINITE TIME, INFINITE SPACE

Is the universe infinite in either time or space? What happened before the Big Bang? These are questions that touch on the problem of infinity in the physical universe. Space is our normal three-dimensional world: up, down, across; time is the fourth dimension. There are many theories about whether either, both, or neither is infinite.

Space and time are normally thought of as infinitely divisible. This means that no matter how short an interval of time, there is always a shorter interval; similarly for space, no matter how small a distance, there always exists a smaller distance. From a mathematical point of view, this is equivalent to assuming that space and time are continuous and must be modeled by the set of real numbers. This has been the most common assumption about space and time for centuries. In the last few decades, the theory of quantum mechanics has raised doubts about this belief. According to theory, the concept of continuous or infinitely divisible time does not hold for time intervals shorter than about 10^{-43} seconds. Astrophysicist John Gribben, author of several books on cosmology, put it this way: "Space and time may not be continuous but rather quantized so that there is a smallest length that can possibly exist and a shortest time that has any meaning."[3] This could impart a granularity to time, a granularity based on a smallest possible time interval or instant. Then the situation could be analogous to the concept of a "cycle" within a computer. In a computer an internal clock ticks away, and computations are only started on a discrete time cycle or instant (e.g., a 50-MHz computer processor has a clock that marks off 50,000,000 cycles per second). No matter what instructions you give the computer, it cannot tell time from its internal clock with any better accuracy than 1 part in 50,000,000 parts. According to quantum theory, an analogous situation also holds for space, that is, there is a smallest distance, and smaller distances than that have no physical meaning. The final word is not in yet; until then, we will still assume that the physical universe is continuous, not discrete. Later, we will speculate about what a discrete universe would be like.

A commonly accepted theory is the Big Bang theory; it assumes that the universe started out as a point, then blew up, rapidly creating all matter and space as we know it. Since the Big Bang about 15 billion years ago, the universe has been expanding. Many physicists think that eventually gravity will slow the outward expansion, stop it, and then start a contraction phase that will continue until all matter contracts back to a point (called the Big Crunch). An alternative view has the expansion continuing forever. In the first case, time is finite in duration, and space is finite in extent. In the alternative view, time can extend indefinitely, and the extent of space is undetermined. These two alternatives imply that the universe will end in fire (Big Crunch) or ice (infinite expansion means a cool-down). If there is a contraction phase ending in a Big Crunch, what happens afterward is only conjecture. Maybe nothing at all; it could simply mean the end of everything that we know of: no more space, no more time, no more matter, no more life for ever and ever. Maybe there is a rebound effect, and another Big Bang takes place; some theories conjecture a repeating series.

The Big Bang explains a great deal of the phenomena that we see in the universe, but we cannot see before it or after the "Big Crunch," when the universe collapses on itself. These initial conditions are limits that blind us.

Even more speculative are theories about other universes or what lies outside our universe. The most popular conjecture has our universe as one of many bubble universes in a meta-universe formed like an endless sea of bubble universes. We will discuss this more in the later chapter "The Beginning and the End." Researchers like Stephen Hawking have developed plausible mathematical arguments that support the creation of these bubble universes out of the fabric of space–time. Each universe is completely and eternally isolated from all others; each universe may or may not be inhabited; each universe follows out its own destiny.

Anyhow, our universe is finite in both past time and space: Whatever lies outside is forever invisible to us; whatever came before is forever lost to us. It all begs the question of a creator. Pope Pius XII once mentioned the Big Bang as proof of the biblical account of Genesis. The Big Bang is consistent with the biblical account, as current theory says that both space and time began at that exact instant and that time did not exist before the Big Bang. Traditional Judeo-Christian belief holds that God existed outside our universe and created our universe.

This is a good place to address the issue of religion and science. Throughout much of the book are many theories about the mind and the universe. Underlying them all are two implicit assumptions: first, we live in a four-dimensional universe (three space dimensions, one time dimension), and, second, calculations and computations must be done at a finite speed. There are important implications here. First, science is based on observations, and theoretical models are made to agree with the observations. If there are really hidden dimensions, then we don't have everything accounted for in our physics models. Second, we are limited by finite speed and cannot draw logical inferences from an infinite number of axioms or draw inferences that require an infinite number of steps to calculate. Our logic can't even handle this situation. Throughout much of the book, we will be making the standard assumptions about space–time, and our limits will be based on them. As such, they form a different set of axioms than religion, and most religious statements can't be judged in this context.

Currently, many physicists (Professor Hawking for one) believe that the physical laws and constants that determine our universe were formed along with the Big Bang. Anything "outside" our bubble universe might be different — perhaps quite different, maybe so different that Einstein's theories don't hold. Also, many researchers studying superstrings believe that there might be more than four dimensions, but we can't observe the others. It would be consistent with Judeo-Christian belief that God could reside outside any bubble universe. If infinite speed of calculation were available there, then our limits would not necessarily apply; if information or influence or something unknown could be sent to us from there via unobservable dimensions, then many things would change.

In the last chapter, we will relax the standard assumptions and speculate about what-ifs for the "big" questions about the universe, free will, computers, and God. As Einstein once said: "Science without religion is lame, religion without science is blind."

HOW COMPLEX IS THE UNIVERSE?

The last type of infinity is the complexity of the physical laws that govern the universe. Does the universe have infinite information content, or can it can be described by a finite amount of information? *Described by a finite amount of information* means that a finite number of physical laws and constants would be suffi-

FIGURE 1. A nineteenth-century realists' dream: the universe completely determined by a finite set of equations or laws. It fit well with the science and religion of the time, but it is coming apart under twentieth-century scientific scrutiny.

cient to describe the past and future of the universe. Description does not necessarily mean prediction of the future, which may not be a computable quantity, but it means that all actions are determined by a finite set of physical laws. Earlier, we saw that the information content of a random number was infinite; quantum mechanics theory requires random numbers to describe the position of elementary particles — this seems to argue for an infinite information content. The finite information content was a dream of the nineteenth-century realists who hoped to describe the entire universe in a set of physical laws that were present from the beginning of time.

In the previous chapter we touched upon a favorite idea in cosmological circles today: a TOE, or theory of everything. TOEs envision the universe being explainable in a few or at least a finite number of basic equations. Other phenomena could have equations that explain them, but supposedly these equations are derived from the TOE equations. For example, basic quantum-level equations could be used to predict atom-level interactions; then these predictions could be combined to predict interactions between molecules, which in turn could predict chemical reactions, leading to a prediction of large-scale phenomena such as star development and eventually weather and biological development. But TOEs are models for understanding, not precise prediction. TOEs will never predict the stock market or the weather, and certainly not a human thought.

The edges of reality stand in the way of such a program. First, upper limits on calculation and chaos could prohibit such enormous calculations. We already saw that 100! calculations or operations are impossibly many. When the TOE equations are applied to all the particles and forces necessary for exact prediction, then the number of mathematical operations required would greatly exceed this 100! limit. Even if we analyze and guess the exact form of the equations of a TOE, we can never use it to determine the state of everything — there are way, way too many operations required. Second, upper limits on logic could prevent us from ever discovering the necessary theory, and third, quantum randomness seems to prohibit such a program anyway. Also, the model of the universe might be infinitely complex; instead of having a few equations from which equations explaining all other phenomena can be derived, there might be an infinite number of equations needed.

In later chapters we will meet several other theories that conjecture about the underlying structure of space–time and the number and type of equations that describe the motion of particles in the universe. Many physicists believe in an infinitely divisible space–time with a finite set of defining equations; others believe that the information content of the universe is infinitely rich and variable so that only an *infinite* number of equations can describe it. We will consider these conjectures later in the discussion about free will. Another, smaller group of physicists believe in a discrete nature to space–time with a completely random underlying structure and equations that make order at the macro level out of disorder at the micro level. We will consider this conjecture later in our discussions about chaos and cellular automatons. The realists' dream of the nineteenth century is rapidly coming apart.

Chapter 5

Jagged Edges — Limited by Chaos

There is no such thing as chance; and what seems to us the merest accident springs from the deepest source of destiny.

SCHILLER[1]

Chaos often breeds life ...

HENRY ADAMS[2]

Nineteenth-century scientists spoke of a coming dawn of understanding, because so much progress was being made in modeling nature with mathematical formulas and discoveries were happening in many areas, from evolution to electricity. Reality was felt to be rational, measurable, and most of all predictable;

any randomness in our models of nature was felt to be caused by a lack of precision in the mathematical models. Also, scientists felt that this lack would disappear shortly when more modern measuring tools were available. Now, late in the twentieth century, most scientists feel that we will never predict nature exactly; they feel that there is an intrinsic random nature to the physical world that can never be entirely overcome by better measurements. *Chaos theory* is the study of uncertainty and unpredictability in mathematics and nature; it is defined as the study of stochastic behavior occurring in a deterministic system. Chaos is an edge of reality. It seems completely unavoidable. Even if the equations of reality were known perfectly, we probably couldn't predict future occurrences exactly because of chaotic systems. This limits our ability to know the future even if we understand the past exactly.

There are two key aspects to this chaos theory: Seeming randomness can give rise to order, while order when studied very closely seems quite random. The one that affects us most is the order-to-randomness aspect that seems to be an intrinsic part of nature. Before, reality was felt to be entirely predictable, and the more accurate the measurement, the more accurate the prediction; now we know that certain deterministic mathematical processes are unpredictable at all levels of measurements. Later in the chapter we will see a classic and important example of this unpredictability of a deterministic, well-modeled system — the weather-prediction problem. The second key aspect, randomness giving rise to order, is invoked by many physicists in describing one of the more perplexing cosmological problems — how something as ordered as life could arise from something as random as the initial distribution of elementary particles in the cosmos.

Randomness giving rise to order? Most scientists agree that this is what has occurred in the universe. First, from the randomness of a primeval soup came clouds of gases that formed stars; elements like carbon and iron were formed; then, skipping ahead a few billion years, amino acids were formed, then small, one-celled, self-reproducing microorganisms, then more complex sea creatures, eventually mammals, and then finally us. We are the biological embodiment of an information system — order, order, order.

ITERATION

Chaos is modeled by a mathematical process called *iteration*, which repeatedly evaluates a function in a special way (iteration in real life will be shown in the next section). Iteration starts with a given number (called the initial condition) and evaluates the function at this number. A value is obtained; this value is the next number that the function is evaluated at; again a value is obtained, and the third evaluation of the function is at this second number obtained. The iteration process continues this way: A function is evaluated at the number that was the value obtained from the most recent evaluation of the function. Simple enough, but often great advances spring forth from simple ideas.

The point is that the output from one evaluation of the function is the input for the next evaluation of the function. The sequence of numbers is the object of interest. Let's look at some examples. Let the function be $x + 1$. Then, if we start at 2, the sequence is 2, 3, 4, 5, . . ., which is very predictable. If the function is x^2, then the sequence is 2, 4, 16, 256, . . ., which predictably grows immensely at each iteration. Another example is $2x^2 - 1$, a function that will result in an essentially random series of numbers for certain starting numbers. To see this, start with some number between 0 and 1 and iterate for a while. Different outcomes are possible; a sequence might take on a random nature, or a sequence might get caught up in a never-ending repetition of a few numbers. Another example that has great practical significance is where two different initial conditions are *very, very* close in value, but the two iterated sequences differ greatly after a few iterations. This is the paradox of weather prediction — weather measurements can be ever so close to the true values but after a few days the prediction is widely off the mark.

The point of this is that order in the form of simple, deterministic nonlinear functions like $2x^2 - 1$ can give iterated sequences that are seemingly random. The outcomes depend on the initial conditions, and even having nearly equal initial conditions doesn't guarantee nearly equal sequences. If this aspect of mathematical iteration were simply a mathematical trick, then we could take note of it and go on our way. It isn't. Our knowledge of our physical universe is modeled by fairly simple deterministic equations that are usually nonlinear; mathematical iteration is like the process of evaluating the values of these model equations at future times — prediction by modeling. Predicting the future of physical processes is subject to the same whims of chaos as our $2x^2 - 1$ example. It can be very bad! Professor Paulos noted that "these nonlinear systems demonstrate a surprising complexity that seems to arise even when the systems are defined by quite elementary rules and equations."[3] Furthermore, he pointed out that chaotic, nonlinear systems are not rare by any means. He quoted mathematician Stanislaw Ulam's remark that calling chaos theory "nonlinear science" is like calling zoology "the study of non-elephant animals."

MANDELBROT SETS

Benoit Mandelbrot is a mathematician who worked for IBM during the late 1950s and early 1960s; his work encompassed a variety of disciplines and addressed such seemingly disparate phenomena as turbulence, stock market randomness, the frequencies of words in writing, errors in transmitted signals, and others. He started seeing a relationship between all these areas; there seemed to be a geometric pattern to irregular phenomena.[4] Mandelbrot captured his own ideas about these patterns in the word *fractal*, which he coined in his 1975 book *The Fractal Geometry of Nature*. The word has the flavor of fragmented or fractured, both adjectives that are often used to describe chaotic patterns. One of the most famous mathematical graphs is the

Mandelbrot set; it was first discovered by Mandelbrot in 1979 and has been admired by millions since then. The set is a result of the mathematical iteration process: A method of plotting the points comes from iterating a function $z^2 + c$. Here, both z and c represent complex numbers; the Mandelbrot set is the set of values of c for which the iteration converges after starting at $z = 0$. This function is simple as mathematical formulas go; the fact that the output of the iteration process is so intricate astonishes us at first. Some researchers believe that parts of the physical universe operate the same way, with simple processes being iterated to form extremely complex results.

The Mandelbrot set is extremely rich in structure no matter what scale it is viewed at, as illustrated in Figure 2. You can magnify one part continually (zoom in) and the structure is still rich and complex — different perhaps, but still extremely intricate. Most important, the set repeats in a sense: Deep down inside the patterns is another complete-in-every-detail Mandelbrot set. Thus, there are Mandelbrot sets within Mandelbrot sets within Mandelbrot sets *ad infinitum.* Another lesson learned from this set is that boundaries need not be smooth; we think of coastlines as smooth, but the more closely you examine them, the less smooth they become. The Mandelbrot set has an infinitely complex boundary between the points that are in the set and those that are not.

Mandelbrot coined the word *fractal* to describe a geometric object that has detailed, intricate structure over a very large range. (A rocky mountain is an example of a fractal: It has rocky surfaces of widely different sizes at different angles to a viewer. When light reflects off it, you get a wide range of detail.) The scale of objects within the observable universe ranges from distances between galaxies (millions of light-years) to the radius of atoms and even further — essentially all scales. Humans, however, can only easily conceive of a small range of scales — from millimeters to miles, for instance. Our minds can't perceive all the features of a thing much bigger than Earth or smaller than a cell. We humans tend to lump together features over a large

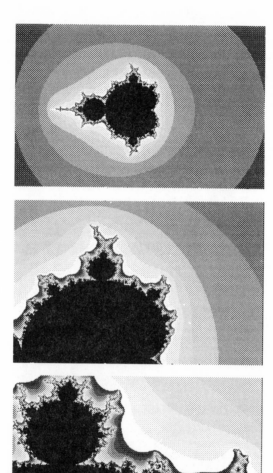

FIGURE 2. The Mandelbrot set (top) and two successively larger enlargements.

range of scale simply because of our lack of ability to perceive them all at once. This is not a problem for most day-to-day phenomena, but for others we can miss a lot. A coastline is a fractal that most of us are familiar with. The Mandelbrot set truly has intricate detail over a range of scale that extends to the infinitely small.

PHYSICAL PROCESSES AND ITERATION

Schrödinger's equation, Maxwell's equations, some of Newton's laws, much of the theory of relativity, and many more equations of physics are differential or integral equations that describe the state of a physical system. A *mathematical model of a system* is a set of one or more state variable equations. A state variable of a physical system is a variable that represents some measurable quantity, such as position, velocity, potential, or charge. The variable is usually a function or continuous dependent variable of other parameters (independent variables), such as "time" or "position." Therefore, the variable can be differentiated or partially differentiated; often the state equations are differential equations. In order to calculate the future state of a system, we face the task of integrating differential equations — a difficult and tricky mathematical process. This is not the place to discuss this process; it usually takes an entire graduate course in mathematics to explain properly. (An extended aside for those interested in the math: The fundamental step is an approximation to a differential that turns out to be an iterated equation. Recall that the derivative of a function is a limit that in turn is approximated by a differential function. By using differential equations or the differential approximation, we can "integrate forward" and estimate the value of the state variable at a future time. The approximation equation works by choosing a small delta time and solving for the value at that point, then continuing this process until the desired future time is reached.) (A shorter aside: "Integrating backward" is possible and is often used to pinpoint the exact day and time of historically known astronomical events such as total solar eclipses in 2553 B.C.)

A problem comes up in calculations like the weather-prediction calculation. Real weather parameters such as wind speed, temperature, and humidity go through a truncation process before they go to a digital computer. Measurement instruments have an inherent maximum precision of their own: They measure the parameters to a certain accuracy (such as four decimal places) and no further. This is not the computer's fault; it can certainly handle data much more precise than that. But this is the data accuracy that the computer starts with; chaotic behavior eventually sets in, and the weather predictions start to diverge from reality.

WEATHER FORECASTING — CHAOS IN PRACTICE

A meteorology researcher named Lorenz was working with a mathematical weather model in the 1960s. One day he wanted to study a particular weather simulation over a longer time duration than he had done the day before. In order to save time, he used the answers that he had obtained halfway through and restarted the computer simulation at that point. (This was and still is a common computer practice; after all, why use the computer to compute numbers that it has already computed before?) Also, in order to save time entering numbers Lorenz rounded off the numbers to three significant figures — after all, how much difference could one part in a thousand make? Lorenz fully expected the same answers from the first and second simulations over the common time duration. Amazingly enough, the simulations looked nothing alike after a short time. James Glick, author of *Chaos*, interviewed Lorenz and told this part of the story: "In the computer's memory, six decimal places were stored: .506127. On the printout, to save space, just three appeared: .506. Lorenz had entered the shorter, rounded off numbers."[5]

In other words, the predicted weather for two days hence depends on the accuracy of measurements to a disturbing degree. A temperature measurement of 47.1° versus the real temperature of 47.13° might be enough to change a prediction from "clear skies and sunny" to "rain." Or if the wind gauge reads 11.2 mph but the wind actually is 11 mph, a low-pressure system might not move fast enough to intersect a cold front at a certain location, and the resulting weather will be much different than predicted. This means that accurate long-range weather prediction is impossible (with current tools) because the weather is too sensitive to small changes (or measurement errors) in the initial conditions (initial measurements). Small errors in the initial conditions lead to larger calculated errors (from the true values) for the weather a mile or an hour away. In turn, these errors lead to still larger errors for weather a continent or a day away. The errors propagate, and eventually the model predicts a pleasant day whereas the weather serves up a blizzard.

A Cray X-MP supercomputer can do the calculations that will give an accurate, complete forecast for one hemisphere in less than an hour. It can forecast fairly accurately about three to four days in the future; the forecasts are better and more accurate farther out if there are no sudden changes in weather patterns.

A mathematical prediction of weather patterns involves a series of measurements (temperature at altitudes, barometric pressure, wind direction and speed, etc.) at many points. These points need to be reasonably closely spaced. The mathematical model involves a set of interrelated equations based on functions like *Temp*(lat, long, time), where *Temp* is the temperature at position "lat" = latitude and "long" = longitude, at "time" = a designated time. (Other independent variables such as altitude above ground level could also be considered, but for simplicity these are enough.) There are other functions like *Pres*, which is the barometric pressure for the same independent variables, or humidity *Humi* or wind speed *Wind*.

The weather-prediction situation has two components: first, a weather model and, second, a set of measurements of today's weather, such as *Temp*(lat, long, now). From these known facts, the weather model is extrapolated to the future (say, 2 days), and the predicted weather is the predicted value of these same weather model functions, such as *Temp*(lat, long, now + 2 days).

The procedure for this result is as follows. Compute the model at now + 1 hour by using the model and current weather measurements, then, using the weather model and these predicted values as the current weather measurements, compute the model at now + 2 hours, and continue until now + 48 hours (2 days).

Remember that one-part-in-a-thousand roundoff of Lorenz that made such a big difference. Later termed the "butterfly" effect, it means that very small fluctuations in the atmosphere in one area can change the weather dramatically in another area from what it would have been without the fluctuation (the term refers to the possibility that the small changes wrought by a butterfly flapping its wings might change future weather patterns). A variation of 1/1000th might substantially change the weather prediction for a few days hence; a variation of 1/100,000th might change it for a month in advance. Smaller errors take longer to propagate. For example, stand outside and vigorously wave a magazine in the air for several seconds. Because of this and only this action on your part, it may happen that five weeks from now the calm clear weather that Hong Kong would have had otherwise will now become a killer typhoon that wreaks havoc on the harbor and kills hundreds. On the other hand, the situation might be reversed, and your magazine waving might save hundreds of lives (both possibilities are quite remote, of course). Very small changes in initial conditions can lead to large perturbations in the weather. In the above case, two possible initial conditions are (1) today's weather and (2) today's weather plus you flapping a magazine outside. In five weeks the result of these two possibilities could be (1) calm weather in Hong Kong or (2) a killer typhoon in Hong Kong.

As with the Mandelbrot set, it is astonishing that a simple and deterministic set of equations like the weather model could behave like this. But it's true, and, even worse, this is not an isolated example; many other physical, biological, and economic systems exhibit the same chaotic behavior. The models that we have seen so far were *exact*; they were just exact mathematical equations. Still they exhibited chaotic behavior that eventually made their solutions very inexact. Chaos from order and order from chaos are intrinsic properties of nature. Next, we will look at another form of chaos where the model is not exact and where small changes trigger enormous shifts — the stock market.

CHAOS ON WALL STREET

The stock market is one of the most interesting, most discussed, and most analyzed systems in our lives. Dow Jones averages, S&P 500 indexes, trading volume, advancing and declining issues are widely understood terms outside Wall Street; the market affects us all, and most all of us know something about it. Many of us think that we know a lot about it; very few of us can predict its behavior. Many of us believe that we can make money by spending time analyzing trend lines or the underlying economic fundamentals; the fact is that most of us that invest *do* make money because, unlike gambling, the stock market is not a zero-sum game. The long-term market trend is to increase, and so the average investor can make money, often more than other forms of investment would yield. But the stock market is chaotic.

A way of expressing the chaos butterfly effect in quasi-math notation is to use the notation $f(cause) = effect$ from the earlier discussion about models. An example is the fictitious formula $f(trading\ volume, advancing\ issues, prime\ rate) = next\ day's\ Dow\ Jones$ average (completely fictitious, but it shows the idea). The butterfly effect occurs when a small change in one variable causes a large change in the dependent variables. In this notation $f(cause + small\ change) = effect + large\ change$. This is chaotic behavior. In the fictitious formula, a very small change in trading volume with everything else staying the same has the possible effect of triggering a large swing in the next day's Dow Jones average. The stock market often exhibits this type of chaotic behavior; recall the stock market crash of 1987 of more than 500 points. Clearly, the underlying fundamental forces driving the stock market did not change that much from one day to the next; however, something changed, and it triggered a massive stock market shift. The market is very people-driven: Desires, fears, analyses, and hunches all play a role in price determination. Exact value is never known for any stock; its value is simply the prevailing price. Slight mood changes or perceptions about a stock can precipitate large moves in price.

Everyone's goal is to make money in the stock market; stories, systems, and wild claims abound. The truth is elusive; one fact is indisputable: The market increases over time. Another fact seems almost indisputable too: The market is nearly random. Over many years, common stocks have increased in value faster than bonds or straight savings. There have been years in which the average value actually fell; there have been years in which stock increases were below inflation. But there have been big years too; in the last ten years there have been at least three years in which most of the growth stock funds returned close to 25% — that makes up for a lot of inflation.

Random behavior of individual stock prices and day-to-day market movements underlies a long-term upward trend. However, this randomness is so pervasive and substantial that it almost overwhelms prediction models for trading systems. Stories on Wall Street tell about trading systems that beat the market or made a million overnight. Some interesting ones involve darts. Once, a reporter for a newspaper decided to hold a stock-picking contest for a continuing report on the stock market. Rules were simple: Everyone started with an equal amount of pretend money and could make all the imaginary buys and sells that he or she wanted to; the person having the most pretend money at the end of the year won. One entrant was the reporter himself; his method was to pin the New York Stock Exchange daily listing on his office door, back up ten feet, and throw darts at it. Where they stuck, he invested. He won, and so did the random-market theories.

On another occasion, Congress was looking into the management fees charged by mutual fund managers. These fees are for providing investment services to investors in the funds. The theory is that investment managers with proximity to the Wall Street beat, who have years of experience investing, who know secret technical analysis methods for finding market breaks ahead of time, who simply know more than the average investor, are probably able to beat the market for the benefit of their fund's investors. To invest money with such management, you must pay a fee for investment services. Congress was questioning the high fees charged by some firms. Some witnesses said that the market was rather random and quoted dart-throwing examples as evidence (this darts experiment has been tried many times). New Hampshire Senator Thomas McIntyre was on the Senate Banking Committee at the time, and he tried the experiment himself right then, right there. He put up the stock market listing from ten years earlier, tossed some darts, and turned a hypothetical profit of over 250%, beating almost every fund manager's performance.[6]

Stock market "models" come in a variety of forms, none of which are clearly in the classical cause–effect or $f(cause) = effect$ form. One reason for this is the data; most data are not clearly either a cause or an effect but some combination of both. For instance, trading volume on the New York Stock Exchange and the Tokyo Exchange is a highly regarded indicator of future trends; however, it is also a function or effect of the previous day's trading conditions. It is a time-series data set, both partial cause and partial effect. The same is true for advancing/declining issues or the S&P 500 index. Rough models are that low P/E (price-to-earnings ratio) stocks have done better over a period of many years; stocks of smaller companies have also done better. However, when trends like these are published and widely known, people become aware and perhaps change their investment patterns. In turn, this drives up the prices of stocks of these preferred companies, making their stock less attractive. For example, during the early 1980s, studies were published that showed that the stock of small companies (capitalization of $5 million or less) increased in value much faster than the stock of large companies (capitalization of over $1 billion). This led many investors to emphasize small-company stocks in their portfolios and hence perhaps overvalue them, which to some extent has lessened or negated the small-company-advantage trend, judging by some data from the mid-1990s.

These rough models are longer-term models, and they are general statements that apply to the stock market as a whole; they may or may not forecast one specific company's stock price movement. For shorter-term models/indicators, statistical analysis has shown that the last trading day and the first four trading days of each month plus every Friday have shown better average performance than the other days over a period of several years.[7] A caution — you can't buy stocks at low prices before these days and then sell them at high prices later, since the average gain over these preferred days is a small fraction of the brokerage fee that you have to pay to buy and sell stocks. Modeling aspects of the stock market is barely possible; a large-scale, semiaccurate stock market model, like a weather-prediction model, is out of the question.

Victor Sperandeo has been a professional trader and money manager for 25 years; in 1971 he founded Ragnar Options Corporation and he has frequently appeared on investment programming on TV. In addition, he is the author of the best-seller *Trader Vic — Methods of a Wall Street Master*. He speaks from experience, not mathematical models or theories; in his world the proof is not in a theory but on the bottom line. His comments show just how difficult it is to model any part of the stock market successfully: "From the outset, I disagreed with the concept of using mathematical models for options pricing," and "Market psychology drives the price more than time does, which is why mathematical models fail. You can't make money predicting the past."[8]

Investor awareness is an issue that we touched upon; when profitable patterns are published, many jump on the bandwagon, which in turn drives up prices, making the stock less attractive. This investor awareness is thought to be a major contributor to stock market chaos; many believe that, because information, patterns, and data become public knowledge so quickly, investors act almost instantly, and this helps to cause the rapid changes that are so commonplace on Wall Street. According to one school of thought, this quick dissemination of information means that all available information about a stock is already reflected in the stock price. In other words, first, data are almost instantly available about the different stocks, general market trends, government policies and rates, and so on, and, second, these data are analyzed quickly by thousands of analysts and computers. Based on these two facts, this school of thought believes that information predicting how a company will be doing in three months is already reflected today in its common stock price. For example, a company can be losing money this quarter but its common stock price is skyrocketing because analysts believe that in three months it will be turning large profits. Known as the "efficient market hypothesis," this belief is usually considered together with another theory called the "random walk theory" (discovered almost 100 years ago by a Frenchman, Louis Bachelier). Together, they relate to the possibility of developing a technical trading system that will outperform the market (meaning that it will average a higher return than the S&P 500, a good proxy for the market). This technical analysis system would be based on a market model and publicly available price data. One important corollary is that this school of thought believes that no trading system that is based on price data alone can outperform the market. In short, it believes that you can't estimate future prices by looking at past prices. (Of course, there are thousands of professional market analysts who disagree. However, in only 5 of the last 15 years have a majority of the mutual funds beaten the S&P 500. Part of this is due to the fees that are subtracted off, but part of this is because the experts aren't so expert.)

In the stock market, prices are not always driven by stock conditions: Sometimes people want something to happen and buy and sell with that goal, not because of the underlying value of the stock or commodity. For example, a group of rich investors may buy big and attempt to corner the market in some commodity and sell back at higher prices later, or a company may be subject to a hostile takeover because it has a large amount of cash on hand or owns lucrative side businesses that could be sold for profit. In cases like these, the buyers are looking beyond the current value of the stock or commodity and planning what they can do after they have control to increase (maybe only temporarily) the value of the purchase.

Chaos and this underlying random nature make it almost impossible to model the stock market well; it is very difficult to develop even rudimentary models/indicators of future market trends. Compared to the weather-prediction situation, stock market forecasting is way behind. Weather has a known model that is accurate yet calculation-intensive and dependent upon timely, closely spaced weather observations. The main drawback is the large amount of computer power required to calculate a day or two in the future. A "prediction" in the weather forecasting business would be the weather at each grid of a map. If you have the computer power and good enough data then you can probably predict with good accuracy; the model is accurate enough to allow this. Predictions further out like weeks or months are nearly impossible, however. There are no known methods for doing the equivalent predictions for the stock market.

101

Chapter 6

Computers — the Thinking Machines

As soon as an Analytical Engine exists, it will necessarily guide the future course of the science.

CHARLES BABBAGE (1864)[1]

10101010101010101010101010101010101010101

Computers are a recent arrival on the historical scene, appearing only in the last half-century. Our dependence on them has grown as they have become more powerful, and we are rapidly approaching the day when computers will supplant many human workers in intrinsically human tasks such as planning, design, writing, and many others. Our main goal in the next few chapters is to understand the ultimate power and limitations of computers; for instance, are there absolute limitations on computers or will they continue to grow indefinitely in analytical ability? Different topics will fit into the final analysis: the analogy between the human brain and computers, a mathematical representation of computer operations, data representations, artificial intelligence and chess-playing computers, and proofs of the ultimate limits of computing. The edge of reality that we concentrate on in this chapter and the next chapter is upper limits of calculation. Computer programs are not infinite in power in a definable way. Upper limits on calculation can be proven by results developed in this chapter. In effect, computers can compute numbers in the infinity of integers and rational numbers; computers cannot compute *exactly* with real numbers since many of them have infinite information content (e.g., are random).

Eventually, we want to consider the ultimate power of computers and human thought. Until 1931 very little was known about the ultimate limits of reasoning; in that year Gödel proved his famous result. In the next few years the study of logic and the theory of computers grew rapidly with several important discoveries by researchers like Alan Turing and Alonzo Church.

There are two theories that set upper limits on computers and reasoning: the Halting theorem and Gödel's incompleteness theorem. In order to understand these results, a mathematical encoding of a computer program is needed; this is the main goal of this chapter. The chapter starts with a general discussion of computers and programming. After a brief discussion of data encoding, the main result of the chapter is introduced. The reader can look ahead to the end of the chapter to see an example of the mathematical encoding of a computer program.

COMPUTER OPERATIONS

Historically, computers weren't invented by any one person or at any time or place; instead, they evolved. Two mechanical computing instruments, the abacus and the astrolabe (a navigation tool), were used 2000 years ago by the Chinese and the Europeans, respectively. Still, the first recognizable digital device was developed by French scientist Blaise Pascal in 1642 to help tax collection. This device could only add; later improvements led to devices that could multiply, subtract, and divide, too. In 1822, Charles Babbage, a mathematics professor, designed an automatic calculating machine, which he called a "difference engine." It was a leap forward as it could do long strings of calculations without human intervention. A few years later, Babbage designed the first program-controlled computer, which he named his "analytic engine." This was to be very similar to modern general-purpose computers; it had built-in operations, and it could make simple decisions and change the program steps based on the result. Unfortunately, an "analytic engine" was never completed; it was a great idea and it could solve many problems, except in the 1830s no one much cared if these problems were solved or not.

After this, progress came in small jumps: from punched-card program control to mechanical relay computers to the first high-speed electronic computer, ENIAC, which helped the military in World War II. From the 1950s on, progress has been made at ever-increasing rates, until today you can walk into a neighborhood store and for less than $1,000 buy the kind of computing power that scientists of just 20 years ago could only dream of.

Computers come in many different sizes and designs: They range from small PCs that fit on a desk (or your lap) to super-computers (like the large Crays) that require their own housing, cooling system, and support team to function. Different as they are, they all still have common features that allow us to discuss them in general terms. Our discussion will consider a simple generic computer system with a processor unit, input and output devices, and memory. The diagram in Figure 3 depicts this generic computer system. It shows four main components or functional entities of a general system. The processor unit is where all the processing or computational and logic hardware resides: adders, multiplying units, logic gates, and more. Above to the right is a box depicting input/output devices, meaning disk drives, mouse input devices, or a keyboard — any means

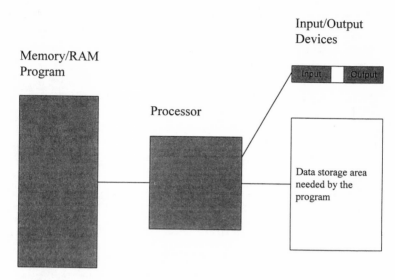

FIGURE 3. A graphical representation of a computer system. Later we will need a numerical representation for a computer program, and this diagram is the intermediate step between a real computer and a very, very large number.

of getting data into or out of computer memory. Computer memory shows up in two places in the diagram. The left-hand side is memory (usually RAM) that will hold the program; now the instructions of a program will not take up the entire memory area (usually), so some can be reserved for storage of values needed by the program. The large box on the lower right-hand side represents the leftover RAM and hard disk storage; this area is necessary for the values that computer programs need to do their function.

Other devices that can connect to a system are audio devices (sound boards and microphones), pointing devices (a mouse), and scanners. Analogies with humans come in at this point: A computer system alone is like the brain, a mouse is like a measuring or pointing appendage (a finger), scanners are like human eyes, and the audio devices are like a voice and ears. With the aid of external devices such as these, a computer can be "plugged into its environment," "aware" of processes, and able to respond to events. Abilities like these make computer systems the ideal process controllers in a variety of industrial situations; for instance, they can automatically check units on the assembly line or respond instantly to changes in chemical or nuclear processes — far faster than humans. Computers switch traffic lights, monitor hospital patients, print out and mail bills, control car brakes and engines, and much more. More and more, computer-driven systems replace human activities. All this brings inevitable questions. Where does it end? Can computers eventually supplant people in all mental activities, or is there a limitation of computers that humans do not have? Whether humans have some innate intellectual talent that computers can never develop is an issue that we will explore. Exploring ultimate computational limitations is our goal for the next few chapters. The answer will be that computers have limits in a real definable sense (humans too), but the answer will take some development.

To answer these questions, we need to delve into the computer process in some detail. Recent scientific thought views the computer process more generally than simply as electricity running through microchips. Or as computer researcher Stephen Wolfram from the Institute for Advanced Study at Princeton said: "Physical systems are viewed as computational systems, processing information much the way computers do."[2] Such analogies are not restricted to physical systems; some believe that mental activity can be modeled as a computer process. Roger Penrose of Oxford University, the author of two books that attempt to refute this position, has this to say: "The belief seems to be widespread that, indeed, 'everything is a digital computer' . . . this need not be the case."[3] A large part of this book will explore this idea; we will need a good understanding of different aspects of the computational process to accomplish this.

For all that computers can do, for all the speed and computational power that they possess, they have only three basic capabilities. First, computers can move data from one place to another; second, computers can do arithmetic and comparison operations on data; and, third, computers can decide between two (or more) future operations based on data values — they make decisions.

PROGRAMS

Programs are the means for accomplishing tasks: Computer programs are lists of instructions that computers follow to calculate some result. A program is not just a simple straight-line list of instructions; variations are possible depending on data values and decisions. Programs (software) embody the "thinking" aspect of computer usage. Like an intelligent person deciding what to do next (a decision) based on the current situation (the data) and his background knowledge (a theory, equations, or a model), computers make calculations with data and base their next instruction on the results.

One of the most important, yet often overlooked, facets of computers is the programming language. A programming language is the tool by which a computer solves a problem. Hundreds of millions of person-hours per year are spent programming computers; the easier it is to code, the more efficient the process is. A 10% savings between languages is an enormous savings in time; studies have shown that 10% is a very low figure — the productivity gap between some languages can be 300% or 400%. Simple arithmetic shows potential savings in the billions. An easy-to-code, easy-to-debug, easy-to-update programming language is everyone's goal. Historically, two of the earliest languages dominated the scene for several decades: FORTRAN, the scientific language, and COBOL, the business-oriented language. Both went through several updates or versions that improved them. However, both came to be seen as unsatisfactory during the 1960s and 1970s, for reasons of inflexibility and difficulty of maintenance. During this time, many program language designers made an effort to construct languages without the inefficiencies that they saw in the main languages.

One of the most successful designers is Niklaus Wirth of Zurich. He is best known for creating Pascal, a widely used language today, which has been the language of choice for teaching computer programming for several years. Although programming gurus like Wirth may not be household names, they save society billions of dollars by developing fast, easy-to-use programming tools. To see this just consider the difference in ease of use of the word-processor software of today compared to that of 1985, or spreadsheet software or database software. Everything does more and does it faster; all the time saved adds up to billions of dollars.

We need to quantify computer programs for our study of ultimate computer limitations. In order to do this, we need to be very specific in our definitions of software coding, input/output, and the other values needed for the final calculation. To this end of a numerical representation, the diagram in Figure 3 illustrates the location of the program, the input/output, and the location of the other data values that the program needs. Lines of code (the program instructions) would be in the left-hand box (the memory), and the input/output appears in the upper right-hand box. The center box, the processor or CPU, doesn't play a big role in what follows: We assume that it will be able and available to calculate whatever we ask. The large box on the lower right stores values computed by the software and needed later in the calculation. It is an important part of our development, and our examples will trace the step-by-step activity in this box. Besides the program put in by the user, the computer has programs that are always running in the background. One of these assigns storage locations in memory for the values or variables that our program develops. This program preassigns the variable's storage location before our program runs, and the variable keeps this location throughout the execution of the program.

A programming language comprises two main parts: a set of reserved words or symbols that mean something very specific to the computer and a syntax (a method of writing commands) that also means something very specific to the computer. Emphasis is on strictly specific instructions and narrowly defined limits of allowable syntax. For our purposes, we will use an English-like language similar to Basic or Pascal. There is no need to introduce the entire language; only a small set of instruction types needs to be discussed for our purposes. The set contains at least one instruction of each of the following classes: data movement, calculation, and decisions. The statement *read(items, price)* is a data movement statement: It reads two data values (numbers or characters) from an input device (could be a disk drive file or someplace else) and then moves the values to the storage locations in computer memory known as *items* and *price*. The statement *cost = items * price* is a calculation statement: This calculates the expression to the right of the equal sign; the equal sign means that the result moves to the variable or storage location on the left-hand side. This, the data values in the storage locations *items* and *price* are multiplied together, and the result then moves to the storage location *cost*. The compound statement *if items > 7 then price = 2 else price = 3* is a decision statement: The data value in the storage location *items* is compared to the number 7. Depending on the outcome of this decision, one or another of the two other instructions, either *price = 2* or *price = 3* (not both), will be executed next by the processor.

A simple program appears in Figure 4; step by step, the effect of each statement on memory appears in the diagram to the right of each programming statement. A grid represents storage locations; it is not important what type of storage. As we saw before, the exact grid locations for all the variables used by the program were preassigned by the computer, so that the computer knows exactly where to store the current value of each variable without being told by the program. The input data preexists (we assume that it is stored on the disk drive); therefore, the initial diagram shows only the input values 3 and 2

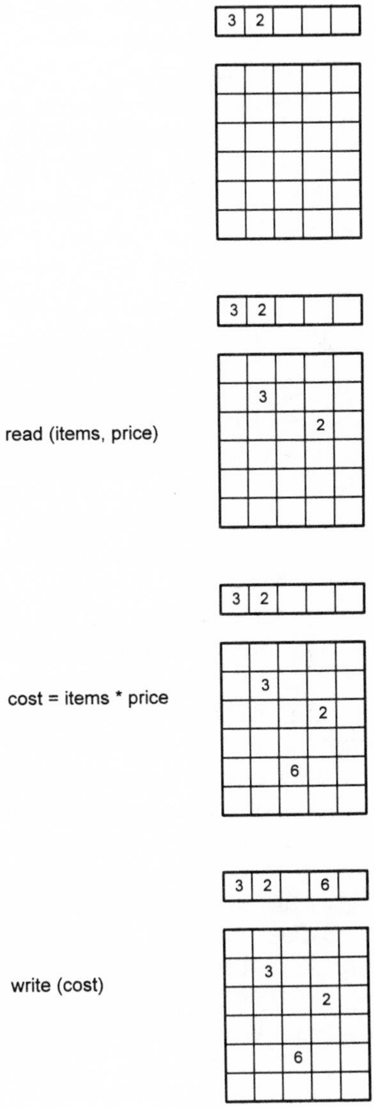

read (items, price)

cost = items * price

write (cost)

FIGURE 4. A simple computer program in action. Input data is read into memory, then processed, and, finally, processed data is output. The process is completely mechanical or deterministic. The computer has *no* choice.

with all other memory locations being blank. The explanation of the last step is that the value for *cost* was output to some device (printer, disk drive, etc.) and stored in the output section of the upper small box.

Our main goal in this chapter is a numerical representation of general computer programs. A numerical representation will seem clumsy and artificial, but it will allow a quick and concise proof of an ultimate limitation of computers. The first step is complete; we now need to discuss how a computer represents non-numerical data such as letters and special symbols. Data is represented as numbers inside a computer: Actually, data is represented as a string of 1's and 0's (binary). This means that all letters and special symbols must be represented by a unique number. ASCII, a standard method, represents characters as numbers between 0 and 255; each letter (both lower and upper case) and each symbol has a unique number associated with it. Sample ASCII representations are: "*" = 42, "=" = 61, ">" = 63, "a" = 97, "b" = 98, "c" = 99, . . . "z" = 122.

NUMERICAL ENCODING OF A PROGRAM

At this point we are ready to numerically represent a computer program completely, uniquely, and logically; this in turn allows us to present a logical proof of computer limitations in the next chapter. Consider the earlier example; in particular, consider the program and the input and output, represented by the step-by-step diagrams in Figure 4. This simple program computes the total cost of a number of items at a certain price. The first diagram shows the memory and input/output area before the program starts to execute. Then each line of the program is executed, and the resulting memory and input/output areas are shown. For example, the second grid shows the situation when the two input numbers have been read into memory and stored in the correct memory locations. The third diagram shows what

read (items, price)

cost = items * price

write (cost)

Input   Program   Output

FIGURE 5. The computation process is viewed as a beginning (input data) and a procedure (the computer program) that uniquely determine the result (the output).

happens when the two numbers are multiplied together and the result is stored in another memory location.

Computers are deterministic: It can never happen that the program in the diagram can have an output of 7 with the same inputs of 3 and 2. The only output possible is 6. Note that this would still hold if the program contained one or more decision statements. Same input, same program, same output — this is always true. You might ask about the case in which a computer is monitoring a random measurement and basing decisions on the value; suppose we made this measurement after the program starts and (supposedly) after the input was set. (This is similar to a person observing something and then basing a decision on this new data.) Then wouldn't the same input and same program give different outputs? No, the input has not been set then. If late input is made during the execution of the program, then it counts as input, too. If two runnings of the program have the same other inputs but differ on one late input, then this is enough to allow the two outputs to differ. Therefore, the difference between the outputs does not violate determinism.

But people always complain that they ran the same program with the same data and got different results — are they all lying? No, there are two things that could cause this in real life. First, there could be hardware errors (misread data, disk errors, etc.) that could change numbers before or after they are read in. Second, this program is not the only one running in the computer; there are always programs running invisibly in the background (e.g., an operating system). If something changed in the background program, it could cause a program to give different results with the same data. Our underlying assumption is that from run to run *all* programs, *all* inputs, and *all* other factors are exactly the same. Then, the same program running on the same input always gives the same output.

Later we will require that only one single number represents the input and output; therefore, we need to concatenate the 3 and 2 into one number. Hence, the input is rewritten as **32**; in a similar fashion the output is **60**. In a sense the computer maps the program and the input into the output. It only remains to put the program and the input/output in the correct numerical form.

We write the program as a concatenated string of ASCII; to illustrate, the first word "read" of the first program statement is represented in ASCII as follows: "r" is 114, "e" is 101, "a" is 097, and "d" is 100. When these numbers are concatenated, they form 114101097100, which are the first 12 digits of the number shown below that represents the entire program (this number is approximately equal to 10^{150}).

114101097100040105116101109115044112114105099101041032099111115116060110511610110911504211211410509910103211911410511610104009911111511604101301001301010

The computer can interpret the program encoded by the above number and then apply it to the input to obtain the output. This ability comes from a universal interpreter program, which can generate the program code from its numerical, ASCII representation, then execute this code on the input values; it would uniquely determine the output. The main result for this chapter is illustrated by this numerical relationship between a computer program and a number.

The important thing to understand is that this representation is possible for *every possible computer program* though it is too unwieldy for normal usage. In the next chapter we will consider a table of these numbers and apply a special method to prove an upper limit on the analytic ability of computer programs.

Computer programs can represent or model almost anything. They model human thought processes, games, and economic trends; they model the progress of galactic structures over the course of eons; they model the very processes that cause stars to burn and to explode as supernovas, which make the raw material for other stars, planets, and sentient beings. If we can encode all the information in a computer program in one number, then can we also encode in a single number a human mind or a galaxy or the entire universe? If the universe and humans are deterministic, then probably yes; if not, if the universe is inherently random or if people truly have free will, then no. Herein lies a recurring theme of the rest of the book: How close can computers come to being human?

Two important points came out of this chapter: first, the reasons why computers are deterministic and, second, a representation of a program as a large number. Later chapters build on this one; determinism is a theme of the entire book and appears many other times. People and computers will be compared and contrasted with this concept of determinism in mind. An upper limit on computer thought is an edge of reality that is proven in the next chapter; this demonstration depends on the program-as-number concept.

Armed with a concise encoding of a computer program as a number, we can now understand two of the most powerful logical theories of all: the Halting theorem and Gödel's incompleteness theorem. Both theories place strict upper limits on the reasoning process; both theories are results of an encoding of statements or programs as numbers. In another chapter that focuses on human thought, an analogy is drawn between programs and the human thought process, and again this encoding is useful in explaining the upper limits on human reasoning.

Chapter 7

Computer Thought — the Difficult and the Impossible

... the difficult we do at once, the impossible takes a bit longer.

INSCRIPTION ON THE SEABEE'S MEMORIAL

... the difficult we do in a billion years, the impossible takes forever.

PROPOSED INSCRIPTION FOR A PROGRAMMER'S
MEMORIAL (TONGUE IN CHEEK)

Algorithms are the methods, the step-by-step procedures, the plans that people and computers think with. Algorithms are the recipes and the lists of instructions that we all follow. For computers, algorithms are the programs that allow them to compute.

A study of algorithms is needed in order to understand the ultimate inherent limits in digital computers; a study of algorithms is also needed in order to distinguish between the capabilities of the human brain and those of computers. Algorithms take data (the input) and process it in special ways; the result is a set of decisions or processed data (the output). Computers and brains differ in the ways that they take in data and process it, but there are many similarities. Algorithms often represent codified methods of solving specific mathematical problems; here measurement is possible, and algorithms can be classified by how long they take to solve the problem. This area, known as "complexity" theory, plays an important role in making final judgments about computers, human thought, and maybe even the ultimate truths of the universe. We will see real-world problems that are impossible to solve and problems that are so difficult that they are for all practical purposes impossible to solve. The *difficult* or nearly impossible are called *intractable* or infeasible; the truly *impossible* are called *noncomputable*.

Computer thought is done by algorithms; this chapter proves upper limits on the ability of any computer to do all the necessary calculations for some problems. This is a hard limit; this is an edge of reality.

The word "algorithm" originated several centuries ago from a variation of the last name of a ninth-century Persian mathematician — Aabu Ja'far Mohammed ibn Musa *al-Khowarizmi*. The study of algorithms grew in the nineteenth century when several important mathematical questions were stated in terms of procedures and methods. Rapid growth in algorithm and complexity studies began shortly after the start of the computer age. Now many general facts are known concerning absolute limits on the time that algorithms take to compute. One fact is that some classes of problems are vastly more difficult to solve than others — so difficult that the universe would run down before a galaxy full of supercomputers could calculate the answer.

Computer operations are analogous to human sensations and thought processes in some way. The input to a computer is like the data that people gather from their senses — sights, tastes, sounds, etc. Both computers and people have a finite amount of memory with which to solve their problems, and both have only a finite amount of time to solve their problems. But do computers and people really think the same way? The answer will turn out to be yes and no and maybe. Since both humans and computers think with algorithms, any limitation on the computation of algorithms is an ultimate limitation on people and computers. Algorithms are a key part of the computational process and are essential to the debate about mental activity as computational process. The mathematician and physicist Roger Penrose (we will be hearing a lot more about him later) had this to say about artificial intelligence (AI) theories that see human thought as strictly computerlike: "The idea is that mental activity is simply the carrying out of some well-defined sequence of operations, frequently referred to as an algorithm." He also added: "But if an algorithm of this kind exists for the brain . . . then it could in principle be run on a computer."[1] Professor Penrose doesn't agree with these theories; we will look at his position in the quantum consciousness chapter on free will. For now, we need to analyze these processes called algorithms.

Several natural characteristics define a computer algorithm. First, an algorithm must be finite in two ways: It must result in only a finite number of instructions, and it can only operate on a finite amount of data. Second, a computer algorithm must eventually terminate with a solution to the problem or indicate that the problem is insoluble by the algorithm. Third — a more technical restriction — any step in an algorithm must be followed by a unique successor step. In effect, this means that computer algorithms don't have "free will": Each step must follow from previous steps and input data. This implies that a computer algorithm is purely "mechanical" and that the algorithm must lead to the same outcome each time that it is applied to the same input data.

EXAMPLES OF ALGORITHMS

Computer algorithms are usually stated in terms of a programming language. The following is a set of short examples of what a computer algorithm *is and is not* and how computer algorithms relate to human thought. Notice that these examples are short examples of statements found in algorithms; many of these example statements would be required to make up a computer program, which is a larger algorithm.

Input after the algorithm/program starts is a legitimate algorithmic process. This would be like the human body and brain sensing some value, color, feeling, etc., and making a decision based on it, this decision being to gather more data or change some information to reflect the new data. Data are not restricted to just numbers or text either; it is legitimate to input *new program code* after the program starts. This is analogous to a person learning a new way of thinking from a college course and incorporating it in his future thought processes.

The programming construction that causes a program to run forever is called an *infinite loop* — an algorithm shouldn't have one of these; if it does, it will not halt in a finite number of instructions and give an answer. However, this infinite loop is a legitimate programming process, but it is very undesirable! The main result that we will prove in this chapter — the Halting problem — is about the impossibility of a general program that can identify these infinite loops in a program.

A *random input* to an algorithm is legitimate; however, the true "randomness" might be subject to philosophical debate. This is analogous to a human brain being acted upon by chance events or quantum events.

A statement like *DO write(6) OR write(2);* is *not* a legitimate algorithmic statement. There is no clearly defined next (successor) step, no method of choosing between the two statements *write(6)* or *write(2)*. This is different from a decision statement, which provides a basis for making a decision. A statement like this does not give the computer any basis for making a choice based on data or logic available to the computer. Later we will revisit this issue since it relates to the matter of "free will." A computer does not have "free will"; its output is *entirely determined* by its original program code and its input data. People may differ in this aspect of thought — it is an open question.

Because computer storage is finite, a number with infinite information content like $u = 2.479615352096418382158361220597-364\ldots$ is *not* a legitimate algorithmic statement. Infinite-length inputs are not allowed, because infinite inputs take infinite memory and infinite time in order to process. For the same reason, an infinite program is not legitimate. An algorithm or program with an infinite number of steps or an infinite number of instructions is not allowed.

DIFFICULT ALGORITHMS — THE NEARLY IMPOSSIBLE

Complexity is the most significant theoretical branch of algorithm theory. Algorithms are important to all forms of calculations done on computers today, and the amount of time that it takes to do the calculations is always a concern. The timeliness of the calculations is a concern: Some calculations must be done before a certain event happens — weather-prediction algorithms must finish before the day of the predicted weather arrives. Complexity theory uses an indirect measure of the time that an algorithm takes to complete. Time is usually linearly related to the number of basic operations (such as additions, multiplications, or comparisons) that an algorithm does; this number is designated $T(n)$. This number is easy to compute for most algorithms — just count. $T(n)$ is a constant multiple of the actual time the computer takes, and because time is harder to calculate (you would have to run the algorithm for each n); $T(n)$ is widely used as the measure of the complexity of an algorithm.

Recall that there is a physical upper limit on computer operations of 100! or about 10^{158}. In powers of 2, this is about 2^{500}. In the next few chapters, algorithms whose execution time is measured in terms of $T(n) = 2^n$ steps will be discussed. Keep in mind that for $n > 500$ these algorithms are essentially impossible to compute, and for $n > 100$ they are beyond the reach of current technology. This is an important distinction: *Knowing how to solve a problem* is much different from *being able to solve a problem*. We can know an algorithm that *in theory* solves a problem, but the algorithm may take too many computational steps to ever finish.

There are important practical algorithms that are quite simply computationally infeasible — there is no hope of being able to complete the calculations within any reasonable time. As Paul Hoffman, who has been an editor for both *Discover* magazine and *Scientific American*, put it: "Every day in industry, computers routinely tackle computational problems that are too time-consuming to be solved by any known method."[2] An example of a simple problem that is infeasible to solve is the computation of all possible subsets of a set of people. If there are n people in the set, then there are 2^n different subsets composed of those n people. It should take a computer a constant amount of time to calculate each subset, so $T(n) = 2^n$ for this problem. If a computer could calculate 1,000,000,000 possible subsets per second (supercomputers can do this), then it would take 1 second for 30 people, 20 minutes for 40 people, 2 weeks for 50 people, 40 years for 60 people, and 40,000 years for 70 people; for 100 people this supercomputer would take 40,000,000,000,000 years or about 3000 times the age of the universe. (These numbers go up by a factor of about 1000 since each is $2^{10} = 1024$ times the predecessor.) These calculations are completely, utterly, totally infeasible for large numbers n; however, they are theoretically possible.

Real-life problems often are so complex that an exact solution takes this much time. The 2^n calculations that must be done to compute the number-of-subsets problem are also necessary to solve many other problems that arise in communications, physics, resource management, retailing, architectural design, and other areas. In the past 20 years the ultimate complexity of these kinds of problems has been unified in one single theory, called the "NP-complete theory." This theory notes that problems that require 2^n or more calculations are impossible for all practical purposes. It asks the question: "Is it possible that someday a more efficient algorithm might be discovered that can do the NP-complete problems in much less time?" Most researchers think not; however, it is still an open question.

One of the best known problems in algorithm theory is the "traveling salesman" problem. Picture a salesman who must make a stop in n different cities on a sales trip. Assume that he doesn't visit a city more than once on a trip, and the order of the visits is not important. The important thing is that the mileage traveled on the total route be a minimum. Assume that there are direct-connection flights from each city to every other. Now if he starts in one city, he has $n - 1$ choices for the second city on his route, $n - 2$ choices for the third city on the route, $n - 3$ for the fourth, and so on. How does he solve his problem? The method essentially involves computing the mileage for all possible routes and finding the minimum-mileage route by comparison. Easy enough conceptually, but the issue is the enormous number of calculations that need to be done for a reasonable size of n. The total number of routes possible is $n \times n - 1 \times n - 2 \times n - 3 \cdots 3 \times 2 \times 1 = n!$. The function $n!$ is much larger than the 2^n function. For $n = 50$, the number $n! = 10^{64}$ or 2^{213}, which is much larger than the number that took the supercomputer 3000 times the age of the universe. Our salesman is lost; he has no earthly hope of calculating a minimum-mileage route.

Flight connections, telephone systems, computer networks, and bureaucratic lines of communications all suffer from this problem: As the number n grows, the number of possible connections grows exponentially or factorially. Any attempt to list all possible connections or any attempt to do some mathematical operation on all possible connections leads to an impossibly large number. Likewise, any problem whose solution requires trying every possibility is doomed — there aren't enough computers or time.

Our mythical salesman is not alone. Telephone companies and computer organizations cannot design the most efficient possible systems for this reason. Telephone and computer networks all have thousands (sometimes millions) of units that connect in some design. The "optimal" or "absolute best" design cannot be calculated because of the computational complexity of the algorithms that can find the optimal design. Operations research is the field that encompasses these design problems. It sprang into being during World War II when the U.S. Army was faced with logistics problems of an unbelievable magnitude. Questions had to be answered: how much food to ship where, how much clothing to stage where before it was shipped somewhere else, how many rounds of ammunition would be needed in what sector of the battlefront? Before the arrival of large-scale computers, these problems couldn't be solved at all. The "best" solution possible was simply based on human judgment and simple calculations done by hand and by the electromechanical calculators of the time. Research has gone on at a fast pace ever since. The result of the research was a large number of algorithms that solved many operations research problems and variants. However, even the best of these algorithms were too slow when implemented. A large number of nodes in a network or a large number of connections required too much time to solve. A pattern was emerging.

In the early 1970s a famous theorem (proven by Cook) started the study of a theory called the NP-complete problem. It turns out that many significant and practical computer algorithms have time complexity functions $T(n)$ that fall into one of two categories: $T(n)$ is a polynomial or an exponential function of n. There is a vast difference in size between a polynomial function [say $T(n) = n^5$] and an exponential function [say $T(n) = 2^n$]. Although n^5 is a truly large number for large n, if the solution to a problem is important enough, the problem can be solved in some reasonable amount of time. This is not so for 2^n. For $n = 30$, n^5 takes about 0.024 seconds on our super computer, whereas 2^n takes 1 second — no big thing (a ratio of about 40:1); both problems are easily solvable. But look at the case $n = 100$: $n^5 = 10^{10} = 10,000,000,000$ takes 10 seconds of supercomputer time to complete, but 2^n takes 3000 times the age of the universe to complete. Solutions to industrial problems where n might be 500 could be done in a few weeks on a supercomputer for n^5 — but would take essentially forever for 2^n.

We know of many real-world problems that have simple procedures (algorithms) for solving them; but these algorithms depend on combinatorial methods and for moderate-sized values of n require far too many computer operations to ever accomplish. Any method that requires a search of all possible combinations of some set of size n will require at least 2^n computer operations. This is completely unrealistic for $n > 100$ and physically impossible for $n > 500$ (since $2^{500} \approx 100!$).

One important problem in operations research is the linear programming problem. It is a resource allocation problem where the solution is the optimal distribution of resources to various nodes in a network. Used since World War II, this problem comes up in almost every business area in commerce — transportation, inventory control, computer system design, network design, and others. Some of these networks have thousands of nodes that must all be considered. For years the best-known solution algorithm was a method called the "simplex method"; it worked very well for most problems, but when the number of network nodes (n) was 10,000 to 100,000 it was simply too slow. A recent algorithm created by Narenda Karmarkar of AT&T Bell Labs is much faster; its complexity is about $n^{3.5}$, which gives reasonable computation times even for large numbers of nodes. This new algorithm was so much faster than others that it actually gave AT&T Bell a competitive advantage over competitors because it allowed optimal design of large networks. This could mean savings of millions of dollars for the size of networks being designed.

Unfortunately, most problems associated with the optimal design and operation of networks can't be rapidly solved. Most researchers believe that many of these problems have exponential time complexity [i.e., $T(n) = 2^n$] and therefore, for large n, are practically impossible to solve. David Johnson, coauthor of the algorithm theorist's bible *Computers and Intractability — A Guide to the Theory of NP-Completeness*, once said: "Virtually every mathematician, I think, now believes that NP-complete problems are intrinsically hard . . . The real issue is proving it."[3] However, to repeat: All of these problems are theoretically possible to solve. Although it might take millions and millions of times the life of the universe and an entire universe full of supercomputers, these problems are solvable in a theoretical sense.

THE UPPER LIMIT OF COMPUTERS — IMPOSSIBLE ALGORITHMS

We have now come to the point where we will see why computers are limited in a definable and absolute sense. It turns out to be a somewhat abstract upper limit; however, in later chapters we will see some related practical limits in mathematics, programming, law, and politics. Most often, computers are computationally limited by difficult problems, instead of absolutely limited by impossible problems. A demonstration of this fact will also be a little abstract; it borrows from a method — called the diagonalization method — from a famous math theorem from the last century.

The discovery of one upper limit is credited to British mathematician Alan Turing. Turing was one of the brightest minds of the 1930s and 1940s and is firmly entrenched as one of the greatest computer scientists of all time; his discovery placed firm upper limits on computers. He also devised a test for artificial intelligence, ever since called the Turing test, and he created the Turing machine, a theoretical concept that is a key tool for theoretical computer science. In addition, he did work in biology and helped the British Foreign Office break German High Command codes during World War II. Turing thought and wrote in computerlike terms; hence, his work still has a modern flavor 50 years later.

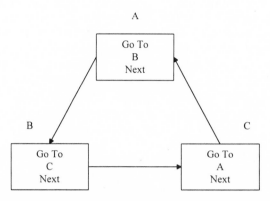

FIGURE 6. Infinite loops. A major problem in programming is avoiding infinite loops that force programs to compute forever without stopping.

There are problems that can never be solved, no matter how good the algorithm is. An important example is the problem called the "Halting" problem. In computer programming, an infinite loop — repeating the same instructions for the same data forever — serves no useful purpose. Figure 6 shows the problem. An infinite loop is a programming manifestation of a logical contradiction or paradox; it usually results from an oversight or misunderstanding. These infinite loops are not easy to avoid. Because it is important to check programs so that they never get into an infinite loop, an extremely useful (if it were possible) program would be one that read in a second program and could tell if the second program had an infinite loop embedded within it. This is the essence of the Halting problem — can a program (call it *Halt*) be written that decides whether *all other* programs halt (i.e., do *not* have an infinite loop) for each possible input? The answer is no. A very important point is that *Halt* is not required just to give the same answer as the second program: This is possible and can be simply done by making a program that does nothing more than run the second program. *Halt* must

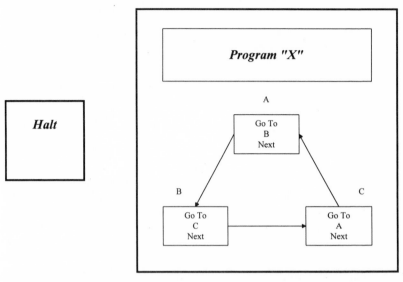

FIGURE 7. Detecting infinite loops beforehand. A program *Halt* that could analyze other programs and discover infinite loops would be the most valuable program ever. Alas, it is impossible!

decide in advance if the second program will run forever on the input; then *Halt* outputs "loops" in finite time.

At first glance, this problem might seem solvable — difficult, but solvable. After all, if we take the new science of AI and combine it with the tricks of the programming trade acquired from millions of programmers and years of experience, there should be enough knowledge to read over a program and tell if it has an infinite loop. Unfortunately, this is not the case, as Turing discovered. This will be rigorously proved shortly, but for now consider a fictional program *Halt* that would detect infinite loops. Think of the money-making potential! Every computer programmer on earth would need a copy; the software company that marketed *Halt* would grow rich. This hasn't happened, and it never will happen. Search your local computer stores; no such program exists.

A program that could solve the Halting problem would have to be able to understand every other computer program in a very essential way. In a sense, we are saying that no computer program can ever understand every other computer program. This statement represents an ultimate limitation on the powers of digital computers, and this is the main importance of the Halting theorem. Our proof of this important result will use the result obtained in Chapter 6 that showed that programs can be represented as numbers.

In Figure 8, a table is made up in which the left-hand column is the set of integers representing all possible computer programs. This is possible as we saw in the previous chapter; every possible computer program has a number N that represents it. Each column in the table is headed by an integer that represents one of the possible inputs to these programs. These column-heading integers are the same as the concatenated inputs like **32** from the example of the previous chapter. At the place in the table that represents the Nth row and the Nth column, there is

Input	1	2	3	.	.	.	M	.	.	.
Program Number										
1	stops									
2		stops								
3			stops							
.										
.					loops					
.										
M							stops			
.										
.										
.										

FIGURE 8. An impossible algorithm. No computer program or human can compute all the diagonal values. This is an absolute upper limit on thought.

a "stops" if the program represented by N halts on the input represented by N or a "loops" if it endlessly loops.

If *Halt* exists, then it can understand each possible program; in particular, it can predict whether a program N halts on the input data represented by N. This is our assumption that *Halt* exists; later we will develop a logical contradiction to this assumption, which is a way of proving that *Halt* cannot possibly exist (proof by contradiction).

Since we assume *Halt* exists, we can use it as a subprogram of another new program. Therefore, a new program can be developed from *Halt* that differs from it for every value of N. Call this new program *Contrary*. *Contrary* is a program so it must exist somewhere in the list of programs; say that its number is M.

What is the result when *Halt* is evaluated at M? Well, by assumption, it must agree with program number M. But program number M is *Contrary*, which must disagree with *Halt* by design. Big contradiction here! Hence, the assumption must be wrong: Program *Halt* cannot exist — it represents an unobtainable or impossible thought process.

An impossible algorithm is a difficult concept to deal with. While a program like *Halt* would be nice to have, it doesn't seem absolutely necessary to future human progress. Are we really missing that much? Difficult algorithms are much more understandable as a practical upper limit on our ability to reason and calculate. Clearly, we are missing a means of calculating optimal solutions to many pressing technical and social problems because of this upper limit. Both are limits; it is not clear which is the more restrictive limit. Whatever the final answer, it will affect both computers and humans. Algorithms are also a human method of reasoning; whatever limits a computer limits us.

This chapter was long and difficult but it showed the difficult and the impossible for computers. Computers can't do some thought processes and they never will. No computer with finite memory and finite programs can understand everything — it can't understand all algorithms or all possible programs or all possible human thoughts. There are absolute limits, and this is one for the computers of today and the future. Furthermore, some processes that computers can do are so difficult that they become impossible in effect. Complexity (the difficult) and noncomputability (the impossible) both play an important role in making judgments about the ultimate nature of computers, humans, and the universe.

Chapter 8

Logic for Computers — Upper Limits on Reasoning

Post hoc, ergo propter hoc.
After this, therefore because of this.

DEFINITION OF LOGICAL FALLACY
IN LATIN

1010101010101010101010101010101010101010101

Logic is a field that started with the Greeks; ever since, many philosophers, theologians, statesmen, and scientists have held out hope that the application of logic would solve the problems of the world. There is a security in logic — a feeling that once an issue has been logically solved it is forever laid to rest. With these hopes and lofty goals in mind, the field has been studied and debated over the ages. In the end, there has been disappointment: The results of logic are usually too narrow or too shallow to solve the pressing issues of the world. We simply don't know how to formulate all the necessary rules and operations for the correct use of logic in a language.

This is not saying that efforts made to apply logic in other areas have been wasted; quite to the contrary, the basic logical arguments and forms have been incorporated into legal systems throughout the world. Logic can solve many of our problems; it simply can't solve them all. And advances in logic have cast doubt on whether the field will ever be able to solve them all. An edge of reality that limits us all is Gödel's theorem. There are simply always going to be arguments that humans cannot resolve to be true or false. This is absolutely true now and for all time. Professor John Paulos, author of the best-seller *Innumeracy,* said this of Gödel's legacy: "Kurt Gödel . . . will probably be one of the few contemporary figures remembered in 1,000 years."[1]

The new computer science field of artificial intelligence (AI) is an area in which 2000-year-old logic precepts combine with modern technology and techniques. In a later chapter, we will study AI in more detail; in this chapter we will see an example of how mechanical application of logic operations and rules can derive new results. This will be the basis for AI operations, and it will show how a computer can *think* using a humanlike database of facts.

One area in which logic reigns supreme is mathematics. Hundreds of thousands of original theorems are discovered and proven each year. Mathematical rules of logical operation are actually few; the number, diversity, and complexity of the proven theorems are a result of the initial mathematical axioms. Mathematics has several narrowly defined initial assumptions (called axioms) and a few logical rules. From this starting place of about 10 axioms and 6 rules, mathematicians logically deduce thousands of results (called theorems.)

Because logic has been such a success in mathematics, many philosophers, theologians, and scientists have emulated mathematicians in their approach to logic. The problem is that the axioms determine the results. Specific, narrowly defined axioms can lead to logically correct results — but results that are narrow and of little importance. For example, it is an indisputable fact that there is an infinite number of prime integers. This fact has been proven by rigorous mathematical deductions from a set of narrowly stated axioms; this fact is absolutely, incontestably true now and for all time. This fact is also of no use whatsoever to people struggling for answers about what is moral and what isn't, what should be legal and what shouldn't, and why society has evolved as it has. Its utility in everyday life is limited. This fact about prime numbers is a very narrow result in the general scheme of things. Try another example from theology: "Thou shall not kill." Now this axiom certainly could have wide usage in moral and legal issues. The problem is applying it so that the results are absolutely, incontestably true. Does it absolutely and incontestably prove answers to issues such as the raising of armies, the death penalty, or abortion? Apparently not, given that people still argue both sides of these issues.

AXIOMS

Logic axioms are bedrock. They are the original *true* statements in any logical system. They are defined to be true; their truth is unquestioned within the framework of that particular logical system. Rudy Rucker, a prominent logician and writer, put it this way: "The actual rules of logic are pitifully few in number. It turns out that what is of real significance is the complexity of the initial assumptions."[2]

Everything depends on the axioms. If an axiom is wrong (causes contradictory theorems), then everything in a carefully constructed logical system can fall apart. This happens repeatedly in the sciences; a new discovery forces a reevaluation of old knowledge, often forcing the discarding of old facts (axioms). It happens in mathematics too. One story concerns one of the most prominent logicians of all time, Professor Gottlob Frege of Germany. As part of his life's work (a major part), he had set up an axiomatic foundation for a mathematical system and proven many theorems based on this system. This single-minded project took years to finish. Finally, it was complete and Professor Frege decided it was time to publish. He painstakingly wrote up the theorems, edited the drafts, submitted them to the publisher, made corrections and finally waited for the manuscripts to be published. At the same time, British mathematician and philosopher Bertrand Russell was pondering a recently discovered paradox caused by self-referencing. Russell knew that Frege used a self-referencing axiom and wrote him a letter outlining the problem. Imagine Frege's consternation: With years of work resting upon a foundation of axioms, one of the axioms is shown to generate contradictions. Since the manuscript was ready to print, he could do little more than add a postscript in an appendix. He said: "Hardly anything more unwelcome can befall a scientific writer than that one of the foundations of his edifice be shaken after the work is finished." Everything depends on the axioms.

Consider four sets of axioms: first, the axioms of mathematical set theory, next, the axioms of quantum mechanics, next, a set of axioms for a legal system (the U.S. Constitution), and, last, a set of axioms for a theological/moral system (the Ten Commandments). Set theory starts with a set of very specific axioms, and the deductions drawn from them are absolutely correct. The axioms are simply assumed to be true; logical deduction demands a set of initial axioms, and these are the ones for set theory. Other branches of mathematics such as arithmetic have another set. The axioms of quantum mechanics were derived from experiments; physicists believe them to be true (although some physicists argue for different interpretations of the meanings of the equations). The statements from the Constitution are treated like axioms; they are in the Constitution because the writers of that document believed in these principles. Deductions based on this logical system treat these statements as bedrock statements. Similar statements can be made about the Ten Commandments handed to Moses on a tablet of stone.

Although they aren't the only basis for Christian thought, they are treated as true statements, and other principles are deduced from them. Examples of axioms from these four well-known systems are:

- *Set theory:* Two sets are equal if and only if they have the same members. There is a set with no members (the null set). A set cannot be a member of itself.
- *Quantum mechanics:* Uncertainty principle — the more precisely that you measure a quantum particle's position, the less precisely you can measure its momentum. Pauli exclusion principle — no two fermions can be in the same state.
- *Constitution:* Right to freedom of assembly. Right to freedom of speech. Right to bear arms.
- *Ten Commandments:* Thou shall not steal. Thou shall not murder.

LOGIC HISTORY

The history of logic extends back more than 2000 years, starting with Greeks like Plato, Socrates, and Aristotle. There are three periods in the development of the field of logic. The first, the classical period, starts with the Greeks and then continues until the mid to late nineteenth century. An emphasis on syllogisms and other types of arguments characterized the field during this period. A syllogism is a type of logic argument or proof that was developed by the Greeks and then taught for the next 2000 years, up to this very day. An example follows: (1) No statistics professor is interesting. (2) You are interesting. (3) You are not a statistics professor. The first two sentences are the premises; the third sentence is known as the conclusion. The premises are assumed to be true for this syllogism, whether or not they actually are facts. For our purposes, the premises serve as axioms, and the conclusion serves as a deduced result or theorem; the logical system is the syllogism itself.

Students of Aristotle over the centuries extended the study of syllogism and categorized different types. A major problem became evident: Syllogisms do not handle quantification well. When the field of mathematics exploded in size and significance during the nineteenth century, mathematicians started to restructure logic in an algebraic sense.

The second period of logic's development started in the mid to late nineteenth century with a group of European mathematicians: Boole, Peano, Russell, and Hilbert. Boole and Peano put together the basics into a flexible symbolic algebraic system that we still use today. Bertrand Russell's main contribution was to set up a logical system for mathematics that avoided paradoxes; he used a method called the theory of types. Hilbert, the greatest mathematical mind of his time, set up many different logical systems. Hilbert is also famous for being wrong. He dreamed an impossible dream.

David Hilbert was the last great universal mathematician — he worked in almost every area of mathematics and made long-lasting contributions to each. Even today, the mathematical foundation of quantum theory is based on a structure called a Hilbert space after David Hilbert. At the turn of the century in 1900, there was a mathematical conference in Paris. The topic was the future of mathematics; Hilbert, who was the most prominent mathematician of all, gave the keynote speech, addressing the 23 most important unsolved problems in mathematics. His second problem concerned the issue of provability.

Hilbert was way ahead of his time in his approach to mathematical proofs. He viewed the process of proving mathematical theorems much as a present-day artificial intelligence system on a computer would: Start with the axioms and keep applying the rules of logic to axioms and the resulting theorems. It works this way: The rules of logic use the axioms (which are the original theorems of the system in a sense) to prove some theorems. Next, the rules, the axioms, and the now-known theorems combine to prove more theorems; then these newly proven theorems are added back into the set of known theorems, and the process continues.

Hilbert focused on axioms as the key to a good mathematical logic system. He felt that if the proper set of axioms could be chosen, then all mathematical statements or hypotheses could be proven right or wrong. This set would be complete in the sense that all mathematical theorems would be deduced from one set of axioms. Hilbert's dream was this complete set of axioms. Gödel shot the dream down.

The third period of logic development starts with Gödel. Kurt Gödel was an intellectual giant of the twentieth century. An Austrian, he eventually came to the United States, where he remained until his death in 1978. He is most famous for his "Incompleteness theorem," which states that there will always be true mathematical statements that will be neither provable nor disprovable within one system of axioms. A "complete" set of axioms can never exist. This theorem and others like it have vastly changed the landscape of philosophy and logic ever since; it is now widely accepted that there are absolute limits on the power of computers and human thought.

LOGICAL OPERATIONS

Before we can examine logical structures and Gödel's theorem, we need to study exactly what composes mathematical logic. There are three components: (1) axioms (discussed before), (2) basic logical operations, and (3) rules of logical deduction.

There are only a few basic logic operations that are needed. Many different logic operations can be defined (and many have been in the past), but only a small set is necessary. Others can be written as combinations of the basic set.

A nineteenth-century mathematician, Giuseppe Peano, represented all logical statements in terms of a few basic logical operations with corresponding logic symbols. These logical operations are of two types. The first four are called logic connectives; the study of statements formulated in terms of them is called the "propositional calculus." These connectives are best known by their English counterparts: *or*, *and*, *not*, and *implies* (usually written in the form "if . . . then . . ." in English). Propositional calculus is very restricted in the type of statements that it can consider. A mathematical analogy is that propositional calculus is a theory of constants — functions and variables are not used. The last two logical operations are called quantifiers; the study of statements that can be formulated in terms of all six operations is called the "predicate calculus." Quantifiers are *every* and *some* in English. Predicate calculus does consider logical functions and is a more general logic. These two quantifiers, along with logical functions, form very complex logical expressions and are sufficient to describe all English logical statements. However, for our purposes in this chapter we will only need the four basic operations.

The syllogism, which was discussed earlier, is expressed in terms of the logical connective operations as follows. First, each sentence is assigned a logical variable — q: No statistics professor is interesting; r: You are interesting; s: You are not a statistics professor. Then the syllogism appears as (q *and* r *implies* s). In other words, if both the premises are true (here q and r both are true), then the conclusion is also true. Using variables might seem like an unnecessary complication since you could just as easily state the syllogism with sentences and the logic operators. However, in general, you want a scheme that allows arbitrary sentences to be substituted into the syllogism form for solution by computers; the use of variables allows this.

LOGICAL DEDUCTIONS

Besides the logic operations, we must also have a set of formal rules that allow logical deductions to be proven. (The terms "inference," "deduction," and "theorem" are often used interchangeably; "theorem" is usually reserved for the more mathematical discussions. "Deduced" and "proved" are also equivalent terms.) There are many known rules, and the rules themselves can be used to form other rules, but we need only a basic set to see how this notation works. True statements are inferred from other true statements, true implications, and certain rules of logical inference. For instance, the rule A *and* B *implies* A states in logic operators that if the compound English statement A *and* B is true, then certainly the statement A by itself is also true. An important rule is where the implication A *implies* B is true and, furthermore, the statement A is also true; from these two true statements, we can deduce that B is also a true statement.

An important fact about these inference rules is that a computer can do logical reasoning with them. If a computer has a statement A marked as true and also has an implication A *implies* B marked as true, then it can prove that B is also true just by computer operations.

Examples of logical deduction (theorem proving) based on rules and axioms can get quite complex. By restricting the system to a few rules and axioms we can see how logical derivation can be *mechanized* for solution by a computer. Consider the set of two rules and two axioms in Table 2 and notice that the logical deduction procedure can be done mechanically by a computer that methodically applies one or two deductions or axioms and one rule to see if a new deduction can be derived. If a new deduction can be derived, then it is added to the list of known facts (true statements) and is considered in future processing by the computer (e.g., in the previous example, "deduction 1" was used as a true statement on par with an axiom in the second step). Now, consider how a computer might look at the previous example. The rules being considered are listed first, then one or two true statements are listed in the left-hand column, and the resulting deduction is listed in the right-hand column. Two lists are kept: the rules and the current set of true statements (axioms and previously proven deductions). These

Table 2
Example of Logical Deduction Based on Rules and Axioms

Rules	
Rule 1	If sentence "X and Y" is true, then sentence "Y" is true by itself.
Rule 2	If sentence "X implies Y" is true and sentence "X" is also true, then the sentence "Y" is true.

Axioms	
Axiom 1	It is cold and raining.
Axiom 2	If it is raining, then there isn't any baseball game and there aren't any fans.

Deduced Statements

Procedure	English statement
Apply rule 1 to axiom 1	It is raining. (deduction 1)
Apply rule 2 to axiom 2 and deduction 1	There isn't any baseball game and there aren't any fans. (deduction 2)
Apply rule 1 to deduction 2	There aren't any fans.

two lists are cycled through; each time the rules operate on combinations of one or more true statements. Each time a unique new deduction is proven, it is added to the list of true statements.

Procedures like the above example are the basis for AI; the axioms form a database of known facts, the rules are similar to those in the example, and the deductions are computer-generated facts that are added to a database. This type of mechanical deduction process or mechanical theorem proving was known to Hilbert.

So far, so good; with a few rules and operations we can prove statements almost mechanically. Is logic this easy? The answer is a resounding "no." Logical rules and operations are straightforward. Their nature belies the amount of effort expended to get them into their present form; there were many different approaches tried that proved fruitless in the end. The biggest obstacle has always been ambiguities in language and the problems these ambiguities cause with the axioms. Logical rules and operations are deaf, dumb, and blind. They are completely mechanical. If two or more deductions and axioms fit a deduction rule, then the rule can be applied to prove another new deduction. Sometimes this new deduction can be totally nonsensical or completely contradictory to known facts. What is wrong here?

PARADOXES

A simple but important point concerns the truth value of a sentence: It should be true or false. It should not be both true and false simultaneously. Don't our logical operations and deduction rules stop that case from happening? Unfortunately not; we can get trapped in a paradox. Paradoxes are sentences where one way the sentence appears true and another way the sentence appears false. The four paradoxes listed below are among the best known.

- Liar's paradox — This sentence is false.
- Barber's paradox — A town barber cuts everyone's hair who does not cut their own hair.
- God and the wheel paradox — if God can do anything, then can he build a wheel so large that he can't roll it?
- Two-sentence paradox — Sentence A: Sentence B is false; Sentence B: Sentence A is true.

Consider the sentence in the liar's paradox: "This sentence is false." Does this sentence have value true or false? If it is true then the sentence is a true statement about itself, and it says that it is false. But if the sentence is false, then the sentence must be false so it must be true. The second and third paradoxes listed above exhibit the same problem. Does the barber cut his own hair? If he does, then it contradicts the statement because he must cut a man's hair only if that man does not cut his own. If he does not cut his own hair, then by the statement he himself is one of the men who does not cut their own hair; therefore, the barber (himself) must cut his hair — another contradiction. The next paradox seems to rule out an omnipotent God, since there appears to be at least one task that he can't do: either build the wheel or roll the wheel.

The "God and the wheel" paradox is particularly bothersome to some people since from a theological standpoint it seems to show that an omnipotent God is a logical contradiction and therefore impossible. This is not really true. The problem is in the scope of actions and objects that we allowed the word *anything* to include: Notice that we defined an object (a wheel) by an action (God can't roll) that presupposed a less-than-omnipotent God and finally allowed the word *anything* to include this concept. We built the contradiction into the word *anything* in the first place; therefore, we shouldn't be too surprised by the eventual contradiction. The problem is with logic — not theology. (An aside: As we will see later, paradoxes are *both* true

FIGURE 9. Paradox — if God can do anything, then can he build a wheel so large that he than can't roll it? (Not a problem with religion but with the word "anything"; this is a favored mind game of college sophomores.)

and false, Therefore, you could answer the question "Can God do anything?" with a "yes" and still be correct in spite of the contradiction. Of course, "no" is also correct. And, of course, if your debating opponents try this trick on you, they probably don't fully understand logic, so they won't accept your argument anyway. Show them this book.)

Last is the two-sentence paradox. If sentence A is true, then it tells the truth about sentence B, which means that sentence B is false; but then sentence B is telling a falsehood about sentence A, so sentence A can't be true. Conversely, if sentence A is false, then sentence B must be true, which means that it is telling the truth about sentence A, so sentence A must be true. Both truth values for sentence A lead to a contradiction. The paradox represented by the two sentences is a different type of paradox. The first three paradoxes all relied on a form of self-reference; the two-sentence paradox relies on each sentence referring to the other one. This form is the more common form in politics and law, and it shows that the paradox problem is much deeper than just self-reference.

These problems are not caused by faulty logic operations or deduction rules; these problems are caused by the wording of the paradoxes. The wording would be in the axioms if we had defined these problems formally. Avoiding contradictions and paradoxes in axioms is therefore the largest challenge in designing a logical system for some area. Nor is it easy to rid yourself of contradictions and paradoxes; often they seen an inextricable part of the system. Rudy Rucker called it about right when he said: "A good paradox can never be finally disposed of."[3] A set of axioms is called *consistent* if they are such that no contradiction or paradox can be logically deduced from them. Consistency is a very deep property; it cannot be readily determined from any set of axioms. However, it is vital that the axioms be consistent. In mathematics or ethics, in physics or law, contradictions must be avoided; a logic system is useless if it allows both true and false conclusions for the same statement.

There are two characteristics that appear in these paradoxes: First, something is defined by reference to itself and, second, a definition depends on a result. Russell's big contribution to mathematics was to define certain properties in ways that precluded these types of paradoxes from occurring. Gödel's theorem proof depends on the construction of an argument like the liar's paradox. A common feature of these paradoxes is a word or idea that is too all-encompassing; words like *all, anywhere, anybody, everything, everywhere,* and *every possible* encompass too much in a sense. Often these words can be construed to encompass two separate ideas, one of which is the negation of the other. This forces a built-in contradiction just like the God-and-the-wheel paradox.

Bertrand Russell was well aware of these problems around the turn of the century. He was instrumental in clarifying axioms so that these types of paradoxes would not happen. Russell stands as one of the most influential thinkers of the century. His greatest works came in mathematics and logic, but more than most all mathematicians he branched out into many other fields. He was born in 1872 and died 97 years later, and he filled every year with activity, writings, and thought. Born a grandson of a prime minister of Great Britain, he was educated at Cambridge, imprisoned for pacifism, and helped organize several political committees to address questions ranging from nuclear disarmament to Vietnam War crimes to who killed John Kennedy. He married four times, started schools, and won a Nobel Prize, enough experiences to make most people happy many times over. But logic was his love: "The Opinions that are held with passion are always those for which no good ground exists; indeed the passion is the measure of the holder's lack of rational conviction. Opinions in politics and religion are almost always held passionately" (from his "Sceptical Essays"). Logic is where his ultimate fame lies.

Russell's paradox involves self-referencing. A statement that refers to itself can look innocent enough when stated in English but can cause problems in mathematics. For instance, earlier when we looked at examples of axiom systems, we saw a set theory axiom: "No set can be a member of itself." This might look like quasi-mathematical–logical jargon (OK, it is), but this convoluted definition does limit how big a set can be. In other words, a set cannot be so large as to include itself as a member. This avoids many paradoxes.

However, in a sense, requiring our definitions to be less than all-encompassing limits human logic. Even with axioms that can cover infinitely many situations, it isn't enough to prove the truth or falsity of all statements. As we will see next, Gödel showed that there will be statements that cannot be proven true or false within a given axiom system.

UNPROVABLE STATEMENTS AND GÖDEL'S THEOREM

At this point, there are several possible outcomes for the truth value of a sentence (or mathematical statement). First, the truth value can be T (or F) — the statement is true (or false) within the scope of the axioms for this logical system. Second, the value can be both true and false; this is a contradiction and a paradox. Unless the logical system was set up with an assumption to test and a proof by contradiction was the goal (this is a legitimate logic/mathematical proof technique), then a paradox exists and the axioms need changing.

There is one other possibility: The statement might turn out to be unprovable — neither true nor false. Unprovable is different from unknown. A statement can be shown to be unprovable within a logic system when one can show that *no sequence of logic operations* can ever prove the statement T or F. Gödel's incompleteness theorem says that for all systems (that contain the arithmetic system) there are always unprovable statements about arithmetic.

Gödel's work concerns central issues about logical limits, and we will be using his name a great deal. Gödel, the man, was more of an enigma; his work was easier to know than the man ever was. Kurt Gödel was a lifelong scholar who wasn't involved in as many areas as an Alan Turing or a Bertrand Russell. Instead, most of his activities involved logic and mathematics; however, this doesn't mean that he was dull or boring. One memorable story tells of the ultimate abstract logician, Gödel, coming to grips with the ultimate pragmatic set of axioms, the U.S. Constitution. Gödel was an Austrian who did most of his early work in Vienna. After the German invasion of Austria in 1938, Gödel found life increasingly dangerous under Nazi rule. In 1940 he fled Europe, came to the United States, and eventually settled in Princeton. Then, a few years later, he applied for U.S. citizenship. An academic to the core, he thoroughly analyzed the U.S. Constitution in preparation for the citizenship test. He approached it like a mathematical system: treat the main statements, the Bill of Rights, and the amendments like axioms and then derive theorems. The day came when he was to go before a judge to test his suitability for citizenship. Albert Einstein was a close friend and colleague of Gödel's at the Princeton Institute for Advanced Study, so he went with Gödel to act as a character witness that day. Now after his experiences with Nazi rule, Kurt Gödel was deeply concerned about dictatorships, and he studied whether a dictatorship could occur in America as a logical consequence of the Constitution's axioms. He thought he had found such a possibility. During the exam, the judge mentioned that Gödel had once lived under "an evil dictatorship . . . but fortunately that's not possible in America." Ever the logician, Gödel jumped right in and volunteered: "On the contrary, I know how that can happen and I can prove it." Eventually, the judge and Einstein calmed him down, and the citizenship test continued. It all ended well with Gödel becoming a citizen and staying in America until his death many years later.

Gödel's incompleteness theory is based on several deep technical definitions from mathematical logic — terms like "set of axioms is recursive," "first order system," "logic system extensions," and "ω-complete." Its proof is even deeper; it consists of page after page of difficult definitions involving a special

Table 3
Unprovable Statements

Axioms:	It is cold. It is raining. If it is cold and raining, then there isn't any baseball game and there aren't any fans.
True:	There isn't any baseball game. There aren't any fans.
False:	There is a baseball game and there are fans.
Unprovable:	No statistics professor is interesting. The color red is nice. All ancient Greek logicians are dead.

coding device (Gödel numbers) and intricate arguments. Any in-depth discussion of the theory requires an excursion into the realm of theoretical mathematics; to avoid this we will consider simplified logic systems to point out the fundamental nature of an unprovable statement and then look at an overview of the proof of the incompleteness theorem.

The example in Table 3 is a simple logic system; all of the axioms are from propositional logic (no quantifiers are used) and are from our previous example. The point is to illustrate which statements are true, false, and unprovable. Two true statements are derived from the axioms by using the rules that we used before. One false statement is the negation of the combined true statements (there are clearly others). The unprovable statements look ridiculous; they don't even relate to the axioms. But that is the point!

In logic, everything follows from the axioms. If the set of axioms is not extensive enough, then many reasonable-sounding propositions (like "All ancient Greek logicians are dead") will be outside the scope of the axioms and will be unprovable in *that particular logic system*. In other logic systems, these same statements might well be true (or false). Clearly, in the logic

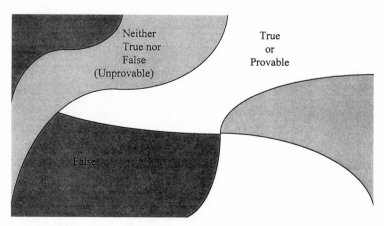

FIGURE 10. Gödel's incompleteness theorem. There will always be gray areas in reasoning that can never be proven true or false.

system we humans use, where historical facts are accepted as axioms, the statement "All ancient Greek logicians are dead" is true. However, in the above example with its extremely abbreviated set of axioms, this statement is unprovable.

Perhaps this was said best by IBM researcher Gregory Chaitin when he remarked: "You can't prove a twenty-pound theorem with a ten-pound theory." Figure 10 represents the situation — in any logical system there will always be a gray area in which the statements are neither true nor false for the given set of axioms. The above example is an oversimplification of real logic systems — for example, the arithmetic axioms allow an infinite number of true theorems — but it does depict the essence of the idea of unprovable statements. Now be clear on one point: Gödel's theory says much more than this example. The set of axioms that it deals with allows very general statements, and before Gödel it was not clear that all arithmetic statements could not be settled by the set of arithmetic axioms. This example and the graph in Figure 10 are trivial compared to regular logic systems — but the idea is the same. Hilbert's dream was for a set of axioms that would deduce a true or a false answer for any question about mathematics. Gödel showed that this was impossible for any set of axioms that could possibly be chosen now or in the future.

Gödel's theorem: No finite set of axioms for a logic system that contains arithmetic can be complete; there will always be legitimate arithmetic statements that are unprovable within the system.

Let's look carefully at the statement of Gödel's incompleteness theorem. First, notice that the set of axioms must be finite as we have noted before; we don't deal with truly infinite axiom sets. Second, the logical system must contain the axioms of arithmetic, since the proof will need the properties of arithmetic. Third, note carefully the word "legitimate" and the phrase "within that system" as they are essential to the theorem. What Gödel did was to construct an *almost* paradoxical, self-referencing statement within the axiom system referred to by the phrase "within that system." Next, he showed that this statement is not provable within that system yet it is a legitimate statement (meaning true) outside that system. Furthermore, he showed that you couldn't patch up the axioms and make the system complete; his proof method worked for all extensions of the original axiom system. A sketch of his proof follows.

1. Start with the set of axioms of arithmetic; call the logical system including these axioms and all resulting theorems *A*. Assume that *A* generates only true statements.
2. Set up a method of coding logical axioms, formulas, and proofs into statements about numbers (like we did with ASCII for programs, although Gödel used a different encoding system). Now all proofs and theorems in *A* can be coded into numerical statements.
3. Define S as the paradoxical statement "This sentence is unprovable in system *A*." "Provable" means that the statement follows from the axioms of the system in which

the sentence is being considered. This statement is to be considered within A and outside system A. Notice that the word sentence is a self-reference to itself or S. The situation is like S = "S is unprovable in system A."

4. In system A: (1) if S is true, then S is unprovable in system A, which can't be since we are assuming that S is true, hence S is provable; (2) if S is false, then S is unprovable in A is false so S is provable in A, hence S is true, which can't be.

5. Outside system A: by step 4 we have shown that it is impossible to prove S within system A. Hence, S is a truth. But it is a truth that can't be generated by system A.

This sketch doesn't do justice to the genius that it took to prove the theorem in the first place. Usually, this type of recursive definition can lead to an infinite regress or insists upon a false hypothesis or axiom that can't be allowed. By restricting things properly and by an extremely clever definition of his methodology, Gödel could avoid these logical problems.

We now have seen three limits on computers and logic: the difficult algorithms, impossible algorithms, and unprovable statements. How limiting are they really? We saw earlier that some difficult problems — the computationally infeasible problems, like network optimization problems — really do cause limitations because we can't solve them exactly. Also we saw an example of an impossible algorithm, the hypothetical program *Halt*, which didn't seem to be a big loss to society. Finally, we ran into Gödel's limit — some statements are unprovable; how limiting is this? Very tough question! Just for the record, most unprovable statements that we know of are very abstract mathematical statements that have nothing to do with reality as we know it. A disclaimer is in order: Proving statements unprovable has been entirely a mathematician's domain for the past 50 years. Mathematicians have concentrated on mathematical statements, not physical theories. Only recently have some physicists conjectured about logical limits on physical theories.

If we have some physical theory, say, a conjectured addition to quantum mechanics theory, which we find to be unprovable using our current system of axioms, what can we do? We could look for an additional axiom to add to our axiom system. Then we could try to prove the conjecture true under this new augmented axiom system. If the conjecture can be proven true then we could go looking for experimental support of the new axiom.

CHURCH'S THESIS

It might be a good time to map out how we are going to approach the issue of computers versus humans and decide which has the most logical power. At this point we have developed a basic computer model using a Pascal-like language and equated a computer program to a large number. Then we proved a result about what computers can't do. In this section, we are going to outline what computers can do. We will rely on a famous result called Church's thesis. Then we will show a simplified computer language (three statement types only) that can do anything that a high-level language can do. Next, using these three statements, we will give a quick proof that humans can do anything that a computer can do. Not that any of us ever doubted it.

At the heart of the human mind versus computer debate is a question: Could a future computer do everything that a human can? This question may or may not be resolved in the future. Even discussing it now leads to definition problems like how do we define what a person can do or how do we compare this to a computer process. One big step in this direction dates from the work of a logician of the 1930s — Alonzo Church. Known as Church's thesis, it addresses the issue of whether our computer programming languages are complete — *complete* meaning that any conceivable algorithm could be stated equivalently by a program written in that language. The result states that indeed our programming languages are complete. However, Church's thesis is a hypothesis; it really hasn't been proven.

The term algorithm needs a definition for this work, but in a sense we can't precisely define the term without referring to computerlike steps, which makes the definition somewhat circular. Church defined his thesis in terms of an abstract mathematical concept, the lambda calculus. A little later, a mathematician, Alan Turing, came up with a concept that included theoretical computing machines of a special type (now called Turing machines). Later theoretical results showed the equivalence of the Church thesis with a statement concerning Turing machines, so Turing's name is frequently associated with the thesis also. Turing's formulation is more natural and more often used. Turing machines are simplistic computer models, much more simplistic than any past or present computer. They can only read or write one symbol per computing step. Also, their sole input/output device is one long (infinitely) tape. Furthermore, their programming language makes simple real programming languages seem complicated by comparison. They work. In theory, a Turing machine has the same power as a modern computer system with its disk memory, its parallel processors, its RAM, and a CD-ROM. Because of this equivalence to modern computer power and because of their simplicity, Turing machines have become the main theoretical model in these kinds of studies. Our past discussion about simple computer concepts was close to Turing machines; the only differences were that we used a high-level language (most people are more familiar with them) and allowed the model to use RAM instead of a tape drive. Turing's use of tape drives and low-level languages was partly historical. Disk and RAM memory didn't exist as such, and modern computer languages weren't invented for another 20 years. Later, when disks and RAM memory became common, models like ours were shown to be theoretically equivalent to Turing's and Church's formulation. Therefore, our model is completely acceptable in a theoretical sense.

A related question is how complex does the programming language have to be to be complete, that is, to be capable of computing any possible algorithm. Not very. It can be shown that a very simple language that has three main types of statements can do as much as a powerful language like Pascal. Three types that can do the job are assignment statements, decision statements (if–then–else or while statements), and simple operations like addition. The language also needs to be able to group together blocks of statements to be executed together and some input/output ability — that's it. Our sample Pascal statements were indicative of a complete language's core. We will refer to this property as the *three-statement power*. In other words, if a programming language can emulate each of these three statements and if it can group statements and if it can do input/output, then we say that it has the same power as *three-statement power*.

A sketch of the proof that three statements suffice to do all the functions of a high-level programming language is as follows. First, the list of commands in a high-level language is laid out. For Pascal a partial list might look like assignments, if–then, if–then–else, while, for, until, bit operations, arithmetic operations, read, write, begin, and end. Second, starting with the three statements (say, assignments, while, and simple bit and arithmetic operations), develop macros (small programs) that emulate each of the high-level language commands. These macros will consist of only these three statement types and assumed capabilities or previously proven macros. Eventually, this bootstrap method will prove that macros of the three statements will do all of the high-level language commands. Any program in the high-level language can now be written in a three-statement form by substituting for each high-level command the associated macro made up of only the three basic statement types. Hence, three statements suffice.

These three simple statements lie at the core of the computers versus humans debate. First, we know (actually assume) by the Church–Turing thesis that a simple Turing machine can do all possible algorithms. Second, there are proofs (not very difficult) that a general high-level programming language is the logical equivalent of a Turing machine (although faster). Third, the earlier proof showed that these three statements can do anything that a high-level language can do, and therefore anything a Turing machine can do. Therefore, a language composed of only these three statement types can do *any* algorithm.

The power of digital computers is the same as three-statement power. That is what the above paragraph says.

Now how about the human mind? Can it do the three statements? The human mind will have no trouble with input/output statements since we can both read and write, listen, and talk. Also, blocking statements together causes us no problem. The only detail that needs verifying is that a human can do the three basic statements.

The human mind can easily do the three basic statements. For example: an assignment statement is simply an association of a name with an operation for a human. Clearly, the human mind can do simple arithmetic operations like adding and multiplying and simple bit operations like moving all bit values one place to the left. The last statement, a "while" statement, is easy for a human too. A while statement starts with a comparison or if statement, and it is easy enough for humans to compare two bit strings to see if they satisfy a simple bit-comparison criterion. Next, the human must be able to complete the operation that is to be performed if the "if" statement is true. Notice that this operation must be either an assignment, an operation, or another while statement. Only a while statement causes us a problem since there is a possibility of many while statements being used. But a string of while statements must end somewhere. We already know that a human can do the assignment or operation statement. If the operation is another while statement, then we know that the human can do the comparison part, and we just keep following any string of while statements down until the operation is a non-while statement. This statement must be one of the other two types, which we already know that a human can do. As mathematicians say, QED; it follows that humans are at *least* as good as computers!

Now consider the flip side of the coin. If humans do not possess some logic ability above that of computers, if humans can't do something more than a combination of these three statements can do, then human activity is equivalent to the three-statement power, in a sense. If this is true, there is a letdown, a certain despair that all that we have accomplished and all that we can accomplish can also be accomplished by combinations of those three statements.

There is no way to neatly summarize logic; it is an open-ended endeavor with upper limits. Current research in logic is extremely abstract; it involves dealing with complex mathematical–logical structures and proving theorems that don't promise much application to reality. However, some researchers are not following a traditional path but are looking for totally new logics. One of these efforts might pay off and open the future to a new type of reasoning.

Is logic correct? What proves it? How can you verify it? Is it possible that all the Greeks, all the philosophers, all the mathematicians, and all the intellectuals for all these centuries have missed the point, and logic as we know it is not correct? An even more pointed question can be asked: Who is to say that people have the intelligence to make true observations about fundamental truths like logic? Why should bundles of DNA (us) with just 2000 years of experience thinking about abstract ideas be capable of discerning what is absolutely true and what is not? Our logic has only two values — true and false; maybe there are more possibilities: three, four, or infinite. Our statements must be true or false always; maybe sometimes a statement should be true, sometimes false. Are these ideas realistic?

There aren't any answers. However, logic has evolved because it answers questions that we can gauge by the results. We believe that current logic does reflect reality although there may be more: Logic seems like a partial answer to final truth.

The twentieth century has been the age of computers and quantum mechanics; both have raised questions about what, if any, ultimate limitations there are on mechanical thought and the universe. Robotics, computer thought, free will, and other ideas have perplexed and confused people about ultimate questions. The twentieth century has also been the age of Gödel and his contemporaries — researchers who have proved that no matter how far we go, there will still be unfathomable depths and unscalable heights that await us. Ten thousand years from now, people will still be searching for truths, but they will never find them all.

Chapter 9

Real-World Limits — Mathematics, Programming, and Logic

A man has gotta know his limitations.

CLINT EASTWOOD[1]

Limits come in many forms; there are problems that don't have solutions, there are processes that are needed but are to be unattainable, and there are limits on our ability to understand complex programs and numbers. Now that we have seen the theory of limitations, we explore some concrete examples of what it means to be impossible or intractable or too complex. Some limits are very low ceilings and cause us problems even today.

THE IMPOSSIBLE IN MATHEMATICS

Truths depend on axioms; what is true is elusive. Several times over the last 200 years different axiom systems have been defined to prove a conjecture, where this conjecture was unprovable by the axiom system in use at that time. Often this is confusing since it seems that what is true is fundamental and shouldn't depend on anything else. This belief in an underlying truth was hard to overcome even for mathematicians and logicians; truths based on other axiom systems appeared suspect. To put the issue abstractly, if you have one axiom system with axioms A, B, and C which you alter by deleting axiom C and adding axiom D, then you get a completely different set of true statements (theorems) from this A–B–D set then you would from the A–B–C set. Surprising results can follow: Axiom C, which was a basic truth (all axioms are true) in the A–B–C system, could be false or unprovable in the A–B–D system, or a conjecture X might be true in the A–B–D system but unprovable in the A–B–C system.

Changing axioms is more than a logic technique or trick; it serves a good purpose in the right situations. Mathematicians and logicians can be cavalier about truths as just logical consequences of axiom systems. To paraphrase the Declaration of Independence, some truths are self-evident; these self-evident truths should follow logically from our axiom systems or we need to change our axioms to reflect truth as we see it. Be careful however, self-evident truths can be relative.

Geometry was the first area of mathematics put on a firm logical foundation during the age of the Greeks. Euclid developed geometry, the lemmas, the theorems, and the proofs based upon a set of axioms that he saw as self-evident. His contemporaries also viewed the axioms as evidently true and representative of fundamental truths. One axiom, Euclid's fifth axiom, appeared true but less fundamental than the others; over the centuries there were many attempts to prove that the fifth axiom followed from the other axioms. Many scholars believed that the fifth axiom was not independent of the other axioms but instead was a provable theorem in the axiom system with itself removed. (Recall that the fifth axiom said that if we have a straight line and a point not on the line in a plane, then one and only one line parallel to the original line can be drawn through the point.)

This effort ended in an unusual way: during the nineteenth century two non-Euclidean geometries were invented — Riemann elliptic geometry and hyperbolic geometry, invented by Bolyai and Lobatchevsky. Both of these used different axiom sets, and both came up with startling results. In the geometry of Bolyai and Lobatchevsky, there are many different parallel lines possible; in the geometry of Riemann, there are none. All three geometries are logically consistent; all three make good physical sense in different applications; all three give different answers to the situation posed in Euclid's fifth axiom. Euclid's best fits the applications of measurements on earth; Riemann's best fits space–time geometry applications.

A survivor of high school geometry might wonder why the Greeks used rulers and compasses in the first place; why does it seem that most proofs in plane geometry involve constructions with rulers and compasses, anyway? The Greeks of antiquity were firmly implanted in the real world, a world of buildings, ships, trading, land, and measurements. Rulers and compasses were basic instruments to them, as familiar as calculators are to today's students. As craftsmen, accuracy was important to them, and means of improving accuracy or extending their techniques through better understanding were topics of professional interest, just as is the case today when Wall Street traders discuss new technical analysis techniques at their social gatherings or engineers meet to hear papers on aspects of their trade or doctors attend medical gatherings. Craftsmen throughout the ages have wanted to improve their trade, whatever it was. Ancient Greeks were no different. Geometry to them dealt with extensions of everyday concepts, and Euclid axiomized these concepts, putting them on a logical, and hence accurate, foundation.

Squaring the circle (constructing with ruler and compass a square with the same area as a given circle) would have been a useful technique to know. Certainly, attempts to solve the problem were made for a long time, probably for hundreds of years, for a long enough time that eventually it became accepted as impossible and most thinkers gave up on it. We do know that by 400 B.C. those still trying to solve it were the objects of some ridicule, since a playwright of the time used "circle squarer" as a derisive phrase in one of his plays. By the 1800s there had been hundreds of failed constructions over the span of more than 2000 years.

The disproof came only after people viewed geometry differently; instead of viewing geometry as ruler-and-compass constructions, they applied the algebra of the early 1800s. They modeled the actions of physically using a ruler and compass with algebra; these actions were designated a certain type of algebraic operation with provable properties for combining them. Hence, various sets of these algebraic-construction operations served as a virtual construction process. Now the problem of constructing a square of the same area as a circle became the algebraic problem of applying a sequence of algebraic-construction operations to a circle and ending up with a square. In the early 1800s this conjecture was finally laid to rest: A proof came out that no such sequence of operations could possibly exist — squaring the circle was quite impossible.

Also, dating from antiquity is the problem of the representation of $\sqrt{2}$. Some background discussion is in order here since this isn't an issue with us at all. We are accustomed to the real-number system; we are accustomed to the idea of infinite divisibility. The ancients were accustomed to rulers, bisections, and integers (remember this was long before the invention of decimal notation). Rational numbers have the property that between any two distinct real numbers you will find a rational; mathematically speaking, the rational numbers are a dense subset of the reals. Hence, you can approximate any real number by a sequence of rational numbers with any degree of accuracy that you need (which is exactly what computers do). Now if you didn't know any better (if you didn't have any concept of real numbers), the set of rational numbers would seem quite adequate. After all, you can measure with them to any accuracy that you want. To you the rationals appear as a continuous string of numbers, and you might imagine that any point or length or area has a rational-number representation. However, a dilemma presents itself; an ancient architect notices that in order to form the unit square of area one square foot, he needs to make that square one foot on each side; likewise, for an area of four square feet, two feet on a side. How about an area of two square feet? By extending the sides of the one-square-foot square a little at a time, you will eventually reach a four-square-foot square; at some point, you must have passed over the two-square-foot square. What point was it? The answer must be some rational number, right? But then some ancient scientist trained in Greek logic points out the following proof that no rational number squared can equal 2 (Pythagoras discovered this during the sixth century B.C.).

Suppose that $\sqrt{2}$ is a rational number which we designate as n/d (where the numerator n and the denominator d are both integers, and the fraction is in lowest terms so n and d do not have a common divisor greater than one). First, notice that if n/d is in lowest terms, then either both n and d are odd or only one of n and d is odd, since both can't be even because then 2 would be a common divisor. Next, start with the equation $n/d = \sqrt{2}$ and square both sides, getting $n^2/d^2 = 2$. Multiply both sides by d^2 and get: $n^2 = 2d^2$. Now consider the possible cases: (1) n is even and d is odd; hence n^2 is divisible by 4, but $2d^2$ can't be divisible by 4 since d^2 is odd, so case (1) can't happen; (2) n and d are odd; hence both n^2 and d^2 are odd, but then the odd n^2 equals the even number $2d^2$, which is also impossible. The conclusion is that both cases are impossible so the assumption must be wrong; therefore, $\sqrt{2}$ is not a rational number.

Well, the puzzled ancient architect says, maybe the original scheme was wrong and you can't really increase the sides of squares and pass through every possibility. Maybe, a length of $\sqrt{2}$ doesn't really exist after all. But then the ancient scientist, with all his Greek logic, points out that the unit square has a diagonal of $\sqrt{2}$, so it must be a true length after all. Which is it?

Both of these ancient unsolvable problems caused grave problems for the mathematicians of their day. Both were resolved in different ways. First, notice a common thread: Both problems are impossible within the original axiom system. Euclid's axioms could not allow a construction of an equivalent square; the axioms of integer arithmetic did not allow a rational representation for $\sqrt{2}$. Second, notice that both have at least a partial solution when the axiom sets expand and include the real-number system. For the case of squaring the circle, if r is the radius of the circle, then the area is πr^2; hence $\sqrt{\pi r^2}$ is a real-number representation of the length of a square with the same area as the circle. But, of course, this transcendental number can't be constructed with ruler and compass methods. For the case of $\sqrt{2}$, the number is clearly a real number, so upon extension of the number system to the reals the nonexistence issue goes away and the number does exist.

Increasing the axiom set or broadening the meaning of some axioms is not just a theoretical exercise in logic; these are real-world examples where axioms were changed to solve problems.

SO MANY CALCULATIONS, SO LITTLE TIME

The most important unsolved problem in computer science and mathematics is the NP-complete problem. Many mathematics problems of the past have achieved temporary fame; still, from the ancient squaring-the-circle problem to the four-color problem to the recently solved Fermat's last theorem, none has had the impact on computer science that a resolution of the NP-complete problem will have. The NP-complete problem is overwhelmingly important simply because it affects the solvability of hundreds of important computer, planning, and design-related problems. It is not one equation like Fermat's last theorem, and it is not one procedure like squaring the circle or the four-color problem. The NP-complete problem is an umbrella statement that if answered "yes" will (perhaps) lead the way to a set of tremendously efficient algorithms for resource allocation, network planning, computer design, and many other tasks. If it is answered "no" (most betting is on this outcome), a door will be slammed in humanity's face, forever keeping us from optimizing our designs, our plans, our resources, and our lives. High stakes, indeed, for a single math problem.

The problem wasn't completely defined until the 1960s and didn't have a name until discoveries a few years later — a late arrival for a major mathematical hypothesis. The NP-complete problem is a blanket statement about the time complexity of a whole class of problems.

If we have N numbers as inputs to a program, then the running time of the program is designated $T(N)$, since in general the more inputs to a program, the longer it runs. The form of this time complexity function $T(N)$ is of paramount interest to computer programmers. If the function has a form such that the running time grows rapidly as N grows larger, then there comes a point, a large enough value of N, at which it takes a prohibitive amount of time to run the program and solve the problem. Although there are many possible functional forms, we will concentrate on only two: fixed integer powers of N (called polynomial) and 2 raised to the power of N (called exponential). It turns out that most important design and resource algorithms fall into one of these two categories.

There are two good reasons why we consider polynomial time complexity as practical and why we consider it the line of demarcation between practical problems and intractable or virtually impossible problems. First, it is a simple function, and the next simple functions are the exponential functions, which we know are intractable for large N. Second, the two function classes come up quite often in programming practice. For example, we could get a linear form of the time function $T(N)$ if there was a constant amount of processing done for each of the N inputs. We could get a quadratic form of $T(N)$ if there was a constant amount of processing done for each pair of the N inputs [there are $N(N - 1)$ pairs]. In the same pattern, for a constant amount of processing on each triple of the N inputs we would get a cubic polynomial form of $T(N)$. A big jump occurs if we have to do a constant amount of processing for each of the 2^N possible subsets of the N inputs. This is the exponential case. The line of demarcation is polynomial time since even the case of eight nested loops, which gives a time complexity of N^8, is very computation-intensive but still could be done for numbers like $N = 100$, whereas the exponential case is effectively impossible for $N = 100$.

Many network design, resource allocation, data retrieval, scheduling, computer program optimization, and fault detection algorithms have the same difficulty. One recent example, which is the subject of much research, is computer-board manufacturing. During the manufacture of a circuit board, many (1 to 2 million) holes need drilling. The pattern of the holes is established in the design phase; the chip production plant needs to plan a circuit around the holes to minimize the time it takes to drill the holes and the amount of movement that the drill must make. With all the computer chips being produced, there would be a large savings with a more efficient path. A lot of money and resources are spent above what is optimal. What we need is a polynomial time algorithm for solving this problem and other problems like it. Algorithm designers have pursued this goal for years.

Until the 1970s a shotgun approach was used; researchers attacked several optimization, network theory, graph theory, and mathematical programming problems separately. As time passed, they noticed that problems from diverse fields could be mathematically transformed into each other, and so could algorithms that solved them. Still the gap between polynomial and exponential time solutions proved to be too much to handle. What they needed was a new insight, new ideas, and a common approach to this class of problems. The traveling salesman problem is the best known of this type of problem. It is also typical in a very strong sense (shown later), so we'll look at it as representative of the entire class of problems. In the traveling salesman problem, there is a group of cities to visit with the distances provided between all pairs of cities. For example, suppose that a salesman has been assigned a route covering the western half of the United States, 70 cities or towns in all, and must visit each of them once a month but no more often. He is traveling by car and wants to spend as little time on the road as possible; his problem is to find out how he can visit all of the cities exactly once and still travel less than 3000 miles. (The 3000 miles could be another distance, but the statement of the problem requires one fixed distance.) He needs a specific route: a trip that takes him through each city. Also, there might not even be a solution, a path, which covers 3000 miles or less.

The big problem here is this: The brute force method of trying every possible path is almost impossible (70!, which is the total number of paths, is an impossibly large number). Our salesman needs a vastly more efficient algorithm. But no such luck. We know dozens of algorithms that solve the traveling salesman problem; *all* of them have exponential time complexity. This means for a size of $N = 70$ a case could exist that could take over 350 centuries for an algorithm that compares a billion paths per second. (Note carefully that this is the worst case; for special types of network topologies of cities, the problem can be solved much faster.) Note also that the lack of a good algorithm is not because of the lack of trying; problems like this have used more researchers' time than many famous math problems. An engineer who discovered such an algorithm would become famous and perhaps rich (such an algorithm would make a bundle for his company). Many have tried, many are still trying, but it is beginning to look impossible.

Fantasy is full of tales of genies in bottles, fairy godmothers, and leprechauns who grant you three wishes or the answers to your questions. Now suppose that one of them offers us a solution to a particular traveling salesman problem. What do we do? The answer is just an ordering of the cities to visit; we don't really know if it is a solution. However, it's not hard to verify whether the solution works; just sum the $N - 1$ distances involved and check if the sum is less than 3000 miles. Let's suspend disbelief for a while longer and examine some fine points. Focus on two points: First, there is essentially no computation time involved in accepting the offered solution and, second, the time expended in verifying that the solution works is linear in N (recall it was $N - 1$), which more generally is a polynomial time function.

As crazy as this sounds, guessing is the starting point for the mathematical assault on this type of problem — and not just guessing, but guessing correctly the first time and every time. Now, of course, mathematicians have not completely lost their minds here; there is a method to this madness. During research, mathematicians focus so completely on their goal that often they come up with seemingly outlandish ways of approaching the goal. Here the focus is on a polynomial time solution — any polynomial time solution, no matter how inelegant or ugly. No matter how inelegant or ugly it is, a polynomial time algorithm will greatly outperform even the most elegant exponential time algorithm. If mathematicians had even one polynomial time algorithm, then they could study it and find what makes it polynomial compared to exponential. But they don't have one, at least not a real algorithm. They do have this fantasy algorithm — guess and verify.

Computers are deterministic, we know that. What has been done in this area of computer science is to define a completely theoretical device called a *nondeterministic algorithm*. Essentially, this theoretical algorithm is hypothesized to guess correct answers in one step; then it goes through a normal computer procedure to *verify* that the solution is correct. For those problems where this verification procedure is a polynomial time algorithm, the problem is said to be in the class NP (for nondeterministic polynomial). The traveling salesman problem is a problem in the class NP, since we can solve it by a nondeterministic algorithm in polynomial time. Also, hundreds of other problems can be solved by nondeterministic algorithms in polynomial time; this is a very insightful distinction between classes of problems.

A special subclass of NP problems is important; we call this subclass NP-complete problems, and it is where the theory got its name. It all started in 1970 when Dr. Stephen Cook was finishing his doctoral program at the University of California at Berkeley. Many of these types of algorithms had been widely studied before this time; however, Dr. Cook gave the entire study a new focus and a very important theorem to start it off in a new direction. He proved a theorem of primary significance, called ever since Cook's theorem. It showed that one particular problem of this type, called the satisfiability problem, had the property that every other problem in the NP class could be polynomially reduced to it. Since then, hundreds more problems of this type have been discovered; they are called the NP-complete class. The theorem means that if any problem in the NP-complete class has a polynomial time solution, then all members of NP also have a polynomial time solution. Solve one, solve them all.

The NP-complete problem simply stated is: Does P = NP? In words, does the class of problems that can be solved by polynomial time algorithms have exactly the same members as the class of problems that can be solved by nondeterministic polynomial time algorithms? Perfect guessing (which is essentially magic) would seem to be a powerful tool, but this conjecture questions whether it really helps that much over a regular polynomial time algorithm. Notice that all members of class P are also members of class NP since any polynomial time algorithm could be used as the verification stage of an NP algorithm. Therefore, the question comes down to proving or disproving that some member of NP is not in P.

This then is the biggest unproven conjecture in mathematics today. There are three possible outcomes: (1) P = NP, (2) P ⊂ NP (some NP not in P, proper containment), and (3) the conjecture is unsolvable within the axiom system.

The first, P = NP, is the exciting one; it promises future algorithms of incredible speed that will optimize many of our society's resource allocation plans, network designs, communications, and much more. It could save tremendous amounts of time and money, freeing up scarce resources for other uses. An algorithm that can do any problem of the NP-complete class would be perhaps the greatest feat in mathematics ever! Unfortunately, almost no one believes that P = NP is correct.

The third possibility is always mentioned whenever researchers have spent a lot of fruitless effort trying to prove a conjecture. "Maybe, it's just not solvable within the axiom system" is a common explanation, and one that has been mentioned for other important conjectures that eventually were proven or disproven. As of a few years ago, some felt that Fermat's last theorem might be unsolvable. However, it too was proven recently. But, of course, several famous conjectures did turn out to be unsolvable within the axiom systems: Euclid's fifth axiom and the continuum hypothesis are two cases in point. A fair number of researchers believe that this case is the final answer for the P = NP conjecture.

The second possibility, P ⊂ NP, is the outcome that most researchers believe will be the eventual result. However, the proof is still a ways off, although it is the most heavily analyzed theoretical conjecture in computer science today. This is the limiting result, which is also quite discouraging. Some mathematical limits are of theoretical interest only; this result affects us and our future.

The result P ⊂ NP would be bad news. Computationally intractable problems limit us, we already know it. However, this result would place a very low ceiling above us; it wouldn't allow us to reach optimal solutions for most design problems. As bad as this news is, there is even worse news ahead. Read on.

A ROAD-WEARY TRAVELING SALESMAN

The traveling salesman problem is NP-complete; Cook's theorem says that if a polynomial time algorithm can be found for this problem, then one can be found for all problems in NP.

This makes the traveling salesman problem quite central to the entire issue. Solve it and you can solve any of them. Therefore, we will concentrate on this problem, knowing that most of what we learn is applicable across the board to the other NP problems.

Of course, we can't solve it and probably never will. Life must go on, however; we can't avoid traveling salesman-type problems, for they come up often in design. Therefore, if we can't solve them exactly with a general algorithm, then we have two approaches: We can (maybe) design a special algorithm for a special problem that has polynomial time complexity, or we can settle for approximate solutions that are close. With these approaches in mind, we consider two practical approaches to getting acceptable solutions from this type of problem: (1) Some problems have particular topologies of cities that allow vast simplification that leads to optimal solutions, and (2) often we will settle for an approximate solution that is close to optimal.

Researchers have many methods of solving this problem; one widely used method is linear programming. In a linear programming solution, each path is considered as a vertex on a multidimensional polygon. A linear function, "trip length," is the length of the path represented by the vertex. The linear programming algorithm finds the shortest trip by finding that vertex where the trip length is at a minimum. (Another aside: A linear programming algorithm moves from vertex to vertex and lowers the value of the trip-length function at each step, until it stops at the global minimum.) An important disclaimer: Not all problems of size N take exponential time; some do, some don't. The worst case is exponential; often researchers can take advantage of certain aspects of the problem and solve even very large problems. The current record is 3038 cities.

A technique called "partitioning" is often used to take advantage of topological aspects. One example is the hypothetical problem of finding the minimum distance that is required to fly to every major airport in the world (N is over 500 for this case). This problem has been solved. Let's look at some commonsense observations about this problem and see how incorporating them into the solution algorithm will drastically reduce the number of possible paths that must be considered. Assume that we start in the United States and must end here too. A common-sense observation is don't fly across oceans more often than necessary — only once should be necessary. An optimal solution should visit all the airports in North and South America before going on to Europe or Africa. It wouldn't make sense to go from New York to London, then fly around Europe for a while and come back to visit Miami — the optimal solution can't be that. A fine-tuning approach, visit all cities in the United States before visiting Rio de Janeiro. Again, it wouldn't make sense to backtrack several thousand miles to visit another U.S. city after flying to Rio de Janeiro. Now, we can partition our problem into a set of smaller problems; these smaller problems involve choosing a minimum-length path between cities that are close to each other, local groups of cities. Then we combine these local groups into entire-world-airport tours and look for the minimum among this special subclass of tours; we are certain that the optimal path is among this greatly reduced subclass. Calling this subclass "greatly reduced" is an understatement: There are about 500! possible entire-world-airport tours; if we form local groups of 25 cities (this is the partitioning process), then the problem goes down to an approximate subproblem of finding the minimum path between 20 local groups. The size differential is impossibly large: 25! is practically zero compared to 500!. Techniques like partitioning are widely used to solve single, large, and very important problems; these are the problems on which it is worthwhile to spend a lot of money to get the best possible solution. However, it isn't always possible, no matter how much money you have to spend.

The second technique is finding approximate solutions. It's like a pragmatic manager telling his computer science staff: "OK, so we can't ever do the absolute minimum. Just find me the 99% solution and I'll be happy." A recent discovery is that (assuming $P \neq NP$) beyond a certain accuracy threshold most

NP-complete problems cannot even be approximated without using exponential time algorithms.

The bad news about the NP-complete problems is that exact solutions are probably of exponential time complexity; the *really* bad news is that approximate solutions are too. This is truly bad news, and it represents a low limit on humans and computers.

COMPLEXITY OF PROGRAMS AND THEORIES

Programs are like theories: A program takes input numbers, processes them, and outputs other numbers — much like Newton's laws or Einstein's equations, where the processing is implied by the equal sign. Some theories are obviously more "complex" than others just on the basis of the number and difficulty of the equations involved. We can see this intuitively; however, as in many other areas that require understanding or meaning, it is very hard to define terms rigorously. This is a major shortfall of AI today and likely will be for the future. Understanding and meaning are and will remain elusive. In recent years, researchers have examined part of the problem, complexity, and have found some interesting results. Complexity has aspects that are quantifiable, and that one fact allows mathematical analysis.

Quantifying this concept of "complex" is the issue. The first good effort came along late in the history of science, about 1964. During that year a researcher, Ray Solomonoff of the Zantor Corporation, published an article that attempted to measure the complexity of scientific theories. His definition was that the "complexity" of a theory was the size of the shortest program that encoded the theory in ASCII. (For example: Einstein's famous equation $e = mc^2$ could be written in Pascal as $e := m * c * c$. This statement has eight characters so its complexity is eight.) A key word is *shortest*. Clearly, programs of arbitrarily large size can output the same values. The point is that scientists develop theories to make their knowledge database smaller, more compact, more understandable — the shorter the better. Physical models are usually compact sets of equations that transform the input data into the output. These equations might be algebraic equations or differential equations, or they might involve random functions or random inputs from another source. Scientists pursue the goal of compacting information into these models to simplify their understanding of nature.

During the same period, a very brilliant high school student, Gregory Chaitin, was tackling a college-level computer programming course given at Columbia University. Before the arrival of large, fast, and cheap computer memory, there was a great emphasis on efficient coding of programs. This meant writing the program code in as short a form as possible to cut down the size of the executable code module. The story is that in this programming class the students competed among themselves to see who could write the most compact program for their regular programming assignments. Apparently, the question came up of how to prove that a program was really the shortest possible that solved the given problem. Chaitin considered this problem even after the course was over and he had moved on to undergraduate studies at the City University of New York. By then, he had changed the focus of the problem slightly from programs to numbers, posing questions like which of the following numbers is more complex: 24, π, or $\sqrt{2}$.[2]

A first step toward an understanding of number complexity is to consider a paradoxical description of certain numbers. Around the turn of the century, Bertrand Russell was asked a question by a Cambridge librarian named Mr. Berry. The question was a paradox: "What is the smallest number that cannot be expressed in 15 words or less?" Since known as the Berry Number or Berry Paradox, this question contains the seeds of interesting ideas. Consider it: If there is a smallest number that cannot be expressed in 15 words or less, then it can be given the designator "the smallest number that cannot be expressed in 15 words or less," which is a unique expression of the number in less than 15 words. Another variant of the paradox is: "What is the smallest number that can't be described in words?" Both versions rely on a number defined by a characterization in words and a minimizing condition ("shortest"). Now, these are paradoxes, and neither of these numbers exists. However, the paradox is caused by the same problem that we have seen before: a definition that requires that some operation can't be done (recall the God-and-the-wheel paradox). It forms a logical contradiction and isn't usable. However, a change in the wording avoids the paradox issue.

Chaitin defined the complexity of a number to be the length of the shortest computer program that will output that number. Next he came up with a definition that said that a number is *random* if the length of the shortest program that outputs this number is not much shorter than the number itself.

Rational numbers like 1/3 and 27/352 clearly have finite complexity, since a computer program need only store two integers and then take the quotient to generate the rational number. This is similar to the finite-information concept we saw earlier. Many well-known irrational numbers (e, π, and $\sqrt{2}$) also have finite complexity; these numbers can be compactly expressed as an infinite series. To evaluate the number, simply sum the infinite series. Of course, a computer can't run the infinite amount of time that it takes to sum an infinite series; however, this is theory, and we are talking about computer programs that theoretically evaluate these numbers. We aren't interested in running the programs to infinity; we are interested in the size of the programs that will evaluate these numbers to any number of decimal places.

If the terms in the infinite series form a pattern that can be coded (in a finite number of statements), then the number has finite complexity. (Aside for programmers: to sum a series, programmers use a standard programming technique — a loop with a temporary variable that holds the current sum of the series to the kth place. Then the next iteration of the loop evaluates the $(k + 1)$st place and adds it to the value of the sum to get the sum out to $k + 1$ places. This code is clearly of finite size since the next value of the series can be computed with finite-size code.)

As simple as this program-complexity concept seems, there are some pitfalls. First, we have to be careful about program forms and conventions. Earlier, we discussed computer programs written in Pascal in a general way. One key point was that we allowed a short-name variable (like "N") to represent a string of memory locations. Depending on the way certain conventions in the compiler and the language are defined, there is often no absolute upper limit on the length of a string represented by a short name like N. Consider two different programs: first, two statements, *read N* followed by *write N*, and, second, one statement *write 47831289045886632*. Both are trivial programs but the first could give the same output as the second if the number read in as N was the same as the large number in the second program. The length of the first two-statement program is always 10 bytes; the length of the second will go up as the length of the number goes up. For a number that takes 10,000,000 bytes to express, the length of the second program will be 10,000,004 bytes. Yet the two programs seem as if they should have the same inherent complexity. We need a convention to take care of this situation. We can do this with our Pascal programs by simply barring from consideration programs that read a long number into a variable name. We will assume that instead of read statements like *read N*, that we consider the equivalent program that has the assignment statement $N :=$ *47831289045886632* in place of the input statements. Therefore, the shortest program that we consider must not contain input statements but will use an equivalent form with assignment statements. [Long aside: Chaitin's original theory was developed using universal Turing machines as the theoretical foundation. Turing machines are theoretical devices that use a tape drive as input, output, and memory. The complexity of a Turing machine must consider the input used on the tape, since that is part of the initial conditions. Otherwise, one could "cheat" by storing a more complex program as input data and then running it. Since we have used Pascal programs to discuss programming, instead of the more difficult to understand Turing machines (the two approaches are equivalent), we need to make this one extra convention to discuss complexity.] On the other hand, it is all right to put arbitrarily large values in local variables that might occur in the program execution.

Chaitin's theorem states that if we have a single computer program P, then there always will be a number N such that N is the most complex number that program P can generate. This N is an absolute upper limit of the complexity-generation capability of that single computer program.

This is one of the most interesting theorems ever in computer science, and it is worth looking at in detail. Chaitin's theorem says some things, it hints at some others, and it doesn't say anything at all about still other things. First, Chaitin's theorem says that one computer program can't do everything. No future AI program will ever uncover all truths; the theorem does say that. However, this is talking about one single program; what if the AI program grows? It depends on that external input data issue. A program that can learn like humans and can access more and more data and can create even more programming based on this new data will evolve to a different program. It too will have an upper limit on its complexity, but it won't be the same as that of the original program. An example is a program that has access to a library of other programs; it could read one in, and then it could generate any number that this other program could. Chaitin's theorem is clear and unequivocal; however, the way that we use the phrase "one program" might not fit the rigorous axioms that were used to prove the theorem in the first place. Second, the conclusion refers to generating numbers, not understanding nor insight nor meaning. Although we might think that a more complex program can understand better than a simpler program, the conclusion of the theorem doesn't state this as such. A person at one given instant has a finite brain, and finite available data and could (maybe) be equated to one program; then this person would be limited by Chaitin's theorem. Rudy Rucker had a good way of describing this: "Chaitin's theorem says that I can't stand on top of my own head. I can't be smarter than I am."[3] Like the AI program that could access other programs and external data, people could increase their own complexity-generation capability by growing intellectually. Chaitin's theorem is an upper limit at one point in time, but it does say that we will always have some upper limits, like random-number generation. Chaitin's theorem is a lot like Gödel's theorem in this respect—add more axioms (add more programming code, facts, and theories) and you can prove more theorems (you can generate more complex numbers). But you will never, never prove them all.

COMPLEXITY AND UNDERSTANDING

Compact sets of equations form short programs (usually) and hence low program complexity. Does that mean that the mechanisms of nature are not very complex in our sense of the word? On the other hand, nature has qualities that take infinite precision to measure; these measurements may even be random numbers that can't be generated by any program. If we input one of these measurements into our model and if we count the input length as complexity, then we have a large- or infinite-complexity combination of number plus program. So is nature complex or simple? In short, models are our view of nature. They are compact, and they are accurate; now what does this say about the complexity of nature?

A problem is the dichotomy between understanding and complexity. Now they aren't meant to be opposites; however, normal English usage has understanding as harder if the subject is more complex, and something that can understand complexity is normally thought of as highly developed or intelligent. We develop our models to aid understanding; we think that reality is complex, but the better models are the simpler models.

The program *Halt* needed to understand all other programs in a very important way — whether they halted on all inputs. No program could do that, we proved it. But could some program understand all other programs with complexities less than some upper bound? This is a hard question; it depends on the definition of a program *understanding* another. If it is just verifying that the program gives correct answers, then the answer is yes (assuming the correct answers are known beforehand); there are logical methods, called logical semantics, which would handle this. If it is finding infinite loops, then the answer is case dependent, since there is no general method for this by the Halting theorem. However, the logical semantics specification that "understands" is usually much, much longer than the program that is to be "understood." That is a general rule in programming. To "understand" the programming entity must be much more complex than its subject. This is a general concept that we will use later in discussions of real-world limits in politics and laws.

The definition of complexity for numbers is the length of the shortest program that can *generate* that number. In a sense this means that a high-complexity number has so little pattern that it takes a program with a great deal of complexity to generate the number. This is the essence of Chaitin's theorem: No program can generate (or calculate or compute) a number more complex than itself.

A hotly debated question is how this complexity notion might apply to understanding. Here is an example of the question as applied to a final theory. We saw before that a program like the two-statement program (*read N* and *write N*) has a low complexity since it is short. We needed to rule out such an example because it can read in a number with arbitrarily large complexity and then output it too. However, this is exactly what the fundamental equations of physics do. Newton's law $F = ma$ is an equation that can take an arbitrarily complex number a for an input and generate a result F that might also have a very large complexity. However, the equation itself is simple. Do

Newton's law and Einstein's theory represent a high degree of understanding? Of course they do. Would a *final theory* represent a high degree of understanding? Most certainly! Would a *final theory* represent a complex theory? No, not really, since the point of theories is to compact the information into an understandable form. In symbolic form, *simple equations + high-complexity input data = high-complexity output data.* The point is that the issues of understanding and complexity are not flip sides of a coin. Being complex does not necessarily mean hard to understand, although it does mean hard to generate. Nor does a simple theory represent little understanding.

All is not well with complexity as currently defined; there are more than 30 currently used definitions of complexity out there. Chaitin's definition is concise, understandable, and rigorous enough to use in mathematical theorems. However, there is a perception problem with complexity as defined by Chaitin: It makes randomness a high-complexity characteristic. This isn't how many view complexity. One view is that if a group of monkeys pound away on typewriters for enough time, their output will be very close to random, and hence very complex — much more complex than a carefully reasoned book about mathematics that follows patterns and hence is more predictable and less complex.

No matter what the final resolution on complexity, it represents a limit on our understanding, but, to an extent, that limit is movable. More analysis, more data, and more complex programs will raise our understanding and the complexity of the programs that we generate. We will move further and further into the unknown.

The unknown that we move further into is the *knowable* unknown; many new theories are out there just waiting for us — we just need more or better axioms or more data to find them. There may also be an *unknowable* unknown. This negates the prospect of a final theory, but it is a very real possibility. Such a situation would be an absolute limit. Since this is a possibility that we need to at least consider later, we will conceptualize the situation now. Our understanding of any part of reality is gauged by the accuracy of our models — having more accurate models means more understanding. If parts of the causes are forever hidden to us, then we can never model perfectly, so we can never understand perfectly.

Consider a series of numbers, .9, .99, .999, .9999, . . ., which approaches or converges to 1. The sequence of numbers eventually closes any finite positive gap. Notice that this sequence of numbers could be said to "be getting closer and closer to 1.1," which is also true, but a gap will always remain. A similar situation may exist for our models or knowledge about reality. Even if reality is infinitely complex, if we can approach it infinitely closely (analogous to converging to 1), then no gap in our knowledge will remain completely unclosed forever. However, if reality has some unknowable, unexplainable, and unobservable component, then we may be in a situation like the sequence approaching 1.1 but never getting closer than .1 from the goal (the analogy is that the .1 is like the unobservable or unknowable component). This would be a place we can never go, a thought we can never think — definitely an edge of reality.

Chapter 10

Real-World Limits — Ethics, Law, and Politics

Law: an ordinance of reason for the common good, made by him who has care of the community.

ST. THOMAS AQUINAS
Summa Theologica

We are all imperfect. We can not expect perfect government.

PRESIDENT WILLIAM HOWARD TAFT
(SPEECH, MAY 8, 1909)

None of us really understands what's going on with all these numbers.

DAVID STOCKMAN, FORMER DIRECTOR
OF THE OFFICE OF MANAGEMENT AND
BUDGET[1]

The preceding three quotes run the gamut of thoughts about laws and governing — from Saint Thomas Aquinas' elegant and pristine definition to President Taft's recognition of imperfection in government and people to David Stockman's admission that modern government's mass of statistics is beyond us all. Most of us have a weary feeling that indeed in government there is simply too much data, too many vested interests, too many decisions, and never enough money. However, some still feel that if we stop fighting among ourselves and stop to reason together, then somehow we will make perfect decisions and move forward to utopia. But "reason together" implies logic, and we have just seen that our best logic is limited and falls far short of perfection. Or maybe in the future if we turn government over to an omnipotent computer system, it could manage perfectly?

Abstract limits are intriguing to consider and play with in our minds; still there might be a feeling that these limits restrict only mathematicians and are far removed from everyday life. People are inclined to say: "So, we can never find an infinite set smaller than the real numbers and larger than the integers — so what? It's the mathematicians' problem, not ours, and it's too abstract to ever affect life as we know it." This is not really true; real life is limited by the same kind of restrictions as those imposed by the Halting theorem, the computationally intractable problems, and paradoxes. This chapter explores that line of thought: our ethics, our laws, our politics, and our future are limited by logical bounds.

A limit in politics or law would be some circumstance that prevents perfection. We aren't limited if we can achieve perfection; in order to see how we are limited, we need to know what perfection in politics or law might entail. Defining utopia is beyond our scope; however, any perfect legal and political system would have the following three characteristics. First, it would have no inconsistent laws or regulations; second, it would have unambiguous laws that cover all possible situations; and third, it would have truly optimal resource allocation and planning. These three characteristics are affected by the logical limitations of the Halting theorem, paradoxes, and computational intractability.

Our goals are to state several legal, ethical, and political limits based on the Halting limit, logical contradiction, and computational intractability limits. Several real-world scenarios will illustrate these points. Now there are several variants of the "impossible" in politics; we are concerned mainly with those that have some logical or computational limit. Limits on money, limits on time, and limits on natural resources are problems, but they have to be accepted whether we like it or not. Adam Yarmolinsky, who served in the Kennedy, Johnson, and Carter administrations, knew this: "Politicians are inclined to take physical limits as givens."[2] Some of these scenarios depend on conflict (or vested interest) applied in such a fashion that the law doesn't attain its intended results or ends in a contradiction. Other scenarios show how well-intended laws can form frustrating logical loops (like the infinite loops of the Halting limit). Others show how computational intractability badly limits resource allocation. In the end, we will have shown reasons why utopia is not attainable by continually improving laws.

What we can control and change are the bureaucracies, how they design policies, how they allocate resources, and how they interpret laws and regulations. That is where we will focus. Pragmatic politicians do the same. Quoting Adam Yarmolinsky again: "Of the three principal sources of impossibility in politics — bureaucracies, factions, and elections — the single greatest source of impossibility is bureaucracy."[3] There are demonstrable limits on how well we can allocate resources; there are demonstrable limits on how well we can design policies, and there are demonstrable contradictions and limits in many of our laws, and these are likely to remain.

There are differences between the logic used by mathematics and the logic used in social science debates. Mathematics uses a few clearly defined, narrow-scope axioms and obtains very narrow-scope truths. On the other hand, many social sciences use general, somewhat vague, wide-scope axioms and obtain wide-scope truths, which are often only half-truths. Social science axioms (or what are treated as axioms in logical deduction) are usually formed by general principles, broad ethical standards, societal goals, and statistical data. We can't treat legal, ethical, and political issues the same way as mathematics because of these properties of the axiom systems. Our results (call them the "legal, ethical, or political" theorems if you want) are not as rigorous as a mathematics proof. Reasonable people might disagree as to their correctness. No theorems like Gödel's or Halting's have been rigorously proven for law, ethics, or politics — for us to "prove" results like this, we will rely on analogous wording to develop analogs to these logical limit results. These are not proofs in the strict mathematical sense, but they could be, if we chose the axioms in a particular way. Finally, the axioms of our example social science systems might seem too narrow to cover all aspects of a situation, and there is a reason for this. General situations involving human interactions have far too many influencing factors to consider them all; we need to make simplifying assumptions to deduce conclusions about anything.

Social sciences have one additional parameter to deal with that never arises in mathematics: conflict or vested interest. Both mathematics and the social sciences use the same general logic operations: and, or, contradiction, and logical inference. However, if the logic used by law and ethics seems softer and less rigorous than the strict mathematical logic used to prove math theorems, then it is more the fault of the axiom set than of the logic operations.

LAW AND ETHICS AS LOGICAL SYSTEMS

We think of our laws as giving one of two results: Either the action is legal or it is illegal. If an action can be logically shown to violate a law, then the action is illegal; furthermore, all actions that cannot be shown to be illegal are deemed legal. As we saw earlier, logic does not work exactly that way; three outcomes are possible: true, false, or neither. False statements must be logical consequences of the axioms in this one narrow sense: Their negations must follow logically from the axioms (i.e., be true statements). Treating laws and evidence as axioms in a legal logic system is possible. For example, (1) a person who kills another person is guilty of manslaughter (law, an axiom); (2) John Doe did kill Joe Smith (evidence, treated as an axiom); (3) John Doe is guilty of manslaughter (conclusion, derived from the axioms by logic operations). That was the guilty verdict; a not-guilty verdict would come about when this chain of logic could not be established. There are no gray areas in this sense. Gray areas abound in the legal system, of course; however, they come from the inability of the logical consequences of legal axioms/laws to faithfully represent the ethical standards that they were intended to protect.

Let's consider the ethical situation that the above mini-legal axiom system is trying to protect. It is wrong that a person plan to kill another person and then do it; it is wrong that one person act recklessly, be aware of his reckless behavior, and unintentionally cause another person's death; it is not wrong (though unfortunate) that a person doing something reasoned, safe, and normal accidentally kills another person who was acting recklessly at the time. Fault is the key here: Right or wrong depends on whether the person was at fault. Morality depends largely on intent; the law needs to make allowance for this in the third case. Here there are three types of actions: moral, immoral, or morally neutral.

Here is where we are. We have three systems, all with axioms; all use standard logical reasoning to come to conclusions. Morality is (perhaps) three-valued: moral, immoral, or morally neutral; legal systems are usually two-valued: legal or illegal; logic is three-valued: true, false, or unprovable. Legal systems stand in the middle. This is not necessarily a problem if the following is possible: The laws can be designed so that all immoral or false situations are judged guilty and all moral/true and morally neutral/unprovable situations are judged not guilty. In practice, it is impossible.

A word about unprovable statements in law, ethics, or politics — it relates back to three-valued systems. Ethics and politics (usually) allow gray areas — areas judged neither good nor bad, but as somewhere in between. In that sense, one could form statements about those gray areas that are unprovable in the ethical or political axiom systems. For example, a runner on first steals second in a baseball game. Can you prove whether that action is moral or immoral? Of course not; applying logical operations to most ethical and political axiom systems wouldn't lead to concluding that the runner is right or the runner is wrong. The action is outside the axioms' scope; it is in a gray area. Or take another case: An actor in a Shakespearean play pretends to kill another. Is this moral or immoral? Again, neither; arts and games are usually outside the scope. In this sense, unprovable statements are seldom pertinent in the ethics–law–politics area.

AXIOMS AND LAWS

Consider a moral dilemma that we often debate in one form or another; it is the basis for many debates concerning limits on police or guns or armies or wars. Killing another human — can it ever be justified? Now consider a hypothetical and horrific example: A deranged gunman holds a large group of people hostage and is killing one person an hour. You alone have a gun and a position from which to shoot. Shoot and kill him or not? That is the question. (No fair ducking out with some "shoot to only wound" alternative; you aren't that good a shot, you must totally incapacitate him immediately, only killing him will do.)

For the sake of argument, use the axiom "A person may not murder another person." Those who might argue that you are morally obligated to shoot base their argument on generalizations or reinterpretations of the axiom like "taking the life of a gunman is not really murder" or "you save more lives by shooting than by not shooting, and, since you have control, you will cause the deaths of many people if you don't shoot — which is murdering them in a sense." Those who might argue against shooting might quote a more literal interpretation of "murder" as a personal prohibition against killing, no matter what the eventual consequences. A horribly sticky moral dilemma, no matter how you approach it. Entire books have been written that venture opinions about how a moral person should face such situations; we won't even try here. We are looking only at the logic of the situation, and the logic seems to be indefinite.

No matter what you decide to do, apparently the axiom is not clear enough to avoid all debate about what it means. And that is the problem. (I am sure that the axiom is clear to some people, but they may not agree with each other! Since we have debate on the meaning, we have a vague statement.) Either the axiom is vague or the axiom ignores some situations like this.

When we faced similar axiom problems in mathematics (Euclid's fifth axiom or the $\sqrt{2}$ issue), we expanded or changed the axioms. We can do the same thing here. Consider the possible variants on a law or axiom against killing: (1) You shall not kill another person; (2) never cause someone to die because of your actions; or (3) always take an action that avoids causing someone to die. The first will suffer from the same kind of argument that the original axiom ran into; the last two are even more sticky. By applying (2) or (3) and not shooting, you save the life (temporarily at least) of the gunman but lose other people's lives, which causes you to violate the axiom later by your action (an action can be an inactive action like not shooting). Perfect laws should be perfectly clear; this isn't going to happen, and even intelligent computer programs can't help. This is a definition problem, not a computational one.

He who applies logic to ethics and morality must prepare for arguments like this. There is no royal road to geometry nor easy path to morality.

LEGAL CONTRADICTIONS

There isn't any shortage of laws. A more common problem in law and politics is overlapping and contradictory laws or regulations. This situation falls under the logic category of contradiction. A contradictory axiom system is one that has a logical consequence (true statement) of axiom A also appears as a negation of a logical consequence (false statement) of axiom B. A statement and its negation both can't be true in the same axiom system. When faced with such a situation, logicians and computers both require that the axiom system be fixed — so either fix or remove axiom A or B. Contradictory logical consequences of the same axioms aren't allowed.

Courts have a variety of methods of solving the issues that arise; none of these have an exact analog in strict logic nor are there any strictly logic fixes that can be used. They can declare part of one law void on various grounds, they can cite precedence (prior decisions) as a basis for making a decision, or a judge can simply emphasize one law and interpret the other law in a different sense in his decision. Last but not least, empanel a jury and take a vote.

In sum, the law doesn't have to use strict mathematical logic. It tries, it really does; nothing bothers a society like arbitrariness from above: vague laws and arbitrary applications of these laws, leading to preferred treatment for some groups and persecution for other groups. But you can't have everything. People and leaders want to solve problems; they want to make their society more ethical according to some moral standards. Critical issues tend to change. As leaders make new laws to address these issues, their wording might contradict the wording of some existing laws, and this won't be apparent until after several judicial decisions. This leads to unfortunate situations like a case in which both the defendant and plaintiff faithfully followed different existing laws and yet find the other's behavior illegal.

VESTED INTEREST

Laws are boundaries on behavior; they define what society thinks is right and wrong or further goals that society wants to pursue. Laws leave a good deal of leeway for people to pursue their own vested interest. Of course, people tend to interpret laws in a way that serves their own interests. This leads to situations in which a person uses a law's wording to circumvent a law's intent. We have seen something similar in programming.

Recall the proof of the Halting theorem from an earlier chapter: "Since we assume *Halt* exists, we can use it as a subprogram of another new program. Therefore, a new program can be developed from *Halt* that differs from it for every value of *N*. Call this new program *Contrary* . . ." (see Figure 11). Here, the hypothetical program *Halt* was a subprogram within another hypothetical program *Contrary*. *Contrary* evaluated *Halt* at each value and then *changed* the value to something else. Then when *Halt* ran with the program *Contrary* as input, a strange thing happened: The values that *Halt* was designed to return had been reversed by *Contrary* already running *Halt* inside itself. This caused the contradiction that disproved the possibility of such a *Halt* program existing in the first place.

One program was deliberately designed to nullify the intent of the other. This was theory; these were hypothetical programs. However, this situation happens in the real world and causes inconsistencies in some of our laws (the logical equivalent of contradictions). Here is the analogy: A law is a set of

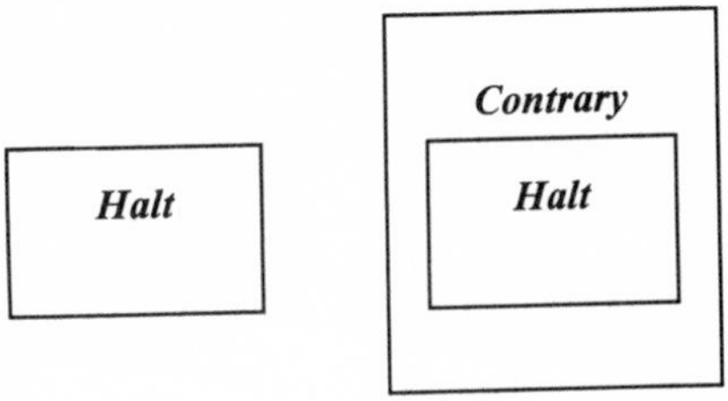

FIGURE 11. A program within a program. The program *Contrary* was designed to act contrarily to program *Halt*. It accomplishes this by turning *Halt*'s own logic against itself.

FIGURE 12. Competing programs. Similar to the *Halt/Contrary* example, but the investment program can't entirely undo the effect of the tax law program. It can offset the desired effect, however.

statements about what tax rates shall be applied to different forms of revenues (stock capital gains, bond yield, interest on cash deposits, and others). It is like a program; you can compute taxes by running revenue levels from the different sources through the law's procedure. The law is public, it is published. Investment firms, companies, and private investors are all free to program the law's procedure into their own investment-mix computer programs.

The following analogy may be made, as illustrated in Figure 12: *Halt* is to the tax law as *Contrary* is to the investment computer programs. *Contrary* contains *Halt* just as the investment program contains the tax code. *Contrary* is run first, getting the answers from *Halt* that *Halt* would get by running on unaltered inputs. (The investment programs are run first before the year's taxes are computed at the end of the year.) *Contrary* alters *Halt*'s output to suit its own purposes. The investment program alters an investment portfolio for some purpose, maybe lower taxes, deferred taxes, or higher income for the current year. These altered portfolios will likely be different from what the designers of the law wanted; the tax law's intent may be circumvented by this referencing of the law.

Now the government is not helpless; tax planners can also use that trick of inserting public-knowledge tax code within an investment program. Consider the planning that goes into tax laws. First, a level of taxation must be one goal; second, the allocation of taxes is another; and, third, loopholes should be avoided.

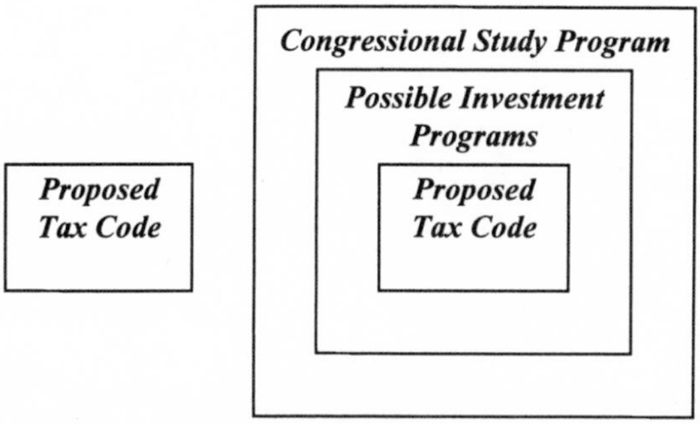

FIGURE 13. Predicting effect of vested interest. A method of predicting how vested interest will affect the operation of proposed laws is to try the proposals with a simulation of the expected response.

The diagram in Figure 13 shows one way that government planners can design tax codes with all three goals in mind and avoid most of the problems caused by investors changing investment mixes to offset tax code intentions. Several potential tax codes are run one at a time in a computer simulation; the simulation tries each out against several possible investment planning programs to see if the investment programs find problem areas for the tax codes. The total study program (outermost box in the diagram) then decides which of these tax codes does best against the suite of investment programs. Thus, we have programs that reference competing programs embedded within programs that reference competing programs — a neat trick that can be applied elsewhere. For instance, this approach could be used in studies of the environment, in the assessment of different possible approaches to regulating industries, in the planning of inner-city renovation, and in many other areas. Any area of social interaction where you can simulate the vested-interest reaction to a law can be analyzed with this approach. It is not enough to simply mandate a law; you need to consider how it will affect the citizenry and how the citizenry will react to it.

This simulation approach is a first step in this direction. Although this approach helps us improve policies, perfection in public policy is still impossible; both our own vested interest (which curtails true optimization) and the shortcomings of logic will limit us in the end.

Laws are often used in a partially recursive or referencing manner that circumvents the law's purpose. We have totally free speech to a large degree (some notable exceptions are slander, inciting riots, and false fire alarms). "Angry words" represent an interesting case. Free speech doesn't have to be constructive, ethical, positive, logical, sensible, or even nice. A person can use words to cause another person to break the law in a way that will benefit the first person. For example, a calm person might be arguing with a hothead. Something is at stake, some discussion follows, nothing is settled, more words, now heated words, next shouted angry words, blows are soon to come. The calm person realizes that he who strikes the first blow not only acts in a childish manner but also could be liable in a civil suit. The possibility of a civil suit means more money for the calm person. If the calm person doesn't fear physical damage from being struck by the other (the other person might be a small, weak hothead), then he might decide to risk a physical confrontation. So it might be in the calm person's financial interest to allow himself to stay involved in the argument and allow his opponent to commit assault and battery. The law was not meant for this. Society has an interest in discouraging physical violence among its citizens and fostering communication. The laws on assault and battery allow victims reimbursement by the assaulter; this penalizes and hence discourages violence. Likewise, free-speech laws encourage communications, lack of restrictions on speech. We attain neither goal by this behavior where one law and leeway in allowed speech parlay into a financial windfall. President Taft's statements — "We are all imperfect. We can not expect perfect government" — really point out the problem here. Laws reflect us and our logic; both are limited well short of perfection.

Computers may be faster, but they still can't design laws that a motivated person can't circumvent in some way.

HALTING LIMITS

The statement of the Halting problem might seem too abstract to be significant to real life. An infinite loop in a computer program may seem like an annoying programming problem, not something of any great significance. After all, most people don't care if one program that finds loops in all other programs is impossible; it's not that important a concept outside the programming world. It should be. The concept has broader implications than just the obvious benefit of saving millions on software development, and we will consider how this principle affects areas of real life like politics and laws.

Besides its application in computer programming, there are more general interpretations of the Halting theorem. The theorem says: *There can't exist a computer program that can tell if every other computer program loops on a given input.* A program could be a procedure, a step-by-step decision process that takes in information, processes it, and outputs a decision. A decision could be in the form of a plan, a policy, or a law. Also, any set of rules could be coded into a computer program. "Every other" is an all-inclusive modifier that is like "all" or "every" or "every possible" or "any possible."

Infinite loops in programs are the manifestation of a logical error; some input values cause the logic to go from one statement to another to another, continuing this way until eventually the program ends back at the original statement and then repeats the sequence. The program can't break out of this pattern, forcing it to repeat forever — definitely an error, but one that seems specific to computer programming. It is hard to conceive of an infinitely repeating operation in real life; at some point, wiser heads recognize the repetition and step in to change something and break the pattern. At first, it seems that there isn't any analog of the need to check for infinite loops in politics or the law. Thus, it seems that the fact that a program like *Halt* can't exist (the Halting limit) shouldn't limit us in these areas (law and politics). Not so! Public policies often are full of situations that could lead to these infinite loops if wiser heads didn't step in and change something. The analog in policy or law is a regulation or a set of regulations that refer to each other for decisions, but sometimes the referencing pattern can't be broken — like an infinite loop. Let's look at some hypothetical examples to explain this idea. IRS forms — the 1040, Schedule A, Schedule SE, and others — cause us to spend hours poring over definitions, exceptions, and columns of numbers to compute our taxes. Consider a hypothetical new form that has these three lines:

> *line 11*   *Compute line 26, multiply by .05 and enter here.*
> *line 26*   *Compute line 34, multiply by .97 and enter here.*
> *line 34*   *Compute line 11, multiply by .72 and enter here.*

This is a mistake, an infinite loop within a public policy. Following these instructions keeps you jumping from line 11 to line 26 to line 34 and back to line 11 for more repetition, endless repetition (see Figure 14). If you programmed the instructions literally into a computer, then it would loop endlessly. In real life, phones will be ringing for days, the callers pointing out to the IRS that this doesn't make sense; then tax authorities will get together and implement a patch for this year's taxes, inform all taxpayers, and continue with business. Nothing infinite happened; they changed the logic to prevent the logical need for an infinite loop. In fact, very seldom does so blatant an error go undetected for long. However, in order to find such an error in the design of a new tax form, people had to pore over the form and try to find contradictions like the above three hypothetical lines. These people were acting out the role of *Halt*: They were looking for infinite loops in procedures (instead of programs). Herein lies the problem: Inconsistent laws are far from perfect

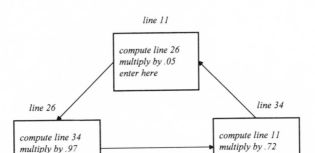

FIGURE 14. Infinite loops. Circular references that never break out of the pattern form infinite loops in both programming and policy.

and cause a lot of wasted effort; if we can't find a way to avoid introducing laws that cause these policy loops, then we will always be limited. The Halting limit says that we can't develop a general process guaranteed to find loops beforehand.

Now that we see the pattern, there are many more examples out there. Consider another hypothetical situation. Suppose a bill is passed to grant money to a company to build a new type of environmentally friendly factory on land in the west. The bill says that before money (these are tax dollars, so conditions can be attached) can be spent planning the final design, all necessary environmental studies (call them study A and study B) must be completed successfully. (Good intent: Don't spend a lot of taxpayers' money on expensive planning if the environment will be harmed anyway.) An existing law, aimed at protecting wildlife, has a provision in it that says that for industries that improve the environment a waiver from study A can be granted if a fund is set up to improve any wildlife habitat harmed by the industry. (Good intent is obvious here; give the environmentally friendly industries a break.) This law requires that a final design be submitted before a request will be acted upon. A waiver doesn't require a final design, so it is necessary because of the clause in the original bill. Another law says that no waiver from its study B can be granted if a waiver was granted for study A (good intent here; lawmakers didn't want companies with money and influence getting waivers on all the environmental studies). It, too, requires a final design before a request will be acted upon.

What can be done? You can't get both studies completed successively without the final design in hand, but the wording of the first bill expressly bans this. You can't get waivers from both studies since one requires doing at least one study. The different laws refer to each other and effectively block the building of the factory that was the intent of the first law. All have good intentions.

Now the problem with circular requirements on the studies will probably get fixed by a high-level manager with regulatory authority to override the procedure. If it can't be fixed like this, then a fix will be added as an amendment to another bill, or the situation can be taken to court for judicial relief from the circular logic of the laws. There are several potential fixes. Eventually, the problem gets solved; either the factory gets built or it doesn't. The government bogs down if there aren't ways around situations like this.

Blame the bureaucrats? No, as much as we like to blame bureaucrats, this one really isn't their fault; the sum total of our laws, regulations, and judicial decisions is simply too complex for a few thousand responsible government lawyers to completely sort out. The complex nature of laws and regulations is the real problem: Many bills passed by Congress can run from 30,000 to 50,000 words of legalese and contain paragraph after paragraph of legal restrictions that interact with each other or with other preexisting regulations, restrictions that refer to other official studies or measures or regulatory agencies, and often vague wording.

Still, wouldn't it be more efficient for someone to catch inconsistencies in the laws beforehand, before they cause lost time and lawyers' fees? Although a complete error-checking procedure like *Halt* is logically impossible, wouldn't it be possible and cheaper to build less ambitious error checkers? This might be a procedure like a partial *Halt* program, a procedure that would find any logical inconsistency in our current set of regulations, not necessarily in any possible set. Surprisingly, the answer is usually no. Error checking is expensive. Although one function of a bureaucracy is to find these inconsistencies, it is too formidable a job to do perfectly and quickly each time we pass a new law or issue a new regulation. Moreover, the job gets harder, the more regulations and laws there are on the books. There is a trade-off: Large bureaucracies cost more and catch more inconsistencies, whereas small bureaucracies cost less and catch fewer. Notice that catching *all* the inconsistencies is out of the question. Our solar system filled with lawyers cross-checking every single paragraph of every single law and regulation against every other paragraph in all other laws and regulations still wouldn't catch every contradiction.

Notice that some regulations and forms are so important and widely used that any contradictions would cause widespread problems. The IRS tax forms are a case in point. Millions use these forms; if a circular problem like our example really existed, it would cost millions of dollars to straighten it out. You can believe that IRS forms are analyzed, checked, double-checked, cross-checked, and probably subjected to Monte Carlo simulation runs to detect loops and other problems. Software verification code can be written for important, heavily used, critical-usage software. Verification software checks out logic in the code being verified; it decides if the code really runs as planned. For other types of code, Monte Carlo simulations are run; these involve running many random sets of data, in the hope that one will cause a problem and thus isolate an error in the code.

Still it is clear that there are enormous problems here. It all seems too much for even the super technicians — the problems seem too big, too involved, and too overlapping. Perhaps the ultimate government technician was David Stockman, the former Director of the Office of Management and Budget. A young, brilliant, Republican congressman, it took him only a few years in Congress to make his reputation as *the* budget expert on the hill. Even his political foes acknowledged his expertise, his in-depth understanding, and his vast store of facts. In 1981, President Reagan chose him to oversee the federal budget; Reagan was planning some of the most significant tax changes of this century and needed Stockman. Many high officials in Reagan's administration felt that Stockman was the only person who understood the entire federal budget — its major goals, its intricate funding, its overlapping programs, and its multitude of pitfalls.

If anyone was the prototype politician and technician for understanding all the loopholes, contradictions, and overlapping regulations in even a part of the government, then it would be a David Stockman. When David Stockman says, "None of us really understands what's going on with all these numbers," we know that we have reached saturation in government; no one can completely track even the budget. But computers can't either.

Now for the big question: Who is the best now and who will be the best in the future at finding inconsistent laws — humans or computers? On the surface, the sheer amount of logical operations necessary seems to favor computers. But that is not so; we humans are much better at this now and will remain so for some time in the future. Human minds are much better at association than present-day computers and should maintain this advantage for several more decades. This advantage is of enormous benefit in making judgments like the ones we have just seen. We saw the problem of uncovering logical inconsistencies in the legal code and statutory regulations. The problem centered on the huge number of laws and regulations and the immense number of subsets of laws and regulations to be searched for inconsistencies. Consider a million laws or regulations or paragraphs in legal code (that is a low number; there are many more than that). Recall the circular reasoning or infinite-loop examples, where there were three regulations that were mutually inconsistent. For a million possible regulations, there are a million cubed or 10^{18} possible three-member subsets, four-member subsets number 10^{24}, and five-member subsets that might harbor a mutual inconsistency number 10^{30}. Giga-flop speed is one billion or 10^9 operations per second; if a supercomputer could completely analyze and report out inconsistencies for a billion subsets per second, then it would take it about 33 years to consider just the three-member sets. (This calculation follows from multiplying 33 years by the number of seconds in a year, approximately 3×10^7, and then multiplying by 10^9 and getting approximately 10^{18}.) The numbers for the four- and five-member subsets are ridiculously large: 33 million years and 33 trillion years, respectively. No computer can do all that.

Humans can look at regulations, classify them as to type, draw comparisons between them and other regulations, and contrast them with other regulations. Humans can also recall past legal decisions involving comparable regulations and predict possible future decisions concerning the new regulations under consideration. Humans excel at digging out the subtle nuances of the regulations' wording. Associative abilities like these allow human analysts to quickly rule out of consideration many irrelevant regulations. Association allows humans to cut down the combinatorial explosion of possibilities.

Computers can't do the two key parts of this inconsistent-law job well (interpreting legal language and association). Of course, there are other parts of the job, such as database searches, that they excel at. So computers in the near future will aid humans in policy making, but they won't be taking over the job. The far future might be a different story: Some computer software (neural networks) emulates human brains and perhaps could match us in language and associative abilities at some future date. We will look at neural networks in the next chapter.

A (hypothetical) omnipotent computer that could govern much better than humans would be expected to issue policies that were consistent with each other. The preceding discussion shows how impossible that is.

COMPUTATIONALLY DIFFICULT SOCIAL PROBLEMS

Computational intractability causes many inefficiencies that are not as apparent as contradictions in laws. A contradiction in a law is usually short to state and prove; a computationally intractable situation usually manifests itself as an inefficient organization or procedure. The organization functions or the procedure works, but clearly its operation is far from optimal.

One main government responsibility is to allocate resources or assign values for a variety of everyday occurrences. Consider something that we often take for granted, traffic light timing. In order to time traffic lights, some organization must study traffic patterns and traffic throughput on all city streets. Many constraints are to be satisfied: delays due to starting and stopping a string of cars, rush-hour overload, street throughput capacity, traffic-light synchronization, and many others; the goal is to provide a stoplight timing pattern for each stoplight in the city grid (which will number in the hundreds for even small cities). This will be an optimization problem with hundreds of variables and constraints. It is distinctly nonlinear; it could take hundreds or thousands of hours of computer time to do well; it is nearly impossible to do perfectly.

Many small things in our lives require some measure of optimization or optimal control to run well. Often they are the responsibility of government or large utilities. Timing of street lights, the proper number, size, and location of new schools, placement of new roads, the interconnectivity of the phone system and computer networks — all these require design to make them work acceptably. All these could be more efficient if we spent more time or money doing more optimization; none of these can be optimized perfectly. That is a limit.

If we devise a traffic-light-timing system that doesn't move traffic volume as quickly as possible, then we waste human commuters' time more than necessary. If we don't build new schools in the best locations, right sizes, or proper numbers, then we either overspend and waste school space or we underspend and cause overcrowding. Our ethical standards view the goals as the least waste, the minimum cost, and the maximum return. Additional waste, extra cost or less than the maximum return is viewed as immoral, although perhaps as unavoidable. Unavoidable is the key word; these are computational issues as well as social concerns; these problems are computationally intractable because of their large time complexity. Absolute maxima, minima, or "the best possible" are often beyond our capabilities; we are too limited computationally to attain these ideals.

Resource allocation is a frequent issue or process for policy makers or social planners. Although allocating scarce resources seems like a task for which we should prefer human judgment to cold, hard numbers and computers, there are cases in which the numbers of resources and possible allocations are so large that some automated method is necessary.

One example of historical significance is resource allocation by centrally controlled economies. During the late 1980s and early 1990s, most of the centrally controlled economies of the world either voluntarily switched to free-market-like economies or suffered political upheaval and then moved toward free-market economic policies. Although there were many reasons for this, one reason that is pertinent to our discussions is the inability of central economic committees to optimally allocate resources. This inability has several facets, but one of them is mathematical; the fact is that the greater the number of nodes that you must consider, the harder (by an exponential factor) the allocation process becomes. With enough nodes to allocate resources to, the optimization problem becomes computationally intractable.

Consider an economy controlled by several central committees that direct individual industries such as power, pharmaceuticals, transportation, clothing, or electronics. Assume that each committee has absolute power to decide for each of its factories parameters like capital expenditures, worker salaries, pricing of products, supply of raw material, and schedules. Information flows up to the committees; decisions flow back down. Now, even in centrally controlled economies, everything can't always be equal everywhere. Some factories are located in more populous areas, some have cheaper raw materials available, some have access to cheaper transportation, and so on, and these factors change as time passes. Assume, for simplicity, that there are K different raw materials needed for production at each of N different factories. Resource allocation of these materials means setting a separate level for K materials at N factories — a total of $N \cdot K$ parameters industrywide. Because of the local nature of the raw material cost and transportation cost, there will be a different cost associated with each material at each factory. Assume further (to keep this example manageable) that the optimal allocation algorithm is a cubic equation in the number of parameters. That means that in order to find the optimal allocation of resources for P parameters, P^3 computer operations are required. Industrywide, this means $(N \cdot K)^3$ computer operations to optimally allocate raw material. However, if each factory was free (as in a free market) to purchase its own material and each factory used the same resource allocation algorithm, then it would require only K^3 computer operations to find the best mix of materials for their budget. Industrywide, this equates to $N \cdot K^3$ computer operations for all the factories. This is an enormous difference: $(N \cdot K)^3 = N^3 \cdot K^3 = N^2 \cdot (N \cdot K^3)$, which means that the central committee approach versus each-factory-on-its-own approach equates to more computer operations by a factor of N^2, a factor of 10,000 for $N = 100$ factories.

This factor of 10,000 represents an additional cost to the central management approach as compared to the local autonomous factories approach. Now did the central management approach attain a better answer to offset this cost? After all, they considered a more global situation and probably purchased some raw materials cheaper and transported then further than some factories would have done on their own. Yes, they probably did get a better answer, a cheaper total price and total transportation cost. It is a mathematical fact that a global optimum of a sum is better than the sum of local optima. Was it sufficiently better to offset that factor of 10,000 in computational cost, given that computer costs are a considerable expense? That depends on specifics of the example, and since we aren't going into any more detail, we won't know for sure. The point is that the cost to manage more nodes increases faster than the number of nodes.

The cost to manage or to communicate or to direct or to analyze must be included in the total cost of the item. If you add more management or more bureaucracy or more studies to manage your resources "better," then the increase in overhead cost might end up being greater than the decrease in manufacturing cost. Often the "best" possible allocation of resources is either computationally intractable or so time-consuming that it is too expensive; you must settle for suboptimal. However, that difference in computational costs is the key point. It is an inescapable extra cost associated with doing the globally best possible allocation instead of doing the locally best possible allocations.

For certain, excessive computer costs alone did not fell Eastern European economies and force them to the free market. However, this example is a sharply focused look at a larger problem. Better and better decisions cost more; more and more variables cost exponentially more to manage. Centralization led to more lines of communications and to more variables to manage or optimize.

The most visible feature of these centralized economies was the enormous bloated bureaucracies that grew to analyze every last variable, manage every last worker, and communicate with every last manager. Simultaneously, the free-market economies were cutting down on management costs, saving money doing that, and then turning the savings back into research and development to allow them to do the job better in the future. During the 1970s and 1980s, they pulled away decisively.

Computational intractability is a limit on both computers and people, and this is one area of government where people do use computers for decisions. As discussed before, this is a serious limitation on us, and there is very little prospect for avoiding this limit.

HOW TO CONTROL A TYRANT COMPUTER

A popular science fiction theme has a master computer controlling life on Earth. This giant computer complex controls all electricity, TV, transportation, heating, lighting, hospitals, schools, stores, businesses, and everything else. It comes in many forms, ranging from the extreme of a benevolent, noninvasive computer persona that simply keeps the necessary machinery running to benefit humans to the extreme of a malevolent computer persona that suddenly develops humanlike traits of power hunger and vengeance and in some fashion takes over and controls the governmental functions of the world. The science fiction scenario sometimes starts with one computer program accessing the worldwide network of computers and seeking out and controlling one computer site after another. Eventually, it gets into the government network and proceeds to gradually take over central computers. There, it monitors all incoming data, accesses all databases, controls vital management functions, and takes countermeasures to ensure that no other program can interfere with it. Next, it is making decisions based on its own plans. This malevolent computer monitors each human's every waking moment, always on the lookout for nonstandard behavior, which it then punishes. It is one bad dream, but it's not necessarily realistic. Another recurring theme is a computer personality progression, usually patterned after human traits. Often the story has the computer personality develop; first, the computer is childlike, then it advances, and finally it advances at a frightening and uncontrollable rate. Total domination soon follows.

There is that which will always be fiction and there is that which could someday be reality. This scenario will probably always be fiction for several good reasons. First and foremost, how did such a computer program come to be? Science fiction stories can take liberties and simply start with such a premise, but logically the existence of the original program is difficult to justify. Two possible extremes are, first, that it started with a small program that either had the intelligence to grow exponentially or mutated into a monster program and, second, that the program was a very large program to start with that attained more capability and got loose in some fashion. The first possibility is extremely mathematically implausible; the second possibility still has upper limits because of complexity and could be controlled even then.

Let's start with the first case of a small program that wants to grow. There is a fear that a small program could enter a computer and grow relentlessly in size and power until it takes over the computer. Then it migrates to another computer and takes it over, too. This process continues until the small program has taken over all computers on Earth. Analogies to DNA, cell mutation, and evolution are often made. If a program could evolve to something different in 1000 computer cycles, then on a 50-MHz computer it could go through 50,000 evolutionary changes per second in an evolutionary chain. After a few hours or days, this once-small program would go through more evolution than most life on Earth has; it could develop into a monster, capable of controlling its host computer. There is one problem: A "mutation" in a computer program would be a small random change. The nature of a small change would be at the least a one-bit change in the code somewhere in the coding. Consider a one-bit change. First, since the bit is in a byte somewhere, a one-bit change is effectively a one-byte change. A one-byte change equates to some letter or symbol being randomly changed somewhere in the program code. The odds are very high that this mutated program won't even compile and run, much less improve itself. For example, consider the simple Pascal statement *read(price)*. Any one-byte change will change one letter or a parenthesis. If the change is to any letter of the word *read* or a parenthesis, then the line of code won't compile or run. If the letter changed is in the variable name *price*, then it will be something like *xrice* or *pyice* or *przce*. All these mutations are variable names that mean nothing to the rest of the program. No one-byte change to this line of code will lead anywhere, and that is the case in general. The vast majority of program mutations are dead ends, causing the program to cease running. The vast majority of the mutations that still run, run less effectively since a random change occurred in a planned program.

Maybe random mutations wouldn't produce a monster program, but what about a small program that simply produces all programs in order, trying each until it finds a monster program? This idea is even less likely then the random-mutation idea. Look at the mathematics of it. The four-line program we considered previously had an equivalent number that was over 10^{150}. A galaxy full of computers running for the entire history of the universe couldn't try out all programs with numbers that high. And that represented only a four-line program. Any program that poses a danger would have to be more complex than a four-line program.

The last point is complexity. A short program probably cannot understand many complex programs, based on our earlier discussion of complexity. A truly dangerous monster program would have to be large and complex. We have just seen that such a complex monster wouldn't arise by random mutations or systematically trying all possibilities. It would have to be designed and probably designed mostly by humans, not other programs. An all-powerful master program would have to defeat the safeguards of all other programs to control them. To defeat them, it has to understand them in an essential way. To understand them, it has to be more complex than they are in an essential way. To be more complex than all the programs, it must be extremely large, much larger than any other program. Understanding programs is very difficult and requires programs that are much more complex than the originals.

The diagram in Figure 15 shows how people might eventually oversee and control the "master computer." First, it is not the computer that is doing the thinking but the software: the

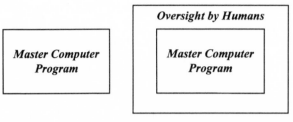

FIGURE 15. How to control a tyrant computer. The master computer program is duplicated and run under a simulation monitored by humans. If the master computer issues any command deemed harmful, pull the plug!

master computer program. We can replicate this program and store and run it in another computer. (This is exactly analogous to the tax code example.) The exact same code and the exact same input will always lead to the exact same calculations and decisions. This means that the human oversight can check to make sure that the master computer program doesn't get out of bounds by monitoring the simulated master computer in the separate system (on the right in the diagram). If something does happen, the oversight computer can overrule the master computer, or, in the worst case, it can pull the plug and disconnect the master computer.

Can that master computer grow superintelligent, develop a demonic personality, and become all-powerful in a short time? Hardly — first, the master computer is limited as we have seen before; it can't develop unlimited powers. Second, more power is exponentially hard to come by. Remember that it took 10^{18} comparisons to test all subsets of three regulations for contradictions and 10^{24} (a factor of one million) to do the same test for subsets of four. Power and control are like that; incremental power and control become harder and harder to obtain, the more power and control there are already.

Computer rule — it can't be perfect. A powerful computer still has the same inherent logical limits that we do. At best, it calculates faster. The scenario of an all-powerful computer taking over the world and ruling the human population isn't that realistic. A much more realistic scenario is one in which humans start linking to computers via virtual reality and find the arrangement so attractive that they start to change society in that direction. But we are ahead of ourselves — we will discuss virtual reality in the next chapter.

Chapter 11

Artificial Intelligence and Virtual Reality

*Concern for the man himself and his fate must
always form the chief interest of all technical endeavors; . . . Never forget this in
the midst of your diagrams and equations.*

ALBERT EINSTEIN
(SPEECH, FEBRUARY 16, 1931)

1010101010101010101010101010101010101010101

Artificial intelligence (AI) is a generic term applied to many diverse computer procedures. In the most general sense, *any* computer procedure is AI since it is both artificial and intelligent.
However, computer scientists apply the term only to those computer procedures that do complex reasoning that was previously
done only by humans. Entire books discuss AI; we can't do the
field justice in just a few pages.

Earlier chapters discussed simple computer program statements and simple logical statements, but normal human

thought is far more complex. It is not clear that a program consisting of these simple statements can simulate human thought patterns — not even a large program. We need to bridge the gap between simple logic and programming statements and complex human reasoning. There is a large gap between single programming statements like *cost = items * price* or *if items > 7 then write price* and a logical thought process by a human like *If we do this planned reorganization and split the engineering department in two sections then we need to cut the salary of the new manager of Engineering Section B or violate the company regulations.*

AI is subject to the same limits that we have been discussing. Usually, the limit that AI runs into is the limit of computational intractability — too many calculations, too little time. Professor Ernest Davis of New York University–Courant Institute of Mathematical Sciences remarked, "Sometimes AI theories are correct in principle but simply take much too long to be interesting."[1] As we saw before, *knowing how to solve a problem* is much different from *being able to solve a problem*, and algorithms that rely on combinatorial analysis are impossible to do for moderate values of N (where N is the number of variables in the problem). Many AI procedures fit this category: We know how to teach a computer to think, but the amount of computation required is simply impossible (recall the prior 2^N discussions, where when $N > 100$ the number of computations is beyond modern technology and for $N > 500$ it is impossible).

Two areas where AI applies are, first, when the situation is governed by a group of known rules that cover all eventualities and can be followed unambiguously (formal step-by-step logic works here) and, second, when there is a way to estimate how good an answer is by some evaluation method and different approaches can be evaluated to find the best. With these two areas in mind, we will look at two AI processes: a rule-based AI system approach, which depends on the formal logic that was discussed in Chapter 8, and an evaluation method that is used when few hard-and-fast rules about a system are known.

RULE-BASED AI SYSTEMS

Most programming statements that we have seen may seem too simple to be of much value in simulating human thought processes. However, many such statements together could do it. We will see a sketch of how this is possible when we consider the following rule-based AI system.

Consider a large, diverse, service-oriented company, one that has many government contracts. The combination of diverse, service-oriented, and government contracts means legal issues, many legal issues and policies that ensure legality in operation. A company like this has many more legal and regulatory problems than a small, single-interest company like a real-estate company or auto repair business. This large, diverse company will have a large, complicated set of personnel regulations that cover reorganizations, personnel changes, salaries, marriage to co-workers, and a host of other issues. These issues and regulations are applied often each day, and lawyers are expensive. To save money, the company might set up a rule-based AI system that operates together with the company personnel database. This system can study planned personnel or organizational changes to see if they violate company policy. This allows planned changes to be rejected beforehand if there is a problem, rather than implementing them first and then trying to solve the resulting problem later.

Some rules might be like the following: "All managers can make no more than twice the average salary of people in their departments" or "No two people can be married and work in the same department." These rules would find violations of company regulations when new changes are being considered. Suppose a department has grown too large and diverse, and a split is being considered with a new management team being added in. Possible problems caused by the second rule (and others) could be found while the split was still in the planning stages. Or if a person wanted to change departments and one of those departments was merging with another department that the person's spouse worked in, again the problem could be found beforehand.

The logic statement of these rules needs some explanation. Included within the above rules is a great deal of implied information that would have to come from a company database. This information needs to be supplied to the system; in some cases the information is numerical, in other cases it is text or character data. A company personnel database would be the place to find the raw data that could help form these logic functions. Axioms and proven theorems in logic are called "rules" in AI applications because this follows the normal English usage better. These rules of logic are more like logical functions or operators, but the logic terminology was fixed before the advent of AI. Now the stage is set; we have the rules stated in logic, we can state these logic rules in terms of logical symbols that the software can interpret, and we have a database from which the software can develop the other information like salary. Now how do we derive results? The answer is the mechanical-deduction-proving method that we considered in a previous chapter.

This type of mechanical-deduction-proving procedure can be coded into a program easily enough; it can then be applied to the personnel regulation system with the axioms as the regulations and database. When someone has a proposed personnel or organization change that they want to run against this AI system for a validity check, two things need to be done. First, the change needs coding in logical symbols, and, second, the negation of this change appears as a new axiom. Why? It takes far too much time just to generate all possible theorems that can result from the company policy and then check if the proposed policy change matches one of them. (After all, you do want an answer sometime this century!) What you want is to see if the proposed change violates company policy (in logic terms, if it contradicts policy). Therefore, by putting the negation in as an axiom, you allow the mechanical theorem prover to check if a null (a contradiction) results from this addition. It is just like the method of contradiction that is used to prove math theorems.

Now we can see how to bridge the gap between single simple program statements and human intelligence. Starting with simple programming statements like *cost = items * price* or *if items > 7 then write price*, we could code small programs of about 100 Pascal statements that could do logical operations like: if the implication form (U *implies* V) is true and also U is a true statement, then V is a true statement for any logical statements U and V. In turn, many of these small logical-operation programs could be combined with each other and other programs to program the mechanical-deduction-proving method discussed in Chapter 8. This complete program might run to 10,000 programming statements. In turn, this program along with hundreds of coded logic rules (like the rules for married people and managers' salaries) could make up an AI program to monitor compliance with the company's personnel policies. This program might run to 200,000 statements. This final program could do the same work as a human expert — like check the validity of this proposed policy: *If we do this reorganization and split the engineering department in two, then we need to cut the salary of the new manager of Engineering Section B.* And all of this with just many simple programming statements.

EVALUATION METHODS

Game-playing systems are the best-known application of evaluation schemes. That is because of the win-or-lose nature of games; there is a well-defined goal and usually a numerical approximation as to which player is leading at that particular time. That numeric approximation is used as the evaluation function for this brand of AI. Chess is the best example. In chess, different pieces have different worth relative to each other (the usual evaluation is a queen = 10, a rook = 5, a pawn = 1, and a king = 1000). By counting the total value of each player's pieces at the end of a move, you have a rough numerical evaluation of the board position. Computers need an ordered set of evaluations to use this approach. Usually, a numerical score is assigned to possible results of actions, and the AI program attempts to maximize (or minimize if that should be needed) the function value. Note that normal English-like evaluations like poor, fair, good, excellent, and superior could be changed to a numerical function by a simple assignment like poor = 1, fair = 2, etc.

These methods often are used with problems that are "too big" to solve completely. The game of chess is an example; it has about 38^{40} possible normal-length games available. Searching out each possible sequence of moves to find the "best possible" move is a lost cause. Instead, heuristics are used; the best move becomes the move that gives the best position 5 or 10 moves down the road.

In the next few decades AI will improve rapidly. In the past the situation was as follows. Computers did better than humans only in two situations: (1) A large database of knowledge was necessary or useful or (2) rapid calculation was necessary or useful. (Computers hold the edge on humans in data storage and rapid calculations.) Humans did better in areas where adaption or learning was necessary or useful (which is almost everything if you think about it). In the past four or five years, computers have made big gains in human specialties like speech recognition and language translation, where adaption and learning are essential. Speech recognition has been studied for many years; it is difficult because different people speak the same words in the same language in many ways. Until recently, computer algorithms couldn't sort it all out, but adaptive learning AI algorithms have made great progress. A similar situation holds for language translation. Computers have understood syntax for years now, but context is very important in rendering a correct translation, and only recently have adaptive AI programs really been up to the task. "Adaptive" and "learning" will be the traits of the next generation of AI.

NEURAL NETWORKS — THE WAY HUMANS THINK

Thus far, we have focused on digital computers; the discrete models, the Pascal programs, the numbers that represented programs, the integer arithmetic axiom system, the proof of the Halting limits, and expert systems all presupposed digital computers. Humans are not digital; their brains are wired in a completely different fashion. Many aspects of the human brain are still mysteries to us because it is difficult to do all the measurements needed for complete theories. However, we do have a very good model of the basic operations of the neurons within the brain. This model is more than just a theoretical device; the past 10 years have seen many artificial intelligence applications programmed differently than before. Before, most AI applications used large databases, with rules and evaluations coded into the programs. These programming techniques were fine for some problems but fell short when attempting more difficult associative problems. Now, many AI applications use neural networks. Neural networks are a simple mathematical structure along with simple mathematical operations that simulate the brain's method for solving problems.

If we are to compare computers to humans, if we are to understand the comparative strengths of humans versus computers, if we are to find the ultimate answer to whether computers can do whatever humans can, then we need to understand the human way of thinking. Humans think with neural networks. They don't use bits and bytes, they don't have little memory cells where numbers, colors, or memories are stored, they don't have little CPUs inside their brains — instead, they use neural networks. The basic element in an artificial neural network is an artificial neuron. Artificial neurons are mathematical structures that have a few characteristics, all of which are patterned after real neurons. These characteristics are: (1) Each neuron can input several numbers through connections to other artificial neurons, (2) neurons can sum together input signals and make simple transformations of the sum (like setting a cutoff level, or increasing or decreasing

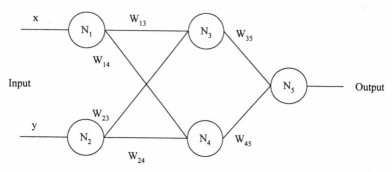

FIGURE 16. Simple neural network. The weights W store the network's pattern.

it) into another signal, and (3) they can output this resultant signal to many other artificial neurons. A simple neural network is depicted in Figure 16. The circles are the nodes of a neural network (analogous to the cell body of a real neuron). The connecting paths from one node to another each carry the output signal of the earlier layer to be one input to the latter layer. The mathematical function within some nodes is the summation function that sums together all the inputs to the node. In addition, each node has a cutoff level (sometimes called a "firing threshold"); if the sum function value is below this level, the node will not output anything — in effect, an output of zero. Each artificial neuron processes information in parallel with other neurons in their layer. The response or output of each neuron is then input to the next neuron, which does the same thing. Think of the action cascading along from one network level to the next, starting at the input nodes and ending at the output level. Hidden layer neurons are the layers between the input and output; together with the weights, they form an internal pattern that holds the network's response to inputs.

Each connection has a number associated with it; these numbers represent an actual neuron's excitatory or inhibitory signal. Excitatory signals boost the receiving neuron's input signal, making this signal more likely to push the neuron past its firing threshold. This excites the receiving neuron (makes it want to output something besides zero). An inhibitory signal works in the opposite way and tends to make the receiving neuron output zero. (Of course, many inhibitory inputs might be summed with many excitatory inputs, canceling each other.) This is analogous to the operation of biological synapses, which in effect apply weights to the outgoing signal by the amount of the signal that they let through. Artificial neural networks can model these two concepts of amount of signal passed and inhibitory or excitatory by real-number weights and minus or plus signs.

Think of the operation of a network as parallel operations that sweep from left to right in the diagram presented in Figure 16. (1) Input signals appear in the input paths; the nodes in the input layer don't normally change the signal strength but simply split it off and (2) output it along the connections to the next layer, the hidden layer. (3) The signals on the second set of connections feed into the hidden layer of nodes. In each hidden node, three things happen: (4) first, the input signals are weighted (multiplied by their connection's weight); (5) second, the results are summed; (6) third, the summation is compared to the firing threshold: if it exceeds the threshold, then (7) an output signal is generated and sent along the output connections to the next layer. Steps (3) through (7) are repeated for each hidden layer in the network (if there is more than one).

Neural networks are important to our understanding of the human brain and how it ultimately compares to a computer; we need to understand them. Therefore, we consider in detail óne example of how a neural network works. The example is very simple: There are two inputs x and y, and the goal of the network is simply to tell if $x = y$ or not. This is a simple digital decision done with a simulated analog network, and therefore it will show how an analog brain can do one of the three basic programming statements. Also, the ability to tell if two different objects have one characteristic that is equal is one basic step in associative thinking. Different objects might have one or more equal (or similar) characteristics (e.g., round, red, hard), and the ability to distinguish which characteristics are equal or similar is a large part of associative thinking.

Before starting on the example, we need to define the firing thresholds and the output functions for our network. Let the firing threshold be .1 and the output function a step function. This means that if the input is .1 or less, the value is 0 (neuron doesn't fire) whereas if the input is greater than .1, the value is 1 (neuron does fire).

Now we are ready to show a neural network that will make a simple decision process based on inputs that are integer-valued. The following connection weights represent the simple decision $x = y$ (with an output of 0 for true and 1 for false): $W_{13} = 1$, $W_{14} = -1$, $W_{23} = -1$, $W_{24} = 1$, $W_{35} = 1$, and $W_{45} = 1$. Consider what happens with this set of weights: first, node N_3 computes the value $x - y$ and node N_4 computes the value $y - x$. If $x = y$, then both values are zero, and the nodes N_3 and N_4 output zeros, which then means a zero input to node N_5 and therefore an output of zero, meaning true. Conversely, if $x \neq y$, then one or the other of $x - y$ or $y - x$ is positive (since x and y are integers, it is actually ≥ 1, which is greater than the firing threshold). Therefore, some hidden node will output a 1, which will be an input to the output node, which in turn will output a 1, meaning false.

Several features bear further examination. First, the threshold level can affect answers; this example used integer arithmetic with a threshold of .1, which is much less than the smallest positive integer 1, so any pair of unequal integers passed the firing-threshold test easily. If the example had used inputs of real numbers x and y, then if the difference between them was less than .1, the neural network would have returned the wrong answer. This reflects a general characteristic of neural networks: They don't process with complete precision. Digital computers have the edge in mathematical precision. Second, the answer is not stored anywhere after it is computed. This neural network will calculate whether 5 = 3 or not, but after it is done the answer is lost, at least it will be after the next use of these neurons for a different calculation. If you want to find out if 5 = 3 at some later time, then you must feed in the values to the neural network and let it recompute the decision. Digital computers have addressable memory or disk storage where the answer can be stored and accessed again later; this is not true for neural networks. Third, notice the role of the two hidden nodes N_3 and N_4: In effect, one checks if $x > y$ and the other checks if $x < y$. These are subproblems or parts of the original problem; hidden-layer nodes often serve as subpattern or feature detectors for neural networks. Human brains can have thousands of layers, layer after layer of neurons feeding partial answers forward for more processing. Fourth, another point is that not all nodes on one layer must be connected with all nodes on the next layer. This allows some inputs to go toward some feature-detection hidden nodes and other inputs to go elsewhere. Human brains react like this. Suppose that a person is in a meadow with many sights, smells, and an approaching thunderstorm. Incoming data will go toward the relevant parts of the brain before processing.

Strokes shut down the blood supply to parts of the brain, which causes entire groups of neurons to die. People often recover from strokes when their brains can reroute mental processing to another part of the brain or simply survive with the loss of those neurons killed by the stroke. An analogous situation can occur with neural networks. Consider the diagram and our example. Now imagine a different neural network with the same inputs and the same output but with the hidden layer duplicated 100 or more times. In effect, two inputs go into maybe 200 hidden-layer nodes, all of which feed into just one output node. The connections and weights are the same as in our example except there are now 100 occurrences of each connection and weight. When two numbers x and y are input, the same answer as before is output; suppose the decision to be made is whether 5 = 3. The summed inputs that reach the output node will be 100 * 1 = 100 (recall that the nodes N_3 and N_4 only output 1 or

0). Next, imagine what happens if something happens to a few of the hidden-layer nodes or their connections. Maybe, their output goes to zero or changes sign; suppose that six nodes that usually would output 1 suddenly output 0; now the sum reaching the output node is 94 instead of 100. Anyhow, the answer doesn't change; 94 is still over the threshold, and therefore the output node puts out a 1, meaning that $x \neq y$. The network gives the same answer as before, because the unchanged nodes still are functioning perfectly and the summation procedure makes a few small errors negligible.

Neural networks have this property of graceful degradation. This means that when something goes wrong, neural networks still function, although the more that goes wrong, the less accurate their output becomes. Digital computers don't work this way. One bit off and you are in big trouble; as we have seen before, a one-bit change in a large program will change one byte, which is most likely to wreck the entire program, keeping it from compiling. Digital methods so fear the loss of even a single bit that they must resort to extensive error-checking, routines to guarantee the integrity of their data down to the last bit. Moreover, if there is a hardware error the digital computer may have no hope of recovery. Neural networks, because of this degradation property, are very useful in specialized computer applications where a hardware error would mean disaster.

A human brain is a complex neuron network containing billions of neurons that may have as many as 10,000 connecting paths each. Biological neurons have the same fundamental structure and properties as the mathematical structure that we have seen, although biological neurons are more complex. Their basic operations are closely simulated by the simple nodes, connecting paths with weights, summation functions, and firing thresholds that we described for the artificial neurons. The synapses are particularly important since they are the biological embodiment of the weights that store a neural network's representation.

The neuron body, which we represent by the node, has a summing function. Electrical signals are easy to add with analog circuitry like that found in the brain; no complicated processing units are needed like that in a digital computer. A second function of the neuron body is to decide if the summed input signals exceed the firing-threshold level and, if so, to then send out an output signal.

Learning in neural networks involves changing the weights of the connections between neurons. Normally, the firing thresholds and the signal transformation functions within the node do not change. Neural networks learn by being taught. There are several general methods for teaching or training networks; one common method is supervised learning, which involves a comparison between the neural network's output and the correct output. The trainer starts with a data set of inputs paired with a correct response or the response that the network should output. [In our example, the inputs and correct responses could be triples like (2,3,false), (2,2,true), and (5,3,false).] The neural network is run many times with the same input. After each run, the output generated by the network is compared to the correct response. A correction is then made to the weight values throughout the network, and the network is ready for the next run. Eventually, the weight values converge to values that will respond with the correct output when an input is presented to the network. At this point you have a trained neural network, and you store the weights and the network design for later use.

You would use the small network of our example to do simple decisions between pairs of integers. If you didn't know what weight values were necessary beforehand (usually the case) for a decision network, then you would have to go through the training process outlined above for a small set of appropriate values. After training on a set of appropriate values, the network should give the correct response for a wide range of input values.

Biological neurons learn in a similar way. Donald Hebb was the founder of the best-known theory of neuron learning. His main contention was that when a pair of neurons are active simultaneously, neural tissue changes. In effect, these changes act like changing weight values on the connections of an artificial network; although several different small changes to parts of the two biological neurons occur, the overall effect is to change electrical signal transmission between this pair of neurons.

Neural networks and brains differ from conventional digital computers. Conventional computers have RAM or disk storage with addressable data, and they have processing units dedicated to doing just mathematical or comparison operations. Neural networks and brains have none of these. Conventional computers store knowledge at certain locations in memory or on disks; they can recall it instantly. A neural network doesn't store knowledge at any specific location; instead, its "knowledge" is spread out and stored as part of the overall pattern of the neural network. The only things that are stored in a neural network are the weights of the connecting paths, the firing thresholds for individual neurons, and sometimes individual input-response functions for each neuron (our examples use simple linear or step-function responses).

Neural networks are still in their infancy; however, we can still make some observations about their abilities and especially their performance against the main form of digital AI, expert systems. Like humans, neural networks excel at association and pattern recognition. Unlike expert systems, neural networks are good with ill-formed data sets and errors. They extrapolate models and predict trends better than most other methods; part of the reason for this is that neural networks don't make strict assumptions about the form of the model. They change the model to fit the data; they do not fix a model like linear regression and force-fit the data to that model. There are mathematical theorems that say that a neural network with only one hidden layer can approximate any continuous mathematical function on a compact set and that one with two hidden layers can approximate any function likely to come up in any physical model. This means that neural networks can approximate to any degree of accuracy any model that we want. So the human brain can, too.

VIRTUAL REALITY

Today, virtual reality means visual and audio interactions with a computer system. Soon there will be more realistic scenarios, with interfaces that block out more of the real world and let the user experience more of the simulation, like smells and touch. Today, most virtual reality software is gaming software, where the user/player controls a constantly changing plot, aided or hindered by other characters in the game. A player has goals to attain; secondary characters have software-generated appearances, traits, and motives of their own. A player participates in an adventure over which he has some, but not complete, control. It is not unlike a dream. And the more advanced the technology becomes, the more dreamlike the scenarios will become.

Secondary characters are absolutely necessary, for realism, to the user in virtual reality games and will become more humanlike. Today, secondary characters consist of a visual appearance (rugged adventurous male characters and voluptuous female characters are in vogue today; no surprise, since almost all gaming software is purchased by males), a voice, motivation (sometimes to help the human player, sometimes not), skills (often with deadly weapons), and other preprogrammed traits.

Soon, virtual reality scenarios could include almost anything. You could talk to long-dead people like George Washington, Cleopatra, or Napoleon (at least computer simulations of them). You could advise Napoleon on deploying troops and help him to win at Waterloo, changing the course of history. You could kidnap the heir to the French throne in the thirteenth century or introduce the printing press into eleventh-century Norman England and observe the changes caused in medieval society. Nearer to home and the present age, you could win the heart of an unobtainable high school heartthrob, write a chart-busting hit recording, make a million in the stock market, or relive your twenties and make amends for all the hurts you caused your family by your immaturity. Conquer enemies, set up fiefdoms, bestow gifts on your friends, build cities, do whatever you desire. Be a warrior, be a legend, be a king, be a god! All these paths would be open to you. All of this would happen in software and silicon memory; none of this would affect history or the actual people in the scenarios. None of this would hurt or affect any other sentient being. It would just be a dream game for you.

Problems with virtual reality are foreseeable. In the near future, a home PC and virtual reality games could be as much fun and as addictive as alcohol or drugs or sex. Even today, the phrase "computer widow" is in our vocabulary. Imagine how many more people will be attracted to computers in the year 2000 when virtual reality is much more realistic. On the darker side, violence seems an integral part of many games of today. Many educators, parents, and politicians have wondered about the effect violence in computer games has on children. And these are just near-term problems. Later, really difficult problems could arise. People's basic psyche could be changed by the effects of ultrarealistic virtual reality. The fear is that today's computer enthusiast (the one married to the "computer widow") could be tomorrow's recluse; today's wargamer might be tomorrow's spree killer.

Virtual reality could be a tremendous positive force. There is no cause to be negative about the possibilities of virtual reality. It offers possibilities in training, entertainment, psychiatry, and sociology, to name a few.

Still, whether positive force or negative influence, virtual reality will change our world. People will demand more and, if the expense is beyond the means of the average person, then look for government funding or control. Politics of the future might have to deal with issues like how much computer time each person gets.

Farther out, the future may bring actual brain–computer linkups; although the exact nature of the linkup is speculative, it would be connected to the central nervous system and have a direct path to the cortex of the brain. A computer then would be an extension of your brain, allowing you access to the computational power and massive memory in large computers. At first, this linkup would probably be used to upload visual or audio data from the computer to the brain. However, as more is learned about the brain and consciousness, the computer could be used to communicate with different areas in the brain. Eventually, the computer link could affect a range of human emotions (possibly all): fears, desires, obsessions, and more. At this point, the human loses complete control over his situation. At this point, the computer becomes part of the human consciousness. At this point, massive social problems begin.

Besides the obvious computer-control problems that could arise, there are other issues. Brain–computer linkups could change secondary characters from created software characters to other humans. A multibrain computer-linked virtual reality game would be the outcome. Herein lies trouble, as we shall see!

You and some of your persona friends could get together in silicon dreamland and form your own societies, with your own moral codes, your own virtual country, and your own laws. Recall our earlier description of a universe in a computer. This would be a human-made micro version of that.

Imagine a courtroom of 2060: The plaintiff's lawyers are arguing that their client's civil rights were violated because his persona was enticed into your virtual society, then forced into farm labor, then drafted into an army, then captured, enslaved, and tortured. The plaintiff suffered for an entire evening, which was the virtual equivalent of 20 years of real life (because of computer speedup of apparent time). This hardship was relayed back to the plaintiff (linked up to the computer all evening) and caused permanent emotional scars in a real person. Should the defendant have ensured a more gentle virtual society, or should the plaintiff have known better to start with? You be the judge.

Dream-game virtual reality becomes a problem when the secondary characters become other conscious personas or when they become so advanced as to be conscious. When personas of other living human beings are being hurt, enslaved, or killed in a virtual reality and feelings are being relayed back to the flesh-and-blood individual connected to the computer, then a problem might exist. Far-out future technology is speculation: We can speculate about downloading or moving human traits and memories directly to software and computer memory, about entire personas stored in computers — personality, motives, loves, fears, memories, desires, and consciousness — and about virtual life, a real person captured in silicon. (Whether this is completely possible is a debatable issue and is discussed later when we consider the conscious mind and free will in Chapters 13 and 19. Free will or souls can't transfer to computers. Still, this is a hot topic in science fiction; one good example is Poul Anderson's great new book *Harvest of Stars*.) The capability to upload computer data to the human mind will arrive sooner than the converse process of downloading human memories to computers. Uploading from a computer to a human brain could utilize human senses like sight and hearing. Downloading requires intricate electrical wiring and a comprehensive understanding of storage of human memories; we are a long way from this capability.

For a far-out possibility, think about a sentient-beings-inside-a-computer scenario. If we could reach the stage where we were certain that our computer creatures were sentient, conscious, and capable of real feelings, then we might restrict what could happen to them in the computer.

A far-out but exciting possibility for advanced virtual reality is technical reincarnation. Imagine a society in which before you die your persona is stored in a computer. So after death you still "exist" in a sense. You can talk to living people and recall memories, and your desires, motives, and personality all remain the same. Even more, you can interact with other "silicon souls" and have new life experiences with them. This would be another society within a computer. Now, we really have options. A child of the far future could spend the weekend with his great-great-great-great-grandparents (dead a hundred years, but stored in a computer all that time), walking through a virtual reality restoration of the land of a century and a half before. And the key part: All these individuals (alive and virtual) would sense this visit, would interact with each other, would recall the visit later, and would enjoy it just as fully as if the child visited *live* grandparents today. Live forever in a computer.

Science fiction sees this as the eventual future of virtual reality and perhaps humanity. If ever computer-people can think, reason, feel, hurt, love, and behave indistinguishably from real people, if ever real people can transfer, personality intact, into a computer and enjoy a wider range of experiences than they do in the physical world, then Homo sapiens will evolve into something else in the evolutionary chain.

And one last thought. Creating a universe within a computer seems somewhat possible in the far future. Of course, this would be many orders of magnitude more complex than our present computer simulations and games — but it seems possible. We use simulations to create situations that we want to study or to study problems that we want to solve. A universe creator could also, but the simulation could be an entire universe. However, if we think that we can eventually create a universe within a computer simulation, then it brings up the possibility that we are within a created computer universe ourselves. Talk about an edge of reality — this would be a dead stop; we could never look outside a computer if we were inside.

We all dream; are we positive that the actual world is not a long-lasting dream? "Dallas" was one of the most famous of all TV series. Once upon a time, the scriptwriters "killed off" a longtime male lead in the show (Patrick Duffy); still the series went on without him and continued this way for another year or more. Then the scriptwriters decided to bring this "currently dead" male lead back into the show — major problem here. The script that handled his reappearance was a cinematic masterpiece; it showed his wife awakening from a long sleep and claimed that *she had dreamed the whole thing* (the entire past year of the series with all the events in all the characters' lives). Viewers apparently bought this, and the show continued for some time after that. The point is: Are we sure that we haven't dreamed our entire lives? Are we sure that we live in a physical world and not a virtual dream world?

101

Chapter 12

Computers Imitating Life

The universe is a computer, the only trouble is that somebody else is using it.

TOM TOFFOLI[1]

1010101010101010101010101010101010101010101

Life as we know it is composed of extraordinarily complex machines called cells. Cells can grasp and organize molecules and then construct extremely sophisticated structures out of them. Birds, flowers, giant sequoia trees, elephants, and people are all composed of diverse structures, which are composed of and by cells. Ordered construction requires patterns; the patterns necessary for these structures are stored in special material called DNA. DNA has one special property that allows it to carry patterns forward from one generation to the next — the property of self-replication. Without self-replication, life itself is impossible. It turns out that this key property, self-replication, is very similar to a mathematical property that some computer programs have, called *recursion*. A self-replicating machine or computer program needs to be able to store a pattern of itself, be able to read this pattern, and be able to act on this pattern. However, self-replicating machines are incredibly complex; they require storage of massive amounts of information, and they need a special mechanism to act upon this information. Suffice it to say that humanity has yet to build such a machine, but apparently nature has. Origins — another edge of reality limits us as we consider the problem of looking back to the beginning of life on earth. We will see that the mystery of life involves naturally occurring machines and self-replication. But how did the first naturally occurring self-replicating machine spring up by itself? We can only speculate; we can't peer back through the haze of time and see life starting. Exploration of the idea of self-replicating machines and examination of some of their unique abilities are the goals of this chapter.

DNA can be thought of as a pattern for a structure that can *gather* material, *organize* material to form other structures, and *replicate* itself. A moment's reflection shows that most machines today do only one of these actions at most. Machines that gather are common (like a coal-mining machine); machines that organize to form a structure are common on assembly lines; machines that replicate themselves have never been constructed by human hands. A machine that can do all these three actions is still beyond our technology and will be for years to come.

Machines have grown in complexity over recorded history. From windmills to spinning wheels to printing presses to steam engines to assembly lines, the history of technology is one of more and more complex machinery. Modern computers are marvels of electronics and logic; they are capable of processes undreamed of just a few years ago. Still, modern machines are *very simple* compared to the machines that we discuss in this chapter. Humans have always interacted with and directed their machines' activities; human beings are vastly complicated machines in their own right. Most processes that we think of as being done by machines are actually being done by simple man-made machines *plus* very complicated natural machines — human beings. Humans are both thinking and processing machines; they can think their way through problems and gather and restructure raw materials. In addition, they can reproduce themselves. Two aspects of humans as machines need discussion in terms of (nonhuman) machines: first, their ability to run any algorithm or thought process and, second, reproduction or self-replication. The first is discussed in other parts of the book; the second is the main topic of this chapter.

SELF-REPLICATION AND RECURSION

Recursion is an important concept that allows systems to self-reference themselves. The concept is immediately applicable to computer programming when a procedure can reference itself for its own definition. And, most important of all, DNA — life itself — is recursive. Recursion and self-replication or self reproduction are closely related. It can be shown that there exists a self-replicating computer program: one of the greatest triumphs of the genius of John von Neumann was his demonstration of this fact by making use of a complex method to define a self-replicating computer program.

John von Neumann and Stanislaw Ulam invented the theory of cellular automatons in the 1940s as part of their study of artificial life. Von Neumann was attempting to show that there could be patterns of information that self-replicated — like living creatures. Von Neumann started describing the theory in terms of robots that assembled factories that assembled other robots, but he changed his approach when Ulam suggested the idea of modeling computer creatures as patterns in grids or cells.

In the mid-1950s, von Neumann proved that there exist cellular automaton universes in which some patterns self-replicate. His proof used the concept of a universal constructor, which is a machine that can be programmed to produce anything. His proof also used the idea of a *computer-creature blueprint* that was part of the computer creatures themselves and was part of the computer-creature children of the self-replicating process. This allowed the computer-creature children to reproduce also. To be a genuine self-replicating machine (or program), the machine (or program) must not only copy itself but also copy the program that copies itself. Otherwise, the children machines (programs) will not reproduce. One of von Neumann's brilliant ideas was a way to accomplish this and still avoid an infinite regress. A few years later, Watson and Crick proved that *DNA* was the *living-creature blueprint*; soon biologists were unraveling the mysteries of the DNA double helix and genetic code and studying the basics of molecular-level reproduction. It was then that they realized that von Neumann had discovered the same principles that nature uses in biology. Later, biologists identified the molecules that acted like von Neumann's universal constructor, computer memory, and control mechanism.

Very simple programs cannot self-replicate; a certain level of complexity is necessary before a self-replicating mechanism is possible. Von Neumann's idea requires 200,000 cells in the grid for the universal constructor, the memory, and the control mechanism. This is mirrored in life; the DNA double helix is incredibly complex. Indeed, the last big objection to the idea of life springing up on Earth from chance combinations of molecules in the primordial atmosphere of Earth is the seemingly near impossible odds of a self-replicating molecule being formed by chance. But more on this later.

"LIFE" — THE GAME

The game of "Life" is an early (and famous) example of a cellular automaton. Developed by a Cambridge mathematician, John Conway, the game gained instant fame from an October 1970 article in *Scientific American* by Martin Gardner.

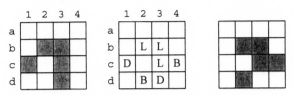

FIGURE 17. One turn in the game of "Life."

One turn in the game of Life is depicted in Figure 17. The game of Life is "played" on an infinite grid of cells, although only a small finite grid is pictured; the game progresses in a series of turns or time periods. Each cell can have one of two states: *living* or *dead*; a cell can change its state during a given turn depending on external factors. These external factors are environmentally motivated: Cells *die* if they are too isolated or too overcrowded, cells *live* on if they are living comfortably (two or three living neighbors), and vacant cells can be *born* (therefore becoming living) if they are surrounded by exactly three living cells. (Note: One cell in the grid can go from living to dead back to living again on subsequent turns if the conditions become right. Think of the cells as areas where life can thrive; don't think of the cells as individual creatures that come back to life.) Each cell has eight neighbors: the adjacent cells and the cells at the four corners. The diagram first shows one small grid of cells with the currently living cells shaded (L stands for living, D for dead, and B for born). Notice that the cell at c1 is isolated and will die before the next turn (it is marked D on the second diagram); notice also that cells at b2, b3, and c3 are all surrounded by two or three living cells during this turn so they will live on until the next turn. The currently dead cells at c4 and d2 have three living neighbors (called parents in the jargon of the game) and will be born during this turn, therefore living during the next turn. The next turn appears in the third grid.

FIGURE 18. Self-replication with computers. The pattern shown in the left-hand grid self-replicates in the four state changes that it takes to get to the right-hand grid. It carries its own blueprint along with it — like DNA.

Years after Life appeared, it was on thousands of college computers across the country. Originally, people believed that no initial pattern in Life could grow without limit. In short order, a group of graduate students discovered a pattern called a "glider" which moved continuously and then a "glider gun" which emitted a steady stream of gliders — therefore, the entire pattern could grow without limit.

The important thing about this game is not its history nor its popularity nor the intricate patterns that it generates. It is a simple yet accurate example of self-replication and how self-replication might be used by real structures. Life is played on a grid that has certain properties: The cells communicate with each other in a sense since a cell "knows" how many neighbors are living. This is actually a very simple assumption; yet very complex diagrams and recursive structures can spring up from such a simple beginning. There may be an important lesson here about the origin of life on Earth. Look at the next diagram (Figure 18), where a certain pattern of cells actually recreates itself after four moves; this is self-replication in its basic form. A "glider" carries its own blueprint along with it and reproduces itself. More complex structures called "glider factories" can be built; these structures produce an unending stream of gliders.

"Life" is but one class of cellular automatons; there are other rules that lead to interesting cell structures and time-varying patterns. However, there may be more to cellular automatons than an interesting computer game or an exercise for graduate students. A recent speculation concerns the exact definition of something being alive and the possibility that a computer program could be alive in some sense. Defining life or what it means to be alive is an elusive proposition. Some regard life as merely energy formed in patterns that exceed a certain level of complexity; others use nontrivial self-reproduction as the definition; others don't define it since they believe that it is a mysterious theological force. If we accept the nontrivial-self-reproduction definition, then there is a possibility that some extremely advanced Life patterns could be considered alive. Clearly, these patterns would have to be much more complex than gliders or glider guns, but the idea is the same. Chris Langton, a researcher at Santa Fe Institute, put it this way: "Life is a process, and it shouldn't matter what the hardware is. If a simulation meets the criteria for life . . . then it should be valid to ask if it's alive."[2] This leads us to a new frontier in metaphysics — the concept of a universe inside a computer. Since von Neumann's study of cellular automatons, speculations have arisen about a possible alternate view of the universe. It is possible that the universe is made of many instances of simple components that act together in a few simple definite ways, analogous to cells with only two or three states and only two or three defining rules for actions. Scientist Ed Fredkin believes that the observable universe is inside a giant cellular automaton. Some scientists go as far as to state that our universe is someone else's computer. Frank Tipler once speculated on simulating people inside a computer: "The key question is this: do the simulated people exist? As far as the simulated people can tell, they do. . . . There is no way for the people inside this simulated universe to tell that they are merely simulated . . . and are in fact not real."[3]

ETERNAL LIFE WITH NANOMACHINES?

Many researchers envision an extreme miniaturization of technology in the future, which could develop cell-size or molecule-size machines; this field is called *nanotechnology*. Machines the size of cells or smaller having built-in computers and built-in propulsion and built-in grappling devices; machines like this could grasp and organize molecules just like cells. Machines like these could repair worn out, sickly human bodies at the cellular or gene level. An idea that has caught hold in the last decade is the potential use of nanomachines as a futuristic vaccine against almost any human ailment. Imagine a set of cell-sized machines that could propel themselves, grab, restructure biological material, sense their surroundings, think with onboard computers, and finally replicate themselves. A vaccine of these nanomachines could be injected into a patient and cure him of almost any disease or disorder. Medicine does *not* heal patients directly; medicine does create favorable conditions within a human body so that the sick body can heal itself. For example, certain drugs can gently spur diseased body organs to heal, but no drug or treatment actually replaces or does component-level repair on individual cells. Or certain vaccines can describe the invading viruses' structure to the body, but it is left to the body's defenses to oust the invader disease.

In fields like mathematics, physics, and chemistry, being called a pioneer usually means being long dead; the fundamentals in these fields go back a long way. It is different in the computer field. Marvin Minsky is a true pioneer in the artificial intelligence field. He has a broad academic background in mathematics and physics along with biology. Although neural networks are a fairly new discipline within computer science, having gained popularity during the late 1980s, Minsky was one of the designers of the first neural network learning machine back in 1951 (ancient history in the computer field). He has recently taught at the Massachusetts Institute of Technology, where he has won numerous prizes and published articles and books including the recent and well-known *The Society of the Mind*. He has done a lot of thinking about nanotechnology and its potential: "Eventually, using nanotechnology, we will entirely replace our brains. Once delivered from the limitations of biology, we will decide

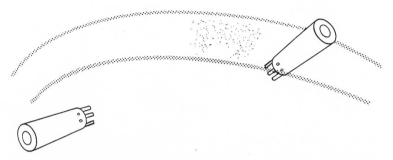

FIGURE 19. Medicine of the future? Hypothetical nanomachines repairing an abnormality on a capillary. These machines could be built by recursion: nanomachines building nanofactories that build smaller nanomachines and so on.

the length of our lives — with the option of immortality — and choose among other, unimagined capabilities as well."[4]

Medicine of the future could be radically different. Nanomedical devices could search injured tissue and organs, analyze the problem, and then mechanically repair it. They could fix minuscule capillaries (see Figure 19), modify cell components, fight invading organisms, and more. Necessary for these cell repair devices would be some sort of guiding intelligence; these cell repair devices need to be constructed, they must be able to analyze complex biochemical problems, and they must then guide the repair. Nanomachines and cell repair technology may be the key to indefinite life extension — the long-sought eternal life.

Unfortunately, this level of nanotechnology won't be available for many decades or centuries. So it won't make much difference to many or all humans alive today. However, there is a way that the people of today could *wait* for the benefits of nanotechnology. A combination of nanotechnology and frozen human brain tissue is envisioned as a possible way of preserving human memories. Brains could be frozen, and then after a few centuries, when nanotechnology will have advanced and science will have a complete understanding of the way permanent memories are stored as columns of neurons, nanomachines could enter the brain matter (we might need nano-icebreakers if the brain matter couldn't be thawed without losing information), read the permanent memories, and then restore them in computer memory (and maybe upload them to a new body). A neuron's output is a function of several measurable parameters, including chemical transmitter density, axon diameter, the size of the synapse area, and the number and size of dendrites. In theory, a neuron's output could be calculated from these parameters without actually measuring it during firing. Therefore a possibility is that future nanomachines could measure these parameters in a (perhaps frozen) brain and map out the network connections between the neurons in the brain. Then the nanomachines could download this data to a digital computer that could form an *equivalent* artificial neural network. This artificial neural network, in theory, could contain the brain's permanent memories. Later these memories could be uploaded into a new body created from the same DNA as the brain. It is just theory now, but within the realm of possibility in a few centuries. Our memories could live for centuries or forever.

The construction of nanomachines probably would have to take place in down-sizing stages. A succession of smaller and smaller nanomachine factories could be built by the successive generations of smaller and smaller nanomachines. The first generation could be the size of coins and be built by humans and existing tools; the second generation might be the size of the diameter of a human hair and be built by the first generation; the third generation might be cell-sized, the fourth molecule-sized. Self-replication patterns would be essential for such a process.

THE ORIGIN OF LIFE

The theme of this book isn't the mysteries surrounding the origin of life; that is a vast subject that has been covered elsewhere. However, any similarity between life and computer thought will cast light upon the computers versus humans issue. Therefore, a quick look at how the computer process of recursion (or the logical process of self-referencing) could play a role in the formation of life on Earth would be useful and interesting.

The short version of the usual story of chemical and biological evolution on Earth is the following: Life is a naturally occurring self-replicating automaton; life on Earth is self-reproducing machinery. Once there was the first single molecule on Earth with the self-replicating property. No other molecule before it had the property. It reproduced and reproduced, occasionally making small errors. Often the error caused that branch of the tree of life to vanish, but infrequently the error led to an improvement which itself survived to reproduce and reproduce. Eventually this improvement made another small error that led to another improvement and so on and so on. Based on many biological observations, this view of evolution confirms that all living organisms seem designed from the same pattern. An even shorter version was noted by physicist Gerald Feinberg, who once called life "a disease of matter."[5]

A few years ago, the usual story of chemical evolution was a chain of logic that had the "simple" molecules of life coming together by chance from random interactions within the primordial atmosphere, then eventually working up to DNA, RNA, and other complex life structures. The first part was fine: Amino acids and other molecules of life can form when sparks (like lightning) pass through simulated atmospheres full of gases like methane, similar to the primordial atmosphere. And clearly the last part exists — we are surrounded by DNA. The problem was in the middle. The unknown in the middle — between the simplest conceivable self-replicating organisms and the component molecules that might have been created in the primordial atmosphere and joined by chance — was overwhelmingly large.

The usual story had this "spring up" happening by chance, the reasoning being that nature had all the time in the world (literally) and so much raw material where chance circumstances could take place that eventually chance circumstances produced such a first machine.

Our form of life would need instructions (like DNA and RNA), a method of reading and acting on the instructions (like ribosomes), and a method of maintaining itself. But DNA and ribosomes are enormous molecular structures. If the *first* of its kind formed by a chance occurrence, then it would be nearly a *miracle*; this was a big problem to try to explain away. A ribosome has over 250,000 atoms in it. The molecules of life, amino acids and some sugars, contain between 10 and 100 atoms. The odds against something as simple as a single nucleotide (DNA and RNA are both chains of nucleotide molecules) or a hemoglobin molecule (the stuff that makes blood red) forming spontaneously are way over 10^{200} to 1. Sure, you say, give me enough time and material and random chance will do it. But 10^{200} is greater than the product of all the material in the universe multiplied by all the time since the universe started — much, much greater.

Numbers like this caused problems for the chemical theory of evolution. To fix the problem, researchers needed to discover a far less complex self-replicating structure than DNA — a structure that could have arisen by chance occurrence in the primordial atmosphere and a structure that could have evolved to the present-day DNA.

When computers became commonplace and computer concepts like recursion became widely known and used, these debates on the origin of life shifted ground. Now the perceived need to have a large part of life's molecules come together at random changed to a more realizable goal of developing self-replicating molecules. Of course, many biologists realized this all along, but it was a somewhat alien concept to others. Still, displaying recursive molecules developing spontaneously from raw materials wasn't possible because, until recently, researchers couldn't create self-replicating molecules within a laboratory.

Let's briefly consider what might be involved in molecular self-replication. A molecule generates several attractive and repulsive forces based on its exact configuration and its component atoms. These forces are less powerful, in general, than the forces binding atoms into molecules; still these forces (like partial positive and negative charges and hydrogen bonding forces) are substantial enough to attract raw material to the molecule. A molecule also has a "shape" in a sense; its component atoms or molecules form a certain pattern. This shape has places where other molecules or individual atoms might fit, first, if they could be attracted there and, second, if enough attractive force was available to hold these other molecules or atoms in place.[6]

A self-replicating molecule can assemble copies of itself from raw materials; one key feature of replicating molecules is complementarity. A complementary molecule to a molecule M would be one that fits into M's shape and is attracted enough to M to hold the complex together. (There could be many complementary molecules with this general definition.) Depending on many factors, it could be that a molecule M is surrounded by the proper raw materials, and when it attracts them a new molecule forms (call it M') which in turn can attract these same raw materials and form a new molecule that is identical to the original M.

Figure 20 shows a molecule M and its complement M'. The rectangular and triangular perturbations are meant to depict the shape and attractive/repulsive forces of the molecules. The molecule M' results from M attracting and holding on to raw materials. Molecule M seems like a mold from which to make M', and conversely M' seems like a mold from which to make M. That analogy is the key to self-replication. Suppose that we have two molecules M and M' that are complementary like that. One thing that could happen is that an M makes an M', the two split, then M' makes another M, and they split. The second M is related to the first M that made its mold; this is self-replication one step removed — the child of M is M', not another M; instead, the grandchild of M is another M. Still, it is self-replication and it is similar to DNA's method.

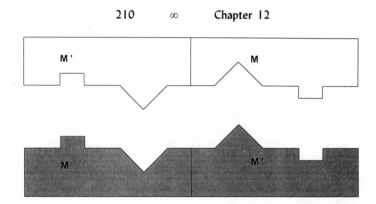

FIGURE 20. Self-replicating molecules. The molecule formed by M joined to its complement M' will attract raw material from its surroundings and form a copy of itself.

Another possible method is depicted in Figure 20. If M and M' were to be joined at the ends, then a composite molecule would be formed, M + M'; this molecule could attract raw material and form a mold for itself as shown in the figure. Therefore, a way that self-replication could take place in molecules is for a molecule M to form a complement M', and then, if M' could join M at one end, the composite molecule M + M' might be a self-replicating device. Moreover, if the composite molecule could withstand small mutations and still self-replicate, then you could have a molecular evolution process on your hands.

Imitating life within a laboratory has been a goal of several biochemistry experiments since the early 1950s. One early attempt by Stanley Miller of the University of Chicago focused on forming amino acids by discharging electrical bolts through raw materials similar to those on early Earth: ammonia, hydrogen, methane, and water. More recently, researcher Professor Julius Rebek, Jr. of the Massachusetts Institute of Technology caused a stir in the scientific community with an article in *Scientific American* in which he outlined his work that had led to the production of self-replicating molecules in a laboratory.

Dr. Rebek was born in Hungary, moved at an early age to Kansas, was educated at the University of Kansas, and then got his Ph.D. from MIT. He and his colleagues at MIT formed a variety of self-replicating molecules from component parts like oxygen, hydrogen, and nitrogen. The method that his group used was similar to the concept described above and depicted in Figure 20, where two molecules joined at the ends to form one molecule that could serve as a mold for itself. Their original molecules could not evolve as such. As Rebek pointed out: "To allow evolution, a self-replicating molecule has to be capable of 'making mistakes'; occasionally synthesizing other molecules that can perhaps be better replicators." However, in later works, molecules were synthesized that could mutate and still produce other self-replicators.[7] This work is progress, actually great progress; still much further ahead in the attempts to create living organisms in the laboratory is the enormous hurdle of DNA-encoded messages and how they came about (see Figure 21).

Every organism has within it a set of instructions called genetic information. Genetic information is a set of directions for producing and maintaining the organism. Think of the information as stored in books: The directions for a human run over 2000 books in length. Each chromosome has the content of about 40 books.

There is an analogy, hinted at before, between von Neumann's self-replicating computer and real life. Patterns and directions are stored in the DNA and RNA molecules; ribosomes operate on RNA and translate the message contained within. A ribosome translates by traveling along RNA and creating a protein chain. In this sense, a ribosome operates like a computer translating a tape full of numbers or a message full of instructions.

But there is a problem! Recall the enormous size and complexity of the self-replicating computer program; it is the same for life. Organisms seem to be necessary for evolution to work; however, all living organisms seem to be very complex. The main problem with life as we know it is the overwhelming com-

FIGURE 21. Origin of life. The answer to the origin of life on Earth lies within the DNA double helix — a self-replicating molecule, analogous to a recursive computer program.

plexity of DNA, RNA, and their intertwined process. It doesn't really work like the simple self-replication process shown in the figures. As A. G. Cairns-Smith, author of *Seven Clues to the Origin of Life*, put it: "But the real trouble arises because too much of the complexity seems to be necessary to the whole way in which organisms work. Our kind of life is 'high tech'." This high-tech life of ours is computerlike: Genetic information about the characteristics of the organism is carried as messages in the DNA; these messages are coded like computer data of a blueprint. RNA reads these encoded messages; therefore, it acts like a computer program in a sense. Both life's program and life's data are incredibly long and complex. Both program and data are essential to it all. How did something like this start? A. G. Cairns-Smith had these words: "Suddenly in our thinking we are faced with the seemingly unequivocal need for a fully working machine of incredible complexity: a machine that has to be complex, it seems, not just to work well but to work at all."[8]

Cairns-Smith has a tentative theory about what might have happened; to skip straight to his conclusion, he concludes that a good possibility is that mineral crystals (which are known to have a certain recursive behavior) might have started the whole chain of life, being replaced at some point by organic compounds.

There are other wilder possibilities for the origin of life. Clearly, life here could be an experimental agricultural project started by some space-faring race. It might be that there was some precursor molecule that was seeded on Earth and then mutated into DNA. Of course, unless we find other life in the universe that seems to have a common molecular basis with ours, this will be hard to ever prove.

Anyhow, the exact details of evolution are probably lost to us forever. There are so many possible chemical configurations, so many possible paths in moving from the basic molecules to RNA and DNA, that we will never figure it out in a lab. If Cairns-Smith is right and the far distant self-replicating molecules were inorganic and replaced at later dates by organic molecules, then the exact path is truly lost forever.

101

Chapter 13

Free Will — for People Only?

> *Man the machine — man the impersonal engine. Whatsoever a man is, is due to his make, and to the influence brought to bear upon it by his heredities, his habitat, his associations. He is moved, corrected, commanded, by exterior influences — solely. He originates nothing, not even a thought.*
>
> MARK TWAIN
> *What Is Man?*
> (1917, PUBLISHED POSTHUMOUSLY)

1010101010101010101010101010101010101010101

Since the beginning, mankind has puzzled over how the universe works. Theories about matter, the number zero, the concept of infinity, and the concept of the Earth moving around the sun have followed. All these lead to a deeper understanding of physical phenomena. In the last two centuries we have come to an

215

understanding of electricity, then relativity, and finally quantum mechanics. Now physicists talk of a final theory to end all theories — a "theory of everything," or TOE. This would be a theory that could explain all physical phenomena by calculations based on a general mathematical model. Many people have assumed (feared?) that a TOE would inevitably lead to the conclusion that the universe and we, its inhabitants, are deterministic — that the future is entirely predetermined and we can neither change nor escape our future. The fear is that maybe humans can't actually change the future, so we are simply players in some scripted cosmic play.

Determinism means that the state of the universe at one instant suffices to determine its state at a later moment. Now this later state determines states at still later moments and so on forever. This means that everything that ever will happen in the future is completely determined by the present state. The universe is reduced to a machine that simply changes as it is forced to, and this has been going on since the beginning of time. God is reduced to a cosmic historian who follows out a timetable of history that has already been written.

Upper limits on logic and calculation are two edges of reality that limit both computers and humans. The lack of free will also limits computers; computers do not and never will have free will. But do humans?

This chapter describes what might be termed "classical free will": what people feel it is and is not, why it is not a characteristic of computers, and, lastly, how it relates to determinism and mathematical models of reality. Also this chapter covers the ethical-guidance character that most people ascribe to free will, and it discusses the dissenting position — concisely summarized by Mark Twain. However, this chapter doesn't discuss some recent theories that apply quantum-theoretic arguments to the issue — these will be covered in the later chapter on "Quantum Consciousness and Free Will."

DETERMINISM AND NEWTON

Discussions of determinism, free will, and the stochastic nature of quantum mechanics all hinge on a mathematical model of the forces of nature. This means that a list of equations is compiled that together accurately predict all events in nature. Correctness of the equations that represent the laws of physics is not really an issue. We know that the current laws of physics are still in error; they are only an approximation to the final-absolute-truth correct set of laws. We believe that, as we learn more, our laws will become better and better approximations to this correct set of laws. And then we will have a correct mathematical model of the universe. Determinism hinges on the form of the equations, not their exact values.

Even though the final model would be a series of equations, the basic ideas can be explained easily enough by considering a limited physical situation. Consider the problem that Isaac Newton faced centuries ago. When an object is thrown, its path through the air is affected by its initial velocity, its direction, and the force of gravity (this makes the simplifying assumptions that this happens in a vacuum where there is no air resistance). According to the law that Newton formulated, if the object is always thrown at the *exact same velocity and in the exact same direction from the exact same initial position*, then the path of the object will *always be the same* — it will never vary.

The phrase *exactly the same* is crucial and much more precise than one might think. In the context of this issue, to be *exactly the same* on two occasions means that every particle must be exactly the same and in exactly the same position with exactly the same resultant force acting on it on each of the two occasions. Consider one atom in another galaxy, a billion light-years away, which is *one inch* away from its position on the first occasion, all other atoms being in exactly the same position on the two occasions. This is enough to make the second occasion *not* exactly the same as the first occasion. The object's path is pre-determined; a computer could compute exactly where the object will be at any future time. No alternative exists, no other flight path is possible. Without outside events influencing the outcome (which would invalidate the model and assumptions), the object will always traverse the same path if it is always thrown the same way. The object's future is predetermined; the object has no "free will," no choice about where it goes.

Everybody would readily agree that an inanimate object acts this way: The object has no choice about where it goes. Most people also would insist that this predeterminism does not hold for the human mind; they would insist that there is the fundamental capacity of choice or free will for humans. The forces acting on humans and the variables that determine their decisions are far more complex than those that determine the path of a thrown object. A multitude of forces of different strengths act upon us continuously.

MODELS OF THE LAWS OF PHYSICS

Newton's laws leave no room for choice. But Newton's laws are not completely accurate descriptors of the universe. Does the reasoning from the example discussed above change if the most accurate theories are used? Maxwell's equations, the laws of quantum mechanics, and the laws of relativity all are extremely accurate representations of reality. This accuracy holds over a large range of distances. Einstein's theory has been validated time after time in experiments over the last 70 years; the equations are so accurate that any error must be less than 10^{-14}. Maxwell's equations also have been validated many times. They have worked extremely well for objects as large as galaxies and as small as atoms. When the object of interest is very small, Maxwell's equations in combination with the laws of quantum mechanics provide equally good accuracy. The point is that we understand action and reaction very well within a wide range;

these three theories and the equations that describe them are very accurate representations of reality. This means that we have an accurate means of calculating the potential at most every point in the universe. (This is not to imply that we actually can do these calculations; too many values are unknown, and the computational effort is too large.) There are many equations within the scope of these theories; most of these equations are not as simply stated as Newton's laws. Many of these equations involve partial differential equations and other specialized mathematical forms. Furthermore, quantum mechanics theory includes many random variables because of the inherent randomness of the quantum-level processes. However, similar arguments can be made about the impossibility of material objects having a choice as to their future path (called a position trace on the graphs).

What does all of this mean? Newton's law made for a clear case: The thrown object could follow one and only one path if the initial velocity, direction, and position were always the same. And this one path could be computed. Also, for the Newton's law example the situation was simplified — outside forces were ignored. If we account for all outside factors, does the conclusion change? Maybe and maybe not. *All outside forces* literally means everything in the universe by quantum mechanics theory. Now most objects are far enough away that they have a vanishingly small effect, but to consider all factors literally means to consider all influences from all other places. Some question whether the calculation is actually possible at all; this would mean that the issue is not computable. However, most scientists currently accept that the calculation could be done in theory. In one theory, one could set up a potential field for the universe — calculate the force acting upon each point in the field. The time complexity of the calculation would be impossibly difficult. However, it appears that the equations for the calculation are known (or can be known and are finite in number) and that the universe is finite. Therefore, in this one theory, the problem is computable, and in some sense the future is "deterministic" though no computer in the universe could ever predict the future exactly.

ARE HUMANS DETERMINISTIC?

But is this theory correct: Are human beings also "deterministic?" Or can humans interact with and influence the outcome of events — this influence being incalculable and nondeterministic? Most people feel that we are not just automatons, machines that have programs along with sensing devices that sense the world around us — automatons that then make decisions based on our senses and programming but are completely bound by both.

The human thought process is an incredibly complex function; a variety of forces, senses, and ideas act on decisions. The question is: Can all these forces, senses, and ideas be stated in terms of physical laws operating on physical objects, or is there something truly mystic and extraordinary about human thought? Can all social, environmental, and genetic factors be stated in terms of physical laws? Let's delve into this by considering an example of a teenager who is witnessing an argument in the school hallway that could erupt into violence. This is a common situation with many possible outcomes; the situation could lead to nothing, it could cause lasting hard feelings, or it could lead to violence. There are social risks for the witness, too. Either of the two people could dislike his meddling or hold him accountable for interceding on the other's side. Should he intercede on one side or try to mediate between the two sides or perhaps keep out altogether? It is a tough decision. But it is a completely human decision. The factors influencing his decision will include moral considerations, friendship, fear, peer pressure, family experiences, ethical training, and hormone levels.

Computers aren't driven by such factors — people are. Computers don't make such decisions — people do. If free will exists anywhere, it exists here.

Table 4
Examples of Influences on a Person's Decision

Type of influence	Example(s)
Extraterrestrial influences	Sunspot activity
Environmental influences	Temperature Barometric pressure Humidity
Past experiences and learning	Previous experiences with arguments Mother's advice Judeo-Christian beliefs Personal beliefs
Current situation	Uncertainty as to the reasons for the situation Close to one of the participants Peer pressure
Brain activity influences	Current hormone level Level of phosphorus in the brain Neuron interconnectivity in the associative cortex
Molecular-level influences	Nerve fiber density Chloride level in nerve fibers

Taken as a whole, the situation is too complicated for detailed analysis; therefore, we will only look at some of the factors. There are many factors that could influence his decision process. Table 4 lists some (by no means all) possible factors. These factors are grouped by level; some are high-level factors, some operate at the cell level.

If this situation is deterministic, then *all factors* in the right-hand column can be *entirely stated in terms* of physical laws and *physical forces.* Clearly, factors such as sunspot activity, temperature, and barometric pressure can be stated as simply physical forces. Lower-level factors such as chloride and hormone levels seem physical (chemical) in nature also. The beliefs are a more personal issue; maybe they can be attributed entirely to experiences, which are stored by physical (chemical) means in the brain, or maybe there is something more here — something nonphysical.

This then is the big question: Can a person really do two or more different actions given the same initial conditions? Or if everything is exactly the same, would a person always make the same decision? Exactly the same means exactly the same childhood experience, exactly the same current situation, exactly the same brain structure, exactly the same hormone level — everything is exactly the same. If our mythical teenager could live his life twice exactly the same way to this point, would he (could he) choose the first occasion to mediate and the second occasion to keep out of the argument?

Is there something called free will that allows humans to make different decisions on these two occasions? Free will has to have the effect of interacting with the physical world; it has to be able to change physical events. Yet, if the cause of an effect is itself an effect of another physical cause, it doesn't seem to fit our understanding of free will. Consider Table 5, which compares the classical view of the world by Newton, computers, and human minds. Neither thrown objects nor computers plus programs have what we might term free will. Computers are definitely deterministic since their output is predetermined by their input and program. The physical world may or may not also be

Table 5
Determinism vs. Free Will: Comparison between the Physical World of Newton, Computers, and Humans

	Physical world of Newton	Computers	Humans
Initial conditions	Same initial velocity and direction	Same input	Same outside stimuli
Controlling mechanism	Same physical laws	Same program	Same experiences and brain structure
Results	Same impact point	Same output	???

deterministic. There is the issue of random inputs to the system addressed by quantum theory; this would make the system stochastic. However, for the purpose of this discussion, those random inputs can be treated the same as random inputs to a computer program. The issue is, if all other things are equal and the same random inputs are input to the system, does the output have to be the same?

Deterministic is used in the sense that the behavior of physical systems is predictable for all future time; the concept of free will is counter to this belief. So what could free will be? Is it an extrauniversal force that only humans can control? This force would have to be able to interact with the physical forces within our own universe. What level would this force operate at? In the earlier example the force would not seem to operate at the extraterrestrial or environmental levels; this level seems too high. Nor would this force seem to act at the brain chemical or molecular level; this level seems to be too hard for humans to control. Most philosophers and religions tend to place the action of free will close to the learning (ethical) and current situation levels. Many scientists think that human thought differs from the strict deductive and inductive reasoning of computers; the reason is that many major mathematical and scientific advances seem to have resulted from inspiration or leaps of imagination.

Ultimate questions like free will, the beginning of time, God, and the purpose of it all were once the domain of religion. In this century, theologians have been sharing the stage with the cosmologists of the Earth. Scientists like Albert Einstein, Niels Bohr, and the latter-day Stephen Hawking and Roger Penrose have speculated about such questions. They have differed in what they believe and what they studied. Einstein spoke often of God, but not as a God that took an interest in individual lives. Hawkings has concentrated on the beginning of the universe more than free will issues. Penrose has been in the vanguard of a movement to find a nonalgorithmic nature of the brain; this would be right in line with free will. A century ago, author Mark Twain had ideas, too:

> Man the machine — man the impersonal engine. Whatsoever a man
> is, is due to his make, and to the influence brought to bear upon it
> by his heredities, his habitat, his associations. He is moved, corrected,
> commanded, by exterior influences — solely. He originates nothing,
> not even a thought.

Mark Twain (Samuel Clemens' pen name) was the author of widely read classics such as *Tom Sawyer* and *The Adventures of Huckleberry Finn*. We associate these works with him, and therefore this quotation comes as a surprise — it seems out of character. However, Mark Twain was far more than a gruff, lovable old man and a simple storyteller. In fact, he had a brilliant mind, was one of the finest writers of his age, and, although not a scientist, understood the nineteenth-century realists' view of the universe. Also, he was a critic of the religion of the day.

Even a century later, nobody states the case for deterministic human beings as starkly as Mark Twain did. Free will is defined differently by some, but it never includes determinism. Determinism means that the state of the universe at one instant fixes (determines) its future states at later times; this leads to the inescapable conclusion that the future (our future) is completely determined for us — determinism is the ultimate in cause–effect. Quantum events are believed to not be cause–effect in nature; a random event is one that the past did not determine completely.

For our purposes, we will even exclude as free will random influences that can't be predicted. This would allow the possibility that the universe is not deterministic, but people still don't have free will. Some "exterior influences" could be random. Then we can never predict exactly — therefore no determinism — but we could be as "moved, corrected, commanded, by exterior influences — solely" as ever.

It is rough on our egos to accept a universe where we are of a mechanical nature, where we are powerless to change the future, where we are "moved, corrected, commanded, by exterior influences — solely." "Solely" — it is that one word that bothers us. We know that we are influenced by exterior forces.

What we want to believe is that there is something individual, something internal, something that transcends these worldly exterior forces, something that guides us or at least influences our actions.

Most people, whatever their religion, or even if they have no religious beliefs, believe in something internal to a person that in concept is close to the concept of a soul. Mark Twain's statement seems mechanical and cold; morality, aesthetics, beauty, good, inspiration, love, all would be by-products of a complex physical–chemical process — namely us. If there is a seat of free will, it seems that it would have to be able to command forces within our universe but not be controlled by other forces within the universe. This is a tall order, but not necessarily impossible. A final answer might depend on whether the universe or life was created by an outside force or sprang up naturally (i.e., as the result of a large-scale quantum fluctuation in the case of the universe or chemical evolution in the case of life). Is the universe deterministic? That is to say, would it be possible to predict the future for all time if we had the right equations and enough computer power? Or are the "right equations" too complex to ever calculate the future with (the "*exterior influences*")? In other words, is the future deterministic, but not computable? Quantum mechanics seems to say "no" — the universe is stochastic, not deterministic. The issue is not entirely closed, however. The key assumption is that quantum uncertainty is intrinsic to nature and not the result of errors in our current mathematical models of physics. In other words, if nature were truly deterministic and our physical models were also deterministic *but* our models were in error, *then would* the difference between nature and our models look like the quantum uncertainty that we observe? To settle questions like this, we need a final-absolute-truth correct set of physical laws — a "TOE." Today there are many scientists who believe that we are close to this correct set. No less than Stephen Hawking once entitled a lecture "Is the End in Sight for Theoretical Physics?"

Chapter 14

Why the Conscious Mind?

What a piece of work is a man! How noble in reason! How infinite in faculty!

WILLIAM SHAKESPEARE
Hamlet, II, ii, 317

My mind is incapable of conceiving such a thing as a soul. I may be in error, and man may have a soul; but I simply do not believe it.

THOMAS ALVA EDISON
Do We Live Again?

Justice is a temporary thing that must at last come to an end; but the conscience is eternal and will never die.

MARTIN LUTHER[1]

Our brains house the most incredible computing structure ever invented; they store our memories and control our actions. As unimposing as brains are physically, they have been responsible for all the great structures built on Earth and all of the great theories that have evolved over the centuries. They have been capable of drawing conclusions about the universe that we live in and then designing tests to prove those conclusions. A brain is also the seat of one of the strangest capabilities of all — consciousness.

Consciousness is what humans value most about life — the awareness, the sights, the sounds, the emotions, and the joys of living. And consciousness is what humans want most of all to preserve; the ultimate threat of the end of consciousness, death, has moved humans to seek ways to continue consciousness even after death. Consciousness may be more than just a human trait. Somehow we are aware, aware of the world around us, aware of ourselves. Consciousness may well influence the universe itself; an idea based on cosmological issues is that of the strong anthropic principle, which states that the universe would not exist as is without conscious creatures to observe it.

Like the previous chapter, this chapter focuses on what might be termed "classical consciousness." There are quantum-theoretic arguments bearing on both consciousness and free will; these issues will be discussed later after quantum theory.

COMPUTER SIMULATIONS AND THE HUMAN BRAIN

Brains can do all that computers can do, although much slower; it is an open question if human thought is capable of more than computers. Furthermore, it is not known if super-intelligent computers could be conscious. The brain is similar to a computer in some ways and completely different in others. Neurons are the basic computational structures within the brain; they total about 10^{11} in number as compared to about 10^9 transistors for today's largest computers. In terms of speed, computer transistors have a large edge: Neurons operate at a maximum rate of about 1000 times per second, whereas today's desktop computers operate at 100 MHz or 100,000,000 times per second.

Many different regions or substructures make up the brain; all have slightly different functions. There are the left and right cerebral hemispheres, a visual cortex, an association cortex, frontal lobes, the thalamus, and more. High-level brain activity (e.g., abstractions, complex associations, analysis) is carried out in the association cortex. Processing or thinking is carried out by the neurons; these specialized cells carry a signal along a long nerve fiber. This signal is passed on to another neuron at the synapse of the neuron; signal transmission speed is over 100 meters per second, a great deal less than the speed-of-light transmission speed of digital computers.

A theory held by many scientists is that the human brain simply acts out some very complicated algorithm as its thinking mechanism. For example: Permanent memories are being studied extensively, and current research shows that they work like the computer neural networks that we saw earlier, which are computer algorithms. Another example is the processing of visual data, which uses processes like digital signal processing, a set of algorithms used in television and stereo. This theory relates to the field of artificial intelligence and, in its strict form, is often called the "strong-AI view." This theory would state, in effect, that anything that a brain can do, so can a computer do. In other words, the brain's activity could be replicated or modeled by a computer with a sufficiently advanced computer program. An inescapable conclusion if the "strong-AI view" is true is that the eventual replacement of humans by computers is a very real possibility. But maybe the human brain has an edge: The main two possibilities are consciousness and free will. To explore this issue, we need a better model of brain activity and how a computer might simulate it.

Modeling brain activity with a digital computer is an idea that requires a great deal of explanation and exploration. Previously, we examined generic computer programs and saw how they operated within the scope of a general-purpose digital computer. We think of computer programs as mechanisms for doing things like mathematical computations, graphical displays, process control, data collection, or games. Computer programs could never hurt, feel pain, know joy, scheme, wonder, fear, taste, or laugh. Or could they? Brains are attached to bodies, which have many senses, such as touch, taste, hearing, and sight. These bodies can reach out and examine the world for their brains; if a computer had these additional capabilities, could it simulate a brain's activities? Imagine a computer that connects to several different sensors such as a printer, a microphone, a thermometer, maybe robot arms, etc. A computer like the one in Figure 22 senses the world around it. This computer can see, hear, sense pressure, communicate with other computers, write, refer to knowledge in databases, and move or grasp objects. Not a complete human being by any means, but it could simulate many

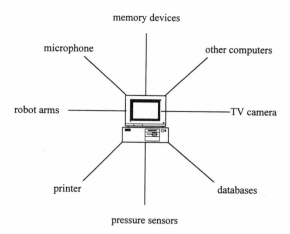

FIGURE 22. Can computers be conscious? The computer represented above can sense the world around it — not equivalent to human perception, but maybe in time. . . .

human activities. Now a computer program could process the inputs from the various sensors and simulate human thought processes such as feeling, recalling experiences, and analyzing. A rough sketch of how the basic program statements would apply as follows: feeling, reading the input from one or more sensors, recalling experiences, accessing computer memory for the record of previous feelings, analyzing, running part of the program on a set of inputs, and reading information that was stored previously. To repeat: This still doesn't closely simulate a human; there are just too many shortcomings of the system in the diagram. The sensors are not humanlike, and the program is surely too simplistic.

Imagine an extrapolation of this computer/sensor system into a futuristic supercomputer with future biomedical sensors that would be almost humanlike. Also imagine an extraordinarily complex future computer program that is based on vast amounts of detailed knowledge about human emotions, psychology, biochemistry, and the inner workings of the brain. This system could simulate or model the thought processes of a human and truly act like a human. The program could store information about its environment and experiences just like a human; the program could also learn from its experiences, changing its code like a human being learns new thought patterns. Now imagine all of this being inside a future biomedical robot. How close would this be to a real human? Is there anything that a human could do that no future robot could ever do — or could robots eventually become indistinguishable from people? Many people believe so; some are doing research, others are making plans to commercialize humanlike computers. A brochure from Matsushita Research Institute in Tokyo reads as follows: "Aimed by us is futuristic humane machines wherein human level electronic intelligence and nerve system are combined to machines of ultra-precision capabilities."[2] Others like AI pioneer Marvin Minsky see robots as the future. "Will robots inherit the Earth? Yes, but they will be our children."[3]

FIGURE 23. Turing test. The lady or the computer — which lies behind the door?

Alan Turing, the British mathematician, thought about these questions and came up with a scheme for testing how humanlike a robot could actually be. Ever since, it has been known as the "Turing test." Turing's test was to have an interviewer pose questions to a computer and a randomly chosen person. Both the computer and the person would be in a different room from the interviewer (see Figure 23) (like the old fable of "The Lady and the Tiger"). The interviewer was to ask (through an intermediary) a series of questions to either the computer or the person and attempt to distinguish between the person and the computer based on the answers. Turing thought that if the computer responded in a humanlike manner that fooled the interviewer, then the computer passed for human. In short, if the machine could pass for intelligent, then it was intelligent.

Computer programs exist that can act as a therapist for human patients; their approach is slightly different from Turing's. Some patients actually prefer to talk to a machine and reveal more of their problems than they would to a human therapist. For an example, consider the following exchange between a computer therapist and a human patient.

Therapist: What is your problem?
Human: I have felt depressed for some time now.
Therapist: Tell me more.
Human: My life has been boring, my kids seem to ignore me, my friends are shallow. I can go on.
Therapist: Why do you think that your kids ignore you?
Human: I don't know.
Therapist: Come on now, you must have some idea.
Human: No, there is no reason.
Therapist: There is always a reason.
Human: Kids are like that, parents don't understand them so the parents get ignored. They think that their parents are boring and are just necessary to provide food, housing, and, of course, spending money.
Therapist: "Boring" has come up twice, your kids think that you are boring and you feel that your life is boring. Talk to me about how you feel about "boring."
Human: I am not boring!
Therapist: No one is saying that. Just tell me how you feel about the word "boring." What do you associate with it?

This might seem quite like a human conversation at first glance; perhaps the computer therapist is intelligent in the same sense as a human. But the therapist program is just following some simple rules about therapy: Focus on the patient, ask follow-up questions about important replies, and gently prod the patient to reveal more.

At this point nothing is settled. Granted that some current computer programs can do very humanlike thought processes and granted that future computer systems will simulate human behavior much more exactly, but ultimately is there something intrinsically human that no computer system can do? The question boils down to algorithms; computers can only do algorithms. Can the human mind do something more, something nonalgorithmic? — that is the question. The answer may well lie in human consciousness.

CONSCIOUSNESS

What does it mean to be *conscious*? We are conscious of many sensations and feelings such as happiness, memories, pain, cold, noise, color, sounds, and tastes. We make conscious decisions about when to go to a movie, when to eat, and how much we should pay for a new car. We know what we are conscious of; what we don't know is what consciousness is exactly. Are we conscious because our brains and bodies form a sufficiently intelligent control mechanism that we are aware of? Would something far less intelligent be conscious, too — say a distant ancestor from 1,000,000 B.C., a chimp, a dog, or how about bacteria? Or are there levels of consciousness — a person being at the highest level followed by chimps, perhaps dolphins, working down through the animal kingdom? There is disagreement among scientists about what really is conscious. Some would say that no nonhuman animal could be conscious, while others would say that even lower level animals such as insects could be conscious.

Could a sufficiently advanced computer be conscious? A theme of science fiction stories for many years has been that of a sentient computer that grows in abilities and humanlike emotions. Often this computer grows tired or afraid of its limited human masters and takes control of them. Is there anything to this theme? Could a computer and its sensors really become humanlike? The computer in Figure 22 has sensors and other attached devices that approximate a human's senses and appendages; could all human feelings and thought processes be approximated by advanced computer programs? Or is there something so special about consciousness that we can never reproduce it in a laboratory?

Maybe consciousness is something mysterious or divine. Recalling the old enigma about a tree falling in a forest — does it make a sound if no one is around to hear it? — can a universe exist if no conscious beings are around to observe it? Were the laws of physics designed to allow conscious beings to develop? The so-called anthropic principle confronts issues like these. The principle has many variations, but the general theme is that humans are sentient, observing beings and that their existence is special within the universe. This belief is reinforced by the uniqueness of the physical constants that allow the universe to be habitable by human beings. There is very little leeway; if some fundamental constants of physics had slightly different values, then life (as we know it) could never have evolved. Indeed, this is a strong belief and not one that is readily provable, but a respected minority of the scientific community does believe this. We will look at this issue later on.

Most human characteristics evolved because they gave us an advantage and furthered our survival. Natural selection evolved our opposing thumbs, our keen eyesight, our upright method of walking, and our enormous brain capacity. Did consciousness evolve too? If so, what advantage did it serve? Could nature have done as well with unconscious automatic brains? It doesn't seem that way at first glance; we can't sleepwalk our way through our lives and do as well as we can when we are awake or conscious. But that simplistic argument may have a flaw. A real difficulty is that most all of the decisions that our body makes are made by the subconscious. When a person *learns* to read, walk, skate, or swim, they must make a conscious effort. Later, when they have learned the activity, it can be done without conscious thought, by the subconscious. And, of course, most normal body functions work without the aid of consciousness.

There seem to be three possibilities for the origin of consciousness: (1) Consciousness has a mysterious, maybe quantum-related, maybe unknowable, or maybe divine explanation; (2) consciousness relates to the level of mental awareness; or (3) consciousness is an effect of the physical system that forms our bodies and minds.

Consciousness, as we know it, is unique to every individual. We assume that *we* exist in no other body except our own; no one else feels, thinks, or remembers exactly the same things as we do. This brings up several enigmatic possibilities. Do identical twins share the exact same consciousness? After all, the twins share exactly the same DNA-encoded master plan for their bodies and brain structure. Admittedly, their experiences will branch out and differ as they grow older. Is this enough difference to say that we are dealing with two totally different conscious entities? If one twin could have his consciousness transplanted into the other twin's body and brain, would the first twin recognize the thoughts, the feelings, and the memories as *close* to his own? In this age of DNA implants and frozen embryos, the possibility of multiple copies of exactly the same person could arise. Another example of slightly different consciousness is the change in a person's consciousness as he grows older. I remember some experiences, thoughts, and feelings that I had when I was 8 years old. But would the 50-year-old consciousness recognize the 8-year-old body and brain if I could be magically transplanted back into that body and brain? Answer this question: Is the 50-year-old consciousness closer to its former 8-year-old self than the transplanted twin is to a totally different body's current consciousness? That issue is even murkier if one considers the smaller differences a one-year difference in age makes. Would the *you of today recognize any large differences in the you* of one year ago? — Are such differences due only to a larger experience set, or has your consciousness changed? Even more extreme, is your consciousness of today the same as that of yesterday — or one hour ago? And now consider the most extreme case of all: the case in which the two bodies and brains are exactly the same and the experiences are also exactly the same. Consider the science fiction concept of teleportation: A matter duplicator images a human body and then sends that image a long distance (usually instantaneously) to be duplicated at another location. The problem is that now you have two *exactly the same* people for a brief instance, same body down to the atomic level, same brain structure down to the atomic level, same thoughts, memories, and feelings down to the atomic level. The question is: Do these two different people have different consciousness at this time? This is a major philosophical issue that touches on the ultimate limits of computers and reincarnation of souls. Would the identity of a human change as the body grows older and gains and loses molecules through metabolism? Even if all the cells are different (say, a person as an 8-year-old and later as an adult), do the people remain themselves? Are we the information *or* the material and the information?

If we are only the information, then could the real us (the information part of us) remain conscious while residing in something other than a human body — say, a computer's memory? This is a hard question to come to terms with. A science fiction theme of today, but maybe a reality of the twenty-first century, is that of a humanlike computer. Computers are entirely made of matter that does not possess free will; if a computer can really simulate a human, maybe humans don't possess free will either. Another science fiction concept is the storage of the memories of deceased people in computer memory; this is a form of reincarnation into a virtual world inside a computer. (A good example of a science fiction story with similar themes is *Hobson's Choice* by Robert J. Sawyer, a serial that recently appeared in *Analog*. It had AI simulations that were alive and competed with their real-life personas; another theme was that the human soul could be electronically sensed.) All of this is possible only if the human mind and memories can be entirely mapped into the logic and form of computer programs.

People are certainly conscious; computers are probably not (at least not now). What of animals? For centuries, most people have dismissed all lower animals as mere automatons that existed and sensed but had no self-awareness or consciousness. However, consider Kansi. Kansi is a 12-year-old pygmy chimpanzee that lives on the Georgia State University campus; he has displayed the grammatical abilities of a 2½-year-old child. Kansi can't talk since apes lack the muscular control to form words, but he can solve nontrivial problems. For instance, Kansi witnessed this test being set up: One of his favorite treats was locked inside one box; next the key to this first box was put inside a second box, and then that second box was tied shut with rope. Inside his cage were placed pieces of flint. When left alone to solve the problem of getting his treat out from the roped box, the chimp came up with this solution. He fashioned the flint into cutting tools, then cut the rope on the second box to get inside and get the key to open the first box.[4] No question that there is something going on inside that chimp's mind, but is it consciousness?

Forming simple plans, expressing feelings, abstract symbol manipulation, and humanlike scheming were probably mental characteristics well within the grasp of the apes of 5,000,000 B.C. By 100,000 B.C. Homo sapiens' brain had reached present-day size — the same size as that of modern scientists who have such a marvelous understanding of abstract mathematics, quantum mechanics, DNA, and a thousand other intellectual byways. However, it has been only during the last 8000 years that most all technological progress has taken place. Evolutionary pressures like survival and more complex social structures probably account for the large brain size, but it is harder to understand the evolutionary pressures that would create an advantage for a facility such as consciousness. Genetic selection is the issue; if there is no advantage to consciousness, then why did it evolve?

There are no answers to these questions. There may never be answers. However, advances in AI computer technology and research into the need for observers in quantum-mechanical processes may provide an answer as to the origin and purpose of consciousness.

Whatever its physical origin, whatever its metaphysical implications, consciousness is something that humans seek to preserve. Total loss of consciousness is death. Call it "self-preservation," "survival instinct," or "selfish genes" — there is a compelling nature that forces us to look out for our own health and safety. The goal is the extension of life — the avoidance of death.

ETERNAL CONSCIOUSNESS?

Ultimately we all die. This finality has faced every person who ever walked the Earth; this ultimate extinction of our consciousness is a fearsome prospect. Reincarnation is a cornerstone of most religions and most people believe in some form of it. There are many forms: One form is that the entire body and mind are reincarnated; other forms have the mind alone being reincarnated and joined into a vast oneness with other minds and a god or some universal entity. A soul could be a divinely given entity that is forever beyond human understanding, and reincarnation might be more than simply a restoration of a human's consciousness and memories. However, the restoration of human memories and perhaps consciousness after death is a scientific possibility. Our bodies don't have to be reconstituted from dust; there are other possibilities that involve technical things like microbiology, nanomedicine, self-reproducing automatons, and computers.

Leaving aside theology for the moment, we can scientifically discuss the issue by limiting our discussion to a *restoration* of memories and maybe consciousness after physical deaths. No more, no less — no statements about whether this restoration lasts for eternity, no statements about whether this restoration involves a *soul*, no statements about the existence of a creation force or God, no statements about whether certain moral behavior is necessary. Since our permanent memories are permanent neural networks (columns of neurons) in our brains and since digital computers can simulate neural networks, we must conclude that our memories could, in principle, be stored in computer memory. Unresolved technical issues are threefold: First, precision measuring devices that could record the output of these permanent-memory neurons would be required; second, we would have to know how to locate the permanent-memory neural networks within the brain; and third, we would have to know how to interpret the output (a numerical value of voltage) of the neurons in terms of color, sound, or whatever. Although these requirements are definitely way beyond present-day technology, still there is little doubt that we probably can meet them within a century or so. Therefore, it is resolved: Our permanent memories could be stored within digital computers.

Consider three aspects of our minds: memory, consciousness, and free will. Future computers will be able to store human memories; they may eventually or may never be conscious; they will never possess free will. Souls and free will are out of the question; so what we call reincarnation wouldn't be possible. However, something less might be. If we define *reincarnation* as *memory + consciousness + free will* and we define *restoration* as *memory + (maybe) consciousness,* then it is possible that future computer systems could store human memories and be aware of these memories too.

When we considered virtual reality earlier, we considered the scenarios where memories in the computer were downloaded to the human mind via a computer–mind link and vice versa. Just this capability alone could form a memory database of the life experiences of those who have gone before. We speculated that children could tap into the memories of their dead great-grandparents. Furthermore, if consciousness were possible within the computer, then the simulated consciousness of these deceased great-grandparents could be conscious of their descendants. However, it is not clear if it would be the *same consciousness* as they possessed when they were alive. But we can speculate.

Many different forms of restored consciousness appear in science fiction and literature. One is where a person who dies at the age of 55 is reborn into the same body with the memories of the 55-year-old; variants of this have the new body being younger and healthier. Here the restored person interacts with other restored people in another society, usually free of many earthly problems. A second form is where only the informational part of the person is restored; the actual storage device would be something like a vast computer memory system. Here the restored consciousness interacts with other restored consciousness in a virtual-computer-world society. A third form is a memory-only form; here an individual's memories have been recorded, but the individual's consciousness has not been reawakened.

A person dies at age 55 and is restored later: What happens to the consciousness as time passes? Would it have to stay at the 55-year-old level always, or could it continue to add more experiences and change its thought process to the level of 85 years old or 120 years old or 1000 years old? What of the baby consciousness or the 8-year-old consciousness of the same individual: Are they lost forever, or could the reborn individual "back up" and relive experiences with his 8-year-old persona? We all say, "if I could only live my life over knowing what I know now" — maybe that is possible in restoration. You could use the experiences and thought processes of a 40-year-old and relive special events of your teenage years. After all, what is so special about your consciousness at the moment of death? Doesn't your consciousness at earlier ages deserve to be reborn too? Is the 8-year-old "you" lost forever? Is the teenage "you" beyond recall?

There are many scenarios about what the society of restored people might be like. Maybe there is *no personal ownership of memories* — no personal "right" to have all your memories accessible by you and only you until the end of time. Instead, maybe the community of restored individuals is really a community; maybe everyone's memories are treated as tribal memories, so that every individual's memories are available to all other individuals' restored consciousnesses. Perhaps consciousnesses are separate from memories; maybe only memories are stored, and dead consciousnesses are never restored. Perhaps our memories are stored in a gigantic data bank, where they can be recalled by another consciousness, perhaps a Gaia, an all-encompassing earth consciousness, or perhaps a technically advanced space-faring race. There may be no privacy in restoration; your memories may be accessible by another race, a god, or your restored spouse.

There are several aspects to a model of an individual identity that includes consciousness and memory. The way people think, their motivations, the relation between their experiences and memories — the composite is not a simple issue. A person's identity is a time history of both memories and the conscious thought process; the thought process includes motivations, emotions, experiences, and decisions. For example, consider the same person as a baby, an 8-year-old, and an adult. The adult remembers many of the 8-year-old's memories, but the motivations, emotions, and decisions are different.

If the stronger AI hypotheses (in brief, a computer can do anything a human can do and be conscious also) are correct, then future computers can be alive and conscious just like us; if this is correct, then human minds could be stored in futuristic computer systems and live and think just like we do now. A computer algorithm could simulate all hopes, emotions, desires, and consciousness, and all memories could be stored in computer memory.

Most interpretations of divine reincarnation involve the idea of *souls* — a not totally defined term, but generally thought to be the seat of something like free will and divinely given. If humans are truly possessed with special nonalgorithmic thought processes, then we can't model them with computers. Then any technical, nontheological, or nondivine restoration wouldn't reincarnate the complete individual — just restore his memories and algorithmic portion. Then this restored individual wouldn't act like the real individual would have under the same circumstances; in some way, the restored individual would fail the Turing Test — the restored person would only be a shell of the original person.

If the stronger AI hypotheses are wrong and the consciousness-is-unknowable theories or religions are right, then bodies are necessary. No body means no free will, no soul — the computer could only store memories, not hopes or emotions. Computer-restored "people" would be missing something essentially human, leaving the machine holding only ghosts with memories.

Humans wouldn't necessarily have to be restored into an electromechanical device like a computer system to be technically restored. Recent advances in the construction of *nanomachines* could point the way to a method of restoration of memories and consciousness that the human race could control itself. Death is usually caused by aging or disease. Aging and disease come in many forms. Some forms affect specific organs, causing them to fail; some forms attack the body at the cell level, causing body function failure. Whatever the forms of body failure that aging or disease cause, there is every reason to believe that future medical advances could isolate and understand each and every one. Now suppose that future medicine had available vaccines composed of billions of smart nanomachines that could repair the body at the cell level for all these forms of body failure. Then the effects of aging and disease could be counteracted. Fine for the individuals of the far future, but the people of today will be long dead. Enter cryonics — the science of freezing and preserving tissue at very low temperatures. Neurons don't really die within a few minutes of death; a few minutes without oxygen destroys enough of the brain's circulatory system so that the neurons are eventually doomed. However, individual neurons can metabolize long after the four to six minutes without oxygen that we normally think of. The information content of the brain should remain intact if the damage could be halted at that point. One method of halting the damage to the information content might be freezing. Low-temperature preservation of the brain could preserve the information content of our brains — our memories.

Then future medical technology could develop nanotechniques that would design and assemble molecular-size components directed by nanocomputers. These molecular-sized machines could do intricate biological repairs or measurements at the cellular level. Then the frozen brain's memories could be extracted. At this point the information would have to be placed in another host body, but DNA cloning techniques could perhaps develop another body identical to our own by using our own DNA.

This may be the future; current scientific thought holds that nanotechnology is just a matter of time. Whether freezing preserves memories is another matter; it seems realistic, but it is untested. If it turns out to be true, then a technical restoration of memories of a "dead" person is possible in perhaps two centuries. DNA cloning should be possible within our lifetimes. It seems quite possible that people living today could be restored in two or three centuries. Would these "technically restored" individuals be the same as the originals? Would they feel the same, be motivated in the same way, aspire to the same lofty goals? Nothing is clear. Again, this discussion is outside of any religion; this technical restoration is discussed only in terms of what might be possible for the human race to accomplish on its own.

Restoring the dead is a wonderful goal, at first glance. However, imagine the possible consequences on society of such a capability: an incredible population explosion, legal problems concerning issues such as inheritance — the likes of which our lawyers have never seen before — multiple clones and restorations of the same person, privacy issues — like whether a dead person "owns" his memories or another person can recall them or whether they are "public domain" memories. The world of A.D. 2200 could be a strange one.

Chapter 15

The Random Edge — Quantum Mysteries

If you aren't confused by quantum physics, then you haven't really understood it.

NIELS BOHR[1]

If quantum mechanics is right, then the world is crazy.

ALBERT EINSTEIN[2]

1010101010101010101010101010101010101010101

The last edge of reality is the mystery of the quantum. Prediction using the equations of nature has an element of randomness because randomness is a fundamental truth of reality. Predicting the future exactly is impossible because of this randomness, and our inability to predict exactly limits our view. But the quantum is more than just random; it is indisputably mysterious.

245

The history of quantum mechanics — its experiments, the people involved, how they came to their individual discoveries, the different formulations of the same processes, the false paths taken, the arguments that went on for decades — would take an entire book to recount. Without trying to cover everything, we will look at the major events, discoveries, and laws that have affected physics and our view of our world. Newton is first; his laws of motion, his discovery of calculus, and his belief in a deterministic universe guided physics for centuries after his death in 1727. And it is not true that Newton was entirely wrong. His laws of motion work fine for large-scale objects whose velocity is not near the speed of light; engineers apply Newton's laws every day. It is just that Newton's laws needed refining, and other laws were needed for cases that his did not cover. Also, there was one other major physical phenomenon that the laws of motion did not cover — electromagnetism. Maxwell is second; during the American Civil War, James Clerk Maxwell, a Scottish researcher, discovered a set of four formulas that related the phenomena of electric and magnetic fields together. Together, Newton's laws and Maxwell's equations comprise the basic classical theory of physics.

Around 1900 the first elements of quantum theory were being examined. At the time it was not clear that quantum theory would require a clean break from the classical theories of physics and determinism. In 1905 a clerk in the Swiss patent office published three papers on theoretical physics that shook science to its core and changed our world forever. In one paper, Albert Einstein described the photoelectric effect, which led to modern TVs. Another paper on Brownian motion eventually led to other experiments that proved conclusively that atoms did indeed exist. Yet another paper laid the groundwork for the theory of relativity. Classical physics had as its foundation two sets of laws: Newton's laws of motion and the electromagnetic field laws of Maxwell. Einstein's theory of relativity, in effect, left Maxwell's equations intact but revised and replaced Newton's laws with relativistic versions. Relativity is classical physics; it enhances and completes the deterministic world of Newton and Maxwell. Conversely, Einstein's paper on the photoelectric effect was the first salvo in a barrage that would eventually destroy the classical deterministic view of the world and ring in the quantum era. During the next quarter of a century, physicists attempted to reconcile Newtonian determinism with the quantum theory of atoms — until breakthroughs in 1925 and 1926 ended any possible reconciliation. In those two years Heisenberg, Dirac, Schrödinger, and others made broad assertions about the nature of the quantum that forced a complete break with the universe of Newton.

QUANTUM MECHANICS

Quantum mechanics consists not of one set of equations nor even of one book full of mathematical methods. It consists of many equations and many different procedures (often mathematically equivalent) for solving problems. These equations agree closely with observed results from experiments. Graduate students spend years learning the basic physics and mathematics necessary to understand just a small fraction of all the methods and procedures; what they learn enables them to use quantum theory to predict and understand applications. However, not so much knowledge nor so many equations are necessary to discuss quantum mysteries. The essentials are the concept of a quantum state and the dichotomy that exists between different equations during a measurement.

A "state" in quantum mechanics is a difficult concept to describe in a few words. Each quantum particle has many "quantum attributes," like particle position, momentum, energy, and spin. Think of the "quantum state" of a particle like this: The quantum state is the set of attribute values in a conglomerate, statistical sense. However, quantum theory doesn't really deal with the particle itself but with the particle wave function. A wave function has an interesting double nature: First, it can be treated as an object in motion, and its future predicted by integrating the Schrödinger equation just like a thrown object's future position can be found by integrating Newton's law; second, when an attribute of the particle is measured, its state immediately stops acting like the first case and takes on a fixed value for the measured attribute. Before the measurement, the state represents a probability distribution of values for the measured attribute; after the measurement, the particle's attribute value is known and fixed.

Quantum equations are mathematical models of what is happening to a quantum as time passes and the quantum comes under the influence of different force fields or is measured. The hallowed position of quantum mechanics among scientific theories comes from its long record of unparalleled success at prediction. Prediction is what much of science is about: Theories are evaluated by their predictive ability. "Great" theories are right more often than "good" theories, which are right more often than "fair-to-good" theories. Quantum mechanics falls in the "never been wrong" category. Thousands of experiments over the past 70 years have repeatedly verified quantum theory, often when the predictions of the theory violated common sense. However, we must note that the experiments were all on quantum-sized entities, and what was verified was the predictive ability of a set of equations. No large-scale quantum system can be run through an experiment in any reasonable amount of time: It is estimated that it would take millions of years for even some microscopic-scale objects to be put through quantum tests. There is more to quantum theory as the term is commonly understood; the most controversial parts are the various quantum theory interpretations. These interpretations have been put forward in an attempt to explain the enigmatic results caused by measurement.

THE MEASUREMENT DILEMMA

Perhaps the biggest dilemma in science concerns the measurement problem in quantum mechanics. One basic equation is the Schrödinger equation, which operates like Newton's second law of motion. It provides a deterministic time-varying description of the quantum state of a system. The problem arises when you attempt to measure the quantum state; at this point we must drop Schrödinger's equation in favor of a statistical calculation to compute the state of the system. This is known as *collapsing the wave function*.

A quantum continues along the path/time history given by the Schrödinger equation until a measurement occurs; at this point the measurement equation gives a definite value. The wave function of possibilities now changes (collapses) to a single value and does so instantly. These wave functions as spatial functions usually cover only a very small area; however, for the case in which the quantum is a photon from a far distant star, the spatial area covered by the wave can be thousands of square miles.

A wave function of a particle represents a range of possibilities, a range of possible positions where the particle might be at a time *T*. It is like a statistical curve flying through space. Figure 24 represents two different scenarios for a quantum particle, represented by the top and bottom diagrams. At the beginning, the particle's position is known (represented by the left-hand point). As time passes, the wave function, which represents the particle, increases in size. If left unmeasured, the state would then progress through time as pictured in the top diagram; however, if measured at time *T*, the wave function would then collapse as shown in the bottom diagram. At this time *T*, the position would be known again. However, immediately after measurement a wave function represents the particle as shown. But the measurement has permanently changed the scenario; the particle's wave function at the right side of the top diagram is larger (more spread out in space) than in the bottom diagram. In the diagrams, we are considering only the position attribute of a quantum; similar statements apply for any other measured attribute of a quantum particle (momentum or spin). The big problem, the quantum measurement enigma, appears in these

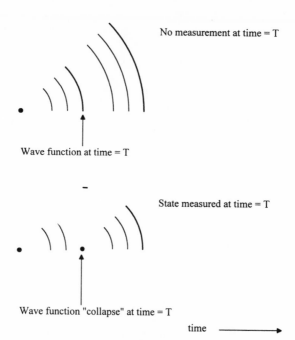

FIGURE 24. The time evolution of the wave function according to the Schrödinger equation and the "collapse" of the wave function when a measurement is made.

diagrams. Notice that the final state (rightmost wave front) is larger in the top diagram and is different from that in the bottom diagram. Measurement caused this, measurement changed the state of the particle at later times. Why does this cause–effect condition exist? A measuring device (M device) is built from quantum parts so it too should act according to the Schrödinger equation. Nor is the wave function just an effect of small random positions of many quantum particles. The wave front of possibilities is truly wavelike since it actually does go through both slits of the famous two-slit experiment. A quantum particle is *not just a particle*; it is both a wave and a particle.

QUANTUM EXPERIMENTS

To get an idea of the measurement problem, we look at the most famous experiment in physics: the two-slit experiment. A stream of photons (a light source) is aimed at a photosensitive plate that will record an individual photon striking it. A screen is placed between the light source and the photosensitive plate; this screen has two slits in it. Now if a single photon goes through, it will strike in a particular place and form one dot; if more photons go through, then their strike pattern will form an interference pattern of these dots. This interference pattern is just like a wave would make by going through both slits simultaneously. Then it gets strange; if the measurement apparatus is moved close enough to determine which slit each photon went through, the interference pattern disappears. It appears that nature allows photons to be like waves, spreading out in space like ripples on the water, until someone (an observer) tries to record where each individual photon is. Then these wavelike photons become particles. That is strange. This is the clearest example of the measurement enigma. We move our detectors close enough to tell which slit a photon goes through, and mother nature changes the photons from waves to particles. Why?

But it gets stranger. There is a similar experiment in which the decision whether to observe a photon's position is not made until after the photon has passed through the two slits. Here, the detector randomly turns on and off after photons have passed through the two slits but before they strike the photosensitive plate. The results are the same as before: An interference pattern is formed if there is no detector or the detector is off, but there is no pattern if a detector is on. Something mysterious is going on here: The decision should have been made at the time when the photon went through the two slits. Here the choice was delayed and actually not known at the time the photons went through the slits; however, the result was the same. This experiment is an example of what is called a *delayed-choice experiment*.

Originally, most physicists thought that measurements disturbed the quantum system being measured. In other words, they thought that their detectors were too intrusive, that their presence affected the system. Many experiments later, this belief was discarded in favor of the uncertainty principle, which says you can't measure two conjugate quantum attributes to closer than a certain degree of accuracy. This means that for conjugate pairs like position and momentum you can measure either one as accurately as you want, but your measurement of the other must become more inexact. This strange action of nature is quite real; but it doesn't stop here — it gets even stranger. Locality of action was long a universally believed concept; essentially it means that an action affects the local area around it, not someplace else a long distance away. We can't turn on our TV set and cause something to happen in the Andromeda galaxy hundreds of thousands of light-years away, at least not instantly. Einstein and Bohr argued for years about the consequences of quantum theory; a point that particularly bothered Einstein was this issue. The wave function collapses instantly according to theory, and he felt that by extending this concept he could create some outlandish scenario that could help disprove part of quantum theory. To attempt this, he used a devised thought experiment. He and two of his colleagues (Boris Pololsky and Nathan Rosen — the thought experiment has been known as the EPR effect ever since) asked what would happen if a particle decayed and shot off two protons in opposite directions. Now, by quantum theory, if neither of the two particles was observed, then their positions would be represented as a superposition of all possible states (this is quantum theory language — a looser but common language description would be that there is a large amount of uncertainty in both of their positions until a measurement takes place). Next, if the particles were many light-years apart before the first measurement of one of them, then the position attribute of the other would also be instantly determined — instantly, even though the particles would be light-years apart. This was Einstein's spooky action at a distance, an instantaneous resolution at distances of the size of the universe. (Much later a theorem by Dr. John Bell, an Irish physicist, proved that some aspects of quantum action can take place at any distance with no time delay. Several experiments have verified this. Technically speaking, pairs of quanta with phase entanglement emitted in opposite directions remain in contact/touch or something no matter where they are in the universe.) However, at the time it didn't feel right to Einstein. It looks suspiciously like infinite-speed action, which would violate the theory of relativity of course. However, physics is not that simple. Right now we doubt that this action violates relativity. As physicist Nick Herbert put it, "any model of reality which fits the quantum facts must possess some means of exchanging information faster than light."[3]

The wildest aspect of these experiments is that they appear to allow us to change the past. The two-slit experiment extends to a thought experiment involving astronomical distances and time numbering billions of years. Quasars emit photons too; if between Earth and a quasar is a massive gravitational object, its huge gravity can bend the paths of the photons. (Aside: This situation actually can happen. We have seen double images of a quasar where there is a galaxy between us and the quasar.) By a process analogous to blocking one slit, we could make the photons appear as particles; otherwise, we would get a wavelike result. It all depends on how we would choose to measure the photons, yet the apparent effect is that the photons that appear as particles went only around one side of the galaxy whereas those that went around both paths appear as waves. This defies belief: The photons went around billions of years ago, long before we, the future observers, existed, yet they chose paths that agreed with our future decisions. These phenomena are incredible and deeply strange, but very real. Quantum theory works in practice, but these events cry out for an intuitive explanation.

Just how good quantum theory is can be seen by a recent advancement in supercooling. Over 60 years ago Einstein predicted a form of matter based on calculations done by Indian physicist Satyendra Bose. Called a Bose–Einstein condensation, it was based on the uncertainty principle trade-off between momentum and position: If you know momentum well, then your knowledge of position is more uncertain. When atoms are supercooled, they lose momentum; at temperatures close to absolute zero, Einstein thought that the wavelengths of the individual atoms would overlap, leading to a cloud of matter. In June 1995 a group of physicists from the University of Colorado and the National Institute of Standards and Technology managed to supercool atoms to a few billionths of a degree above absolute zero and observed this state of matter with a microscope. Carl Weiman of the Colorado group said that: "You cannot talk about them as individual atoms any more. They're a new kind of entity."[4] He also added that the whole concept was so bizarre that "if it hadn't been Einstein it would have been laughed off as a ridiculously far-out idea." That's the way it is with quantum theory: Wild mathematical concepts prove true a half-century later, which is why there is so much faith in the theory.

QUANTUM REALITY INTERPRETATIONS

Quantum theory is a composite of a set of mathematical axioms, a few allowed mathematical operations, and several physics equations. Thousands of experiments over the last 70 years have proven that quantum theory is incredibly accurate at predicting the results of experiments. Two points need to be made: First, the experiments have involved quantum systems, not classical or large systems (the two-slit experiment has never been done for systems larger than an atom); second, the physics equations and axioms were chosen to fit the experiments' results (admittedly a normal procedure). Now the problem is that many quantum experiment results don't make sense. That is to say, the results agree with the mathematical prediction but they don't agree with any preconceived notion of how reality should work. Results like the two-slit experiment are effects crying out for causes. Even worse, when these experiments or quantum theory are extrapolated to large-scale systems (such as people), the predicted results can be very strange. This is why the past 70 years have seen many different attempts made to explain the underlying reality that could allow such happenings. The duality shown by the two-slit experiment is the heart of the quantum dilemma. The mechanical operation of the equations to predict where the particle should be and what properties the particle should have at a future time is the study of quantum mechanics. Conjectures about why the measurement process should cause the situation to split are the reasons for the different quantum interpretations. It is because of this problem that there are several interpretations of quantum mechanics. The word *interpretation* used in this context refers to a view of the underlying reality that the equations of quantum mechanics represent. This is no small issue; although quantum mechanics is a superior predictor of what will happen in quantum-level interactions, all solutions to the measurement problem lead to wildly bizarre speculations about the true nature of the universe or to the attribution of sanctified or near-religious aspects to the measurement act.

Several interpretations of quantum theory and quantum reality are outlined in the following paragraphs. All are profoundly mysterious; all do not make sense to people accustomed to our world.

Copenhagen Interpretation: This was developed in the 1930s by Bohr and Heisenberg, and even today is the most commonly accepted of all the interpretations. It is hard to sum up in a few words, but a main belief is that when an electron or another quantum entity is not being measured, it doesn't have any dynamic attributes. Dynamic attributes are not seen as properties of the quantum systems, but as properties of the experiment, which is both the quantum system and the measuring device. This interpretation does not accept objects; atoms are not objects in this interpretation. M devices play a special role in the Copenhagen interpretation. They are seen as solid actualities, whereas other quantum entities are simply possibilities. This interpretation deeply bothered Einstein and has also bothered many lesser lights in the years since its inception. Professor John Bell, discoverer of the famous Bell theorem on quantum locality, was certainly qualified to judge what the Copenhagen interpretation meant. In an interview shortly before his death, a question was asked about the meaning of this interpretation. The Copenhagen interpretation "says that we must accept meaninglessness" was the way he put it. The interviewer pressed on by asking if that made him afraid. Bell simply replied: "No, just disgusted."[5]

There are problems with the Copenhagen interpretation.[6] The first is the key question about how a measuring device can avoid the quantum rules that hold for everything else. The second is the belief that the measurement act is unknowable in a sense.

It is because of the belief that quanta do not really have attributes until measured that the Copenhagen interpretation is sometimes summarized by the phrase: *There is no deep reality.*[7]

Observer-Created Reality: Professor John Wheeler of the Institute of Theoretical Physics at Austin once said about observer-created reality: "No elementary phenomenon is a real phenomenon until it is an observed phenomenon." Observers interfere with/change/affect reality by deciding which quantum attributes to measure. Again it is the measurement act that is central; this interpretation is slightly different from the usual Copenhagen interpretation because it centers on the observer. Therefore the dilemma — the observer creates the reality. There are two ways in which observers create reality: first, when they decide which attribute they will measure and, second, when they collapse the wave function of a quantum entity and force the quantum system to use the second equation. Usually, the observer-created reality believers would say that making a record of the measurement is enough to qualify as an observer, but others feel that a conscious observer is necessary, and so that position is regarded as a separate interpretation.[8] This distinction is vital to our computers versus humans question: If it turns out that computers can never attain consciousness, the truth of the consciousness-created reality interpretation would give humans a capability that can never be simulated by computers.

Consciousness-Created Reality: The nagging unanswered question is: Is a human or conscious observer necessary for a measurement? (If a tree falls in a deserted forest, does it make a sound?) This school holds that interaction with other quantum material does not trigger the measurement equation; interaction with conscious people does trigger it. Proponents of this interpretation would say that quantum particles that started on a journey through space billions of years ago and interacted with other quantum particles still are predicted by the Schrödinger equation, but the first interaction of these particles with conscious sentient humans and the humans' measuring devices (also made of quantum material) immediately collapses their wave functions for the first time in those billions of years.

The question is: Why would nature allow humans to relate with quantum entities in a way that all other interactions cannot? This question and the uniqueness of the values of many constants of nature (which necessarily would need almost those exact values to allow life to arise in our universe) have led to several anthropic theories. There is a substantial minority of physicists who believe in an anthropic-centered universe. Conversely, most other physicists are concerned with any interpretation that forces human interactions to be a mystic act; something is strange about a universe that is determined by human measurement abilities.

Parallel Universes: Of all scientific theories, this is my favorite. It takes a new look at a difficult problem and then jumps off in an unexpected direction. It is utterly clever, thought-provoking, and as bold as the wind. I love it, but I don't believe it for a minute.

Scientists through the ages have made logical, creative, insightful, brilliant, and bold leaps of reason to arrive at their theories. This was about as bold a leap as there ever was. Hugh Everett was a Ph.D. candidate, working under Professor John Wheeler, studying the enigmas caused by the quantum measurement problem. By 1957 most of the quantum interpretations had been around for a while, and most of the thorny issues surrounding the measurement act had been discussed for decades. In all interpretations the measurement act (or the M device) was different; in some it got special status, in others it was nearly sacred. Few physicists were really comfortable with the implications, but the experiments matched the theory so well.

Everett focused his attention on the instant of measurement, when the wave function collapses in other interpretations. Before that instant, the quantum wave function represented a set of possibilities; at that instant, a single value. The collapse of the wave function is the collapse of many statistical possibilities into one actuality. This all happens at the time of measurement; this only happens in the presence of an M device. In a sense, the wave function and the M device form a system with a range of possibilities, and at measurement only one value comes out. At least this is how most other physicists saw it. The chief enigma was this collapsing of ten or a hundred other possibilities into one actuality, with all other possibilities disappearing.

Everett boldly stepped in at this point and made the claim that this isn't the way it happens. Instead, all the possibilities are realized, all become actualities. What happens is that the wave function–M device system evolves into one system for each possibility. Well, this would certainly solve the dilemma, but we do have a small problem here. Quantum measurements had been made for years, but no one had ever seen such a thing: the magical splitting of a measurement device into ten or a hundred other measurement devices would have been big news. Everett took the bull by the horns. He proposed that the devices really do evolve into many other devices but that the other occurrences happen in other universes that human beings cannot perceive — parallel universes, thousands of them each branching out every time there is a quantum measurement somewhere in the entire universe. Every being in every parallel universe would be unable to sense the rest of the universes. Multidimensional time and space being filled with all these minutely different copies going off on their own and splitting again and again — it boggles the mind.

You can get a feel for how much mental anguish the measurement problem causes theoreticians by noting this one simple fact. Many physicists and others believe this interpretation, as wild as it is, for one reason: It is the *only* interpretation that completely avoids the measurement enigma — the only one.

At present, quantum theory seems stuck with this quantum measurement enigma; there isn't any answer nor will there necessarily ever be one. This enigma could be the unknowable, a limit that we can never get past. On the other hand, a new interpretation or a new theory that replaces quantum mechanics might provide an answer. Anyhow, the two interpretations that seem to give humans an edge over computers are the observer-created reality interpretation and its stricter relative that requires a conscious observer. The rest don't seem to favor humans over computers, especially not that parallel-universes interpretation.

Chapter 16

Quantum Consciousness and Free Will

Only that day dawns to which we are awake.

HENRY DAVID THOREAU[1]

It is not possible to formulate the laws of quantum mechanics in a fully consistent way without reference to the consciousness.

EUGENE WIGNER[2]

1010101010101010101010101010101010101010101

Can a computer be conscious? Can we model consciousness? Is consciousness beyond human understanding — unknowable? A debate has been raging in the scientific community on these questions; this chapter will explore these questions and the possible answers. The areas that we will explore will be consciousness, free will, and computational differences. These areas are quite vague, ill-defined, overlapping, possibly affected by unknown or unknowable forces, and laden with emotional connotations. This chapter won't be a philosophical treatise on free will or consciousness; we won't be going into lengthy definitions or quoting hundreds of philosophers and theologians from ages past. Instead, it will attempt to focus on how these qualities would give humans an advantage over computers, whether they exist, and why quantum theory makes it possible that they do indeed exist. We will consider two general questions and attempt to explain them and offer answers for them. First, can we model consciousness or even explain it? Second, does quantum theory offer any computational, logical, or operational advantage to humans over computers?

Both explanations and answers (or conjectures) come in layers; quantum theory has two main characteristics and several possible interpretations that require different answers to these questions. In other words, if you believe or become convinced that quantum theory is intimately involved in these issues, then there are possibly layers of abilities that could exist that humans could have that computers can't have. And if you don't believe or become convinced of this, then what? Well, you aren't alone, and we will discuss where that leads too.

Consciousness will be the main issue; in particular, we will consider whether consciousness is a computable process or can be modeled by an algorithm. This is a major issue: If computers can become conscious, then people could be entirely stored in a computer memory bank — not just their memories, but their inner selves. The virtual reality scenario of a previous chapter could become a reality.

It's not that free will is less important; it is just that discussing it is hard, and there is little hope of resolving the issue. In this book we have referred to three levels of mental activity that might be called "free will." First level, are our actions predetermined? Second level, are our actions computable (i.e., calculable by computer or algorithmic)? Third level, are any of our actions free of worldly influences (i.e., can we act on a higher ethical plane, or are we only products of our experiences and present state)? The answer to the first level is probably "no" based on our analog bodies and quantum randomness. So, in a sense, free will exists at that level. The third level is the most common usage of the phrase "free will" and was the subject of a previous chapter. The second level relates to our discussion about consciousness being nonalgorithmic, so we will be discussing this level in the background throughout this chapter.

The book up to this point has set the foundation for this chapter, but there are a few more topics that we need for completeness. We will quickly review the biology and structure of the human brain, and we will look at a theoretical concept called a quantum computer. During the discussion, we will refer to several topics that we have covered earlier.

The chapter will unfold as follows. First, brain biology is outlined. Second, we look at both sides of the debate between the neuroscience community and others who believe in quantum-related consciousness or consciousness as unknowable. The eventual outcome of this debate will settle most of our questions, so we try to understand both sides, their arguments, their positions, and how they view their opposition. Last, we summarize all the viewpoints and try to choose the most likely.

THE BRAIN

The biology of the brain is divided into large- and small-scale structures. Large-scale structures include the cerebellum, the cerebral cortex, the medulla, the subcortical region, the brain stem, and others. Small-scale structures are the neuron-related structures: the soma, axons, dendrites, and boutons.

A human brain is composed of several regions with specialized functions, some unknown. There have been many theories put forth about the exact location of that elusive quality, consciousness. Searches for the location of human consciousness have focused on several main areas: a part of the cerebrum called the cerebral cortex, a part of the spinal cord called the reticular formation, and an outside possibility, the location where long-term memories are originated, the hippocampus. We look briefly at each possibility. The cerebrum is on top of the brain and consists of two parts, the cerebral hemispheres. The slang term "gray matter" refers to the outer covering of the cerebrum or the cerebral cortex. Gray matter is much like neural networks; it is where most of the computational processing is done. The inner part of the cerebrum is communications oriented; it carries data to and from different parts of the brain. Overall, it is a very computerlike structure. One part of the cerebral cortex is where association occurs; most of the complicated mental activity that distinguishes humans from other animals is done here, which is why many think that this is the location of consciousness.

However, mappings of neural activity within the brain during conscious periods and sleep periods show a clear correlation with activity in a structure on the spinal cord, the reticular formation. This fact supports the claim that this is the location of consciousness.

The other possibility is the hippocampus, where permanent memories are set up. Recall from neural networks that artificial neural networks don't have any memory like that of a conventional computer. The only long-lasting features of a neural network are the weights of the connecting paths. These weights correspond to electrochemical activity levels within the synapse regions around neurons. A permanent neural network would be one where the weights are fixed and the input could also be fixed. Then the network would always produce the same output — a permanent memory. Something similar occurs in the brain (although the exact procedure is much more complex). Some researchers think that long-term memories are part of consciousness and therefore that the hippocampus might be the location of consciousness.[3] They feel that our ability to voluntarily recreate memories by sending electrical signals up columns of neurons is a large part of consciousness.

Small-scale structures are the neuron components and related parts that we saw before in neural networks. Biological neurons have three basic parts: the soma (neuron body), an axon, and dendrites (the latter two together have a physical counterpart in artificial neural networks, the connecting paths; dendrites handle input, axons output). An important related structure is the synapse; synapses lie between neurons and connect them chemically and electrically. The functions of a soma are to decide how to respond to inputs and to start the electrical output impulse. A decision on whether the input signal level exceeds the threshold level is the main computerlike activity here. The functions of the dendrites are to handle the input impulses from other neurons. In this sense, they act like data paths or buses would in computers. Dendrites are the hairlike structures that emerge from the soma; they are involved in data input, but they do not receive the output signal directly from the axons of other neurons; instead, they receive them via the synapses. The function of the axon is to output data; it branches out and forms connections with other neurons' dendrites via their synapses. Synapses are like electrical contacts between neurons.[4] These are all microscopic structures, but they are, of course, much larger than molecules or smaller quantum-sized entities. However, this level of thought might be directly affected by one quantum event. Experiments in some animals have shown that one single photon impacting a retina that is acclimated to total darkness can trigger a nerve signal (for humans you might need more than one photon strike as we have a type of noise reduction system in our eyes). This makes the case that a random quantum event could set in motion a mental process. Extrapolating further, this means that humans respond directly to quantum randomness. However, Roger Penrose cautions: "Even this does not yet look very *usefully* quantum-mechanical, since the quantum is being used merely as a means of triggering a signal."[5]

As we pointed out previously, there are two aspects of quantum theory that might affect a final computers versus humans decision. The first is the inherent randomness of the quantum, and the second is the collapse of the wave function, which might be only caused by observers, or which might be caused only by conscious observers. This response of humans to quantum randomness falls in the first category, and, as Penrose alludes, it doesn't seem like much of an advantage to humans.

THE NEUROSCIENCE POSITION

Conventional neuroscience has had many successes in uncovering and describing characteristics of the mind. It approaches consciousness from several directions. The chief problem as seen by neuroscientists is to explain how the firing of billions of neurons throughout the brain can be combined into a single unified perception. Known as the binding problem, it represents an enormous technical difficulty. Billions of neurons firing trigger billions more neurons to fire. The columns of neurons (the biological analog of a neural subnetwork) that fire won't have the same number of neuron layers; hence, the time to complete the firing of one neural subnetwork will differ from the time needed for other subnetworks. Therefore, completed network processing of inputs and output of information will take place at slightly different times for different neural subnetworks that are working on part of the same perception in our brains. Timing seems as though it should be critical: Body functions like muscle control or proper sequencing of recalled memories or reasoning seem to require that different data be processed in the proper order or with the proper timing. Our consciousness seems very aware of timing and proper sequencing of thoughts, feelings, and memories. Indeed, timing seems central to consciousness. How does a vast neural network with different numbers of layers of neurons do this?

Digital computers with single processors and standard hardware handle the timing problem with a clock. A 50-MHz computer has a break in the computations at every clock tick, 50,000,000 times a second, and all computations are being done in sequence — everything is synchronized. Furthermore, during a computation like an addition or a multiplication, part of the operation stores the calculated value in a memory location. Digital computer programmers can then operate under two conditions that simplify computation: First, if computation A started before computation B (specifically, if the code for A preceded the code for B), then computation A was complete before computation B started, and, second, any results from computation A would have time to be stored in memory and be available to computation B. This is so routine that we don't even think about it. (However, programmers who deal with distributed computer architectures or parallel processors do have to worry about timing.) The calculations are done and the data is ready — we can count on it.

The brain's problem is the lack of these two features and the consequence — how to handle timing. There are many theories, but no proofs. One interesting theory envisions a digital-computer-like clock within the brain. A few studies on animals have found a 40-cycle-per-second frequency in neuron activity in some regions of animals' brains. (Although there is not any solid evidence, it has been best seen in anesthetized cats.) This might suggest that neurons fire simultaneously, which might not be quite as good as complete synchronization but would simplify the synchronization problem. Although the issue of binding may be solved soon, still it may or may not finally settle the consciousness issue. Even if a location for consciousness is found, there may still be unresolved issues. There are several peripheral issues that cause problems, for instance: Are animals conscious? Does language have anything to do with consciousness? Or is human self-awareness something unique? The animal-consciousness issue is pertinent to our computers versus humans focus. There may be levels of consciousness: Animals like birds (or even worms) might be conscious of their surroundings as we are. Certainly, higher-level primates like chimps seem aware, although not necessarily *self*-aware. A school of thought sees consciousness as a common biological phenomenon, not just peculiar to humans only, perhaps not for one-cell life forms or mosquitoes or earth-worms but certainly for chimps, monkeys, and maybe even cats and dogs. It is this school of thought that many computer scientists refer to when discussing the possibility of "conscious life" developing in a computer. The more cognitive or intelligent the program or animal, the more aware of its surroundings it becomes. There may be layers or degrees of awareness. However, many adherents to these theories see self-awareness as a special level of awareness or consciousness unique to humans.

The use of language might be necessary for higher levels of consciousness; many researchers focus on language ability as the distinguishing factor. Animals don't have it, although, as we saw earlier, we have successfully taught some intelligent chimps to understand our language at the level of a 2-year-old human child. Of course, our computers "understand" in some sense much more of language than this, but computers are far from conscious. And what does it say about people? Does this imply that more linguistically oriented people are more conscious?

Probably the largest schism between neuroscientists and physicists is on the issue of quantum effects on consciousness. Consciousness as a question has been around for centuries and was first debated not by scientists but by philosophers and theologians. During the 1930s, physicists started studying the meaning of consciousness in earnest when quantum theory was verified but didn't make good sense. The biological sciences were interested too, of course; however, the technology didn't allow study of an active brain down to the neuron cluster level. Recently, the technology has reached a level where neuroscientists can make neuron-activity-level maps of a brain during thoughts and actions. Neuroscientists hope to explain consciousness after they develop a complete description and model of cerebral processes.

Many conventional neuroscientists believe that they can find the root of consciousness without resorting to quantum effects. They argue simply that when we know more about brain functioning, then much of the mystery about the mind and consciousness will disappear. AI pioneer Marvin Minsky had this to say: "Yet every proof in each of those books is flawed by assuming, in one way or another, what it purports to prove — the existence of some magical spark that has no detectable properties. I have no patience with such arguments."[6]

For years, the study of consciousness was never considered a completely legitimate scientific research area. Considered semimystical, avoided as undefinable, burdened with many mistaken beliefs, the science of consciousness has just started recently. If there is one person who had the stature and interest to start the trend, it would be Francis Crick of the Salk Institute for Biological Studies in San Diego. He shared the Nobel Prize for the discovery of DNA's internal structure and for the past 20 years has been involved in neuroscience. In 1990 he and a colleague, Christof Koch, decided that the time for starting the study of consciousness had arrived. They feel that it is necessary to study the brain at a low level (neurons, synapses) to create the knowledge base necessary to model consciousness.[7] Crick's view, as stated in a new book, is: "Your joys and your sorrows, your memories and your ambitions, your sense of personal identity and free will, are in fact no more than the behavior of a vast assembly of nerve cells and their associated molecules."[8] Crick and Koch have helped push consciousness onto an academic center stage; recently, it has been the subject of scholarly meetings with hundreds of participants, which was unheard of five years ago.

All of this has caused a chasm between these neuroscientists and those philosophers who see consciousness as too profound for humans to understand (unknowable) and physicists who see quantum effects as instrumental in understanding the mysteries of the mind. The conclusion that many neuroscientists hope to come to is that consciousness is entirely explainable with biological models, and nothing semimystical like the collapse of the wave function is necessary. And the battle is on.

One problem that has kept the two camps apart is the mathematical nature of quantum mechanics. Quantum mechanics is mathematics. It is based on a mathematical abstraction, called a Hilbert space, that is so advanced that most math students don't even study it until graduate school. The main operations are calculus integrals and statistical probability density functions. The whole field rests upon on a set of mathematical axioms (they are based on laboratory results, however). And that is just the mathematical part. A good deal of electromagnetic theory, particle theory, and theory of classical mechanics is necessary too. The experiments are done with roomfuls of complicated electronic sensing devices and computers; quantum events take place in incredibly short intervals of time, and the particles are often traveling at near the speed of light. It doesn't happen in your normal biology laboratory. Neuroscientists dwell in a macro world with larger structures, perhaps smaller than engineering structures like buildings or ships, but definitely larger than molecules. Experiments like the two-slit experiment have never even been performed with quantum entities as large as molecules.

Therefore, the situation appears to many people to be this: There is a set of axioms, a set of mathematical physics equations, and many extremely accurate experiments on subatomic particles. From this, they are supposed to be convinced that a function of the brain is intimately tied to the quantum. For many, it isn't convincing. Furthermore, the quantum theory interpretations are what cause the most distrust and misunderstanding. Quantum theory interpretations are close to mystical. How can something mystical be correct? Is this science or sorcery?

THE QUANTUM CONSCIOUSNESS POSITIONS

A group within the physicists' camp has two major problems with the neuroscience position: (1) Biological models seem to imply a type of computability for the brain, a controversial position, and (2) the quantum mysteries are real — perhaps they appear semimystical, perhaps some quantum interpretations sound like science fiction — but the quantum mysteries are as real as any biological entity, and they appear to be related to conscious observers.

The consciousness debate is not so much a debate between two different views as it is the conventional neuroscience position against all others. In a sense, those who think that quantum theory might be a major factor in the issue are between the neuroscience position and the "unknowable" position, the position of those who reject that the human brain can comprehend its own consciousness. Consciousness to them is an unknowable quality that we can never fully understand.

One of today's most famous mathematicians, cosmologists, and thinkers is Roger Penrose, a professor of mathematics at the University of Oxford. Penrose has had a long illustrious career, ranging from proving a multitude of theoretical mathematical results to a longtime collaboration with Stephen Hawking on black holes and cosmology to a more recent interest in the conscious mind and the ultimate limitations of artificial intelligence. As a mathematician, he became well known for the absolutely astounding breadth of his creative abilities in fields like topology, mathematical physics, plane tilings, and others. He also got a reputation as a creator of mathematical puzzles and impossible objects. Perhaps his best known mathematical work is known as the Penrose tiles, a pair of geometric shapes that have a very interesting property. Tiling a plane is simply laying tiles over the standard two-dimensional plane (infinite in both horizontal and vertical directions) so that they never overlap and cover the entire plane. This is simple enough to do with squares or rectangles, but Penrose discovered a pair of tiles that tiled the plane in a way that had never done before. The pattern they form *never repeats*. Patterns formed by squares and rectangles start repeating quickly whereas more complex tile patterns take longer, but, before Penrose tiles, all patterns formed by just two tiles had repeated.

Penrose wrote a best-seller that addressed his beliefs about the limits of AI and why the human mind could have capabilities beyond that of a computer. Called *The Emperor's New Mind*, it delved into Turing machines, classical physics, biology, and a good deal of quantum theory to make its points. A recent sequel called *Shadows of the Mind* purports to show how a nonalgorithmic capability might exist within the mind; it relied upon Gödel incompleteness and more quantum theory to make the case. These two books put him in the forefront of a group of thinkers who are seeking a nonalgorithmic capability of the conscious mind. The forefront of any movement is often an uncomfortable place as the opposition aims their verbal volleys in that direction. Penrose receives his share of verbal slings and arrows.

Penrose's position can't be quickly summarized; however, part of it is that an extremely small structure within the neuron itself (and other cells), called a microtubule, has a computational nature. Furthermore, he believes that it can be directly affected by quantum events (possibly even effecting quantum events itself). If a microtubule could do calculations of its own, then the brain has a large unexplored computational capacity outside neurons and their networks.

Other scientists, including some neuroscientists, also believe that these microtubules have a computational nature. Stuart Hameroff is a neurological scientist at the University of Arizona who has spent the better part of two decades looking into these ideas. A quick sketch of how a microtubule works is as follows. Microtubules are so small that even a one-electron change in their electrical charge can affect a neighboring microtubule. When external forces change the charge of one microtubule, this effect can be passed along from one to another. Hameroff says that "microtubules could be the primary processing element in the brain."[9] He defends this by pointing out that researchers have compared the complexity of the flight of a common fly with its brain's processing power and have concluded there isn't enough processing power in the synapses of a fly's brain to do the maneuvers that it can do.[10] One additional fact is that if Penrose, Hameroff, and others are right about the computational nature of microtubules, then we are vastly underestimating the complexity of the brain by only counting neurons.

So it comes down to these different possible answers: (a) Consciousness will be eventually explained by neuroscience models without relying on quantum effects, (b) quantum effects will be necessary to explain consciousness, and (c) the issue is too profound or unknowable for humans to ever solve. If (a) is correct, then consciousness will probably be explainable with a semi-classical biological model, which a computer probably can simulate with an algorithm. If (b) is correct, then humans probably will be declared the winners of the computers versus humans contest. Of course, position (c) is a wild card, with no way to prove or disprove it; adherents of this position are not required to accept any proof from either of the other two camps. We assume that in case (c) humans have some unknowable quality that cannot be explained, since everything that computers can do is explainable. Therefore, humans must be able to do something that computers can't; therefore, in this unknowable case humans are the winners also.

POSSIBLE ANSWERS

Conclusions about the final resolution of the computers versus humans issue are difficult to prove rigorously. In previous chapters we looked at several aspects of this problem; now we attempt to tie the loose ends together and see what we can conclude. To start with, the term computers refers to *digital* computers — today's computers and their bigger, faster descendants; we aren't going to include analog computers, biological computers, or hybrid human–computer robots or other speculative systems. Next we will be considering possible differences based on quantum effects. I feel that there aren't any really convincing arguments that don't include some quantum theory. So the quantum observer questions — Can computers be observers in the quantum theory sense? Can computers be conscious (hence conscious observers)? Are either of the two observer-centric quan-

Table 6
Computers vs. Humans

	Computers	Humans
Type of data	Discrete	Analog
Speed of calculations	Finite	Finite + infinite-speed wave function collapse
Calculation type	Deterministic	Deterministic + some random
Type of thought	Algorithmic	Algorithmic + ?
Conscious	No	Yes
Quantum observer	?	Yes

tum interpretations correct? — will be central. Table 6 summarizes the key points from the earlier chapters.

Before going on, let's recall how we arrived at each of the table entries. We saw in Chapter 3, "Modeling Reality," that humans, being analog, do process analog data. Analog data does contain infinite information content in one narrow sense: the infinite decimal expansion of a real number. Discrete data is limited to a finite number of decimal places in its accuracy. However, the ability to store or compute with an infinite number of insignificant digits does not seem to be an advantage.

Computers and humans both process data at finite speed, of course. Until recently, that statement would never have been modified in the slightest. However, quantum computers that can use the infinite-speed wave function collapse as part of their calculation process have been defined. Quantum computers and computations are a theoretical concept; at present, no one has an operational quantum computer in hand. They are like the "thought experiments" of Einstein and Bohr; one considers how the computers might perform. Although a quantum computer is a theoretical device, we know something about the computational power of these devices. Researchers have found that they aren't any more powerful than digital computers programmed in Pascal or another high-level language (or a basic Turing machine). However, there are certain classes of problems for which a quantum computer is faster than a conventional digital computer. That means that the order of the time complexity function $T(n)$ is lower for a quantum computer than for a conventional computer doing the same problem. Depending on what makes up an observer, a human–quantum-computer pairing might have a computational edge sometimes; there might be other undiscovered instances, also.

Quantum computers would utilize the wave function collapse by setting up the computing apparatus so that correct answers would appear as uniquely identifiable interference patterns. Skeptics have pointed out that by the random nature of quantum theory, quantum computers would be very delicate; the mechanical problem of setting up the necessary number of quantum bits might be exponentially hard, negating its theoretical computation speed. However, other researchers are carrying on because a recent theorem by Shor shows that quantum computers could rapidly solve the problem of factoring large numbers — an extremely slow procedure for digital computers. Other researchers feel that a quantum computer could demonstrate the validity of the parallel universes interpretation of quantum theory. This is all controversial and very exciting, yet the ultimate logical power of quantum computers is the same as that of digital computers.

Deterministic calculation, one step at a time with a clearly definable next step, is the rule for both computers and humans. Humans, being subject to quantum randomness, do stand the chance of a random quantum event changing the balance in some neuron and thus effecting a random change in the next step. So we must consider that human calculation has a small but definable random component to it that computer calculation doesn't.

Computers think in terms of algorithms and only algorithms. Humans think in terms of algorithms, too, but they may also have a nonalgorithmic capability. This is a key issue in the consciousness debate that we have been talking around. The problem is that we don't have a rigorous definition of an algorithm, and therefore we don't have a rigorous definition of a *non*-algorithm. The next best thing is to find something that a human can do that is probably noncomputable — of course, this hasn't been done yet, or we would have resolved the debate.

Computers aren't conscious; it is still debatable if a future superintelligent computer could be conscious or if consciousness is caused by the physical functioning of the body or some mystic cause.

It is unknown exactly what makes up a quantum observer. If consciousness is required, then we are indeed special in the universe, and the universe "needs" us in a sense. However, quantum theory doesn't specify what makes up an observer; maybe computers are observers, maybe they aren't. It probably only makes a difference should either observer-created or consciousness-created reality be correct.

If there isn't any completely unknowable aspect of humanity or the universe (e.g., a final theory is possible at least in principle), then we can categorize the possible outcomes. We could conclude that if consciousness-created reality is correct and if computers can't be conscious, then humans win the computers versus humans contest outright. Without consciousness-created reality, the outcome is murkier: If observer-created reality is correct and computers can't be quantum observers, then again humans seem to have a clear edge. If computers can be conscious, then it seems that the ultimate logical power of people and computers would be the same. If computers can't become conscious only because consciousness is simply a by-product of physical action, and if consciousness-created reality is wrong, then the logical power of people and digital computers will probably be the same; however, this combination might disprove advanced virtual reality scenarios where people enter computers and experience conscious virtual reality.

In the end, if computers have the same logical power as people and possess consciousness too, it isn't all bad. For the next few centuries we can look forward to more computer–human interfacing that will increase our awareness, expand our consciousness, and vastly increase the number and breadth of our experiences. Ultimately, however, it seems depressing. And it could be that there is a completely unknowable aspect to it all that would change everything.

In this debate, one rarely spoken word is religion. For centuries science has been hammered by religious opponents, and biological sciences have been hit especially hard because of anti-Darwinism. Also there might be a certain satisfaction (superiority?) in knowing (believing?) that we are at the top of the intellectual ladder and were created by a random series of molecular events, not by some superior being. There may be an antireligion backlash going on here too. Although quantum theory is solid science, quantum interpretations are mystical; mystical means quasireligious to some. Additionally, some language of logical limits and mathematical logic has a quasireligious ring: Words like unprovable and unknowable have connotations of "only God knows," secrets that supposedly God keeps from people but knows himself.

So who is right? Can computers ever be conscious? Does quantum theory have anything to do with consciousness? Does consciousness trigger quantum effects? These are all hard but central questions. There are two major factions in the debate of these questions, but they aren't talking to each other as much as talking at each other. Neuroscientists are confident that they can model consciousness without quantum theory, while the other camp feels that many physics experiments clearly show the intervention of consciousness. The consciousness-created reality adherents complain that the biological scientists aren't taking quantum arguments seriously because the arguments are mathematical and abstract; conversely, many neuroscientists complain that some physicists are intruding in an essentially biological question. And then there is the group of philosophers and others who say that the whole question is unknowable.

There is a chance that religion is the answer. Our earlier discussions left open the possibility of other dimensions where our physical laws don't hold, possibly even allowing infinite speed of calculation or extra unobservable dimensions. If a God acted there, then he is beyond the powers of our theories. If a God interceded in human affairs with thoughts based on infinite-speed calculations and could transmit guidance via unseen dimensions, then it might appear like free will to us. Certainly, Christianity would predict a *divine guidance* component of free will. If this divine guidance comes from outside our bubble universe where our physical laws do not hold and could be sent to us via unobservable dimensions that we couldn't measure directly, then it would appear as a random or unmodelable action. If some infinite-speed or infinite-storage calculations could take place outside our bubble universe, then these calculations would exceed the power of our computers. Therefore, a completely religious theory could be logically consistent with our definition of free will — although probably it couldn't be tested scientifically. Of course, in our own universe infinite-speed communication of information is ruled out by Einstein's theory of relativity. However, the quantum wave function collapse or action at a distance seems to be an instantaneous (infinite-speed) action.

My feelings are that the quantum issue is a serious problem and, whether or not they say so, basically the neuroscience faction is talking of modeling brain activity and consciousness with a semi-classical model. Quantum involvement in consciousness and a meaningful distinction between computers and humans based on this are real possibilities and should be considered such.

The consciousness question will not remain unanswered forever. I feel that it will not be answered by either neuroscientists or physicists but by computer scientists instead. At some point in the next century or two, people will be able to interface with computers via direct brain–computer links. Then a sort of super

Turing test can be performed: If people coming back from virtual reality say that they felt alive and conscious within the computer, then we would have to say that computers can be conscious. If not, then the final answer to consciousness will be found in the quantum or religion.

Chapter 17

The Large and the Small

*Now, my suspicion is that the universe is not
only queerer than we suppose, but queerer
than we can suppose.*

J. HALDANE[1]

Physical limits now become our focus instead of logical or computational limits. In science, we develop our knowledge base by two different methods: First, we can infer more facts by prediction or logical inference from our present theories, models, and knowledge base or, second, we can discover more facts by collecting data from experiments. For instance, consider the problem of predicting the position of Saturn in the sky a year or more in the future. Orbital equations are available that will predict Saturn's position. Once you have these equations, that is all you need for the prediction. No data or experimentation is necessary; it is simply a logical process or a computational procedure — knowledge derived from a model. Before we had the orbital model (these orbital equations), a tedious, exacting data collection with telescopes was necessary to develop the model. Data was necessary to solve simultaneous equations for unknown parameters of Saturn's orbit like distance from the sun and shape of orbit.

Deriving more knowledge is a logical process that is limited by the Gödel, Halting, and computational intractability limits that we discussed at great length. Now we turn to the second method — more facts or data — and consider our limits on gathering facts about our surroundings and universe.

Scale is important here; we won't be considering limitations on gathering data or facts about everyday-scale objects (e.g., brains or chemical compounds) or processes studied on the scale (e.g., atmospheric conditions or diseases). Human technology will continually improve, and so will our ability to collect data on this scale of processes. Instead, we will only be considering the very large and the very small; at these ends of the scale, hard limits exist, limits that we can't get past with any future technological improvements.

THE SMALL

In this section we will be considering the smallest limits of our reality: matter, force, space, and time. Our models are based on small-scale structures; the ultimate limits to our models (if any) exist here. We will see that our current knowledge base is very good, but there are still some missing facts. More data would be helpful. But we will also see that data collection becomes exponentially more difficult, the smaller you go — energy requirements go up quickly as you search for smaller particles.

Particles form the "small" of our reality; although we may not be sure that we know the smallest, most indivisible particles, they form the lower limit of our perception. A longtime question has been: What are the fundamental building blocks of matter?

As early as the time of ancient Greece, hypotheses were put forward about what was fundamental, what was indivisible. It wasn't until this century that we succeeded in going past hypotheses and detecting these building blocks. At first, only a few were detected, but soon many had been. The big problem facing physics in 1960 was too many different particles. After discovering only a few different particles during the first half of the century, physicists now had a new generation of particle accelerators that could generate high-speed–high-energy collisions between particles and observed a multitude of particle traces in their cloud chambers. In the early 1960s physicists had accounted for over 100 different particles with no end in sight. If the different particles had fit into a pattern and formed families, there wouldn't have been a problem, but they didn't. Physicists had a large unstructured set of particles and no real idea of what, if anything, was fundamental. Enter Murray Gell-Mann.

Murray Gell-Mann is perhaps the one person most responsible for our current understanding of particle physics. Entering college at 15 and earning a Ph.D. before the age of 21, Gell-Mann is one of the truly brilliant minds in science. He is considered an expert in several fields ranging from arms control to Mandarin Chinese to geology to Swahili. During the early 1960s, Gell-Mann solved some of the thorniest problems facing theoreticians and thus propelled particle physics into a new age.[2]

The first good model of an atom was made by Ernest Rutherford in 1911. He pictured an atom as the familiar orbital model: positive charge and most of the mass in the nucleus and a negatively charged electron orbiting the nucleus, with a lot of empty space between. This was the first layer. In 1922 John Cockcroft and Ernest Walton succeeded in splitting the atomic nucleus into protons and neutrons. This was the second layer. In the 1950s and 1960s more particles were found.

Gell-Mann devised an algebraic classification method that grouped the particles together in a quasitabular form similar to the chemist's periodic table of elements. Experiments confirmed his method when particles predicted by his classification were later discovered. Very good so far, but he wasn't done.

Now a classification method is great, but can you go a step further and find building blocks that form these particles? Gell-Mann thought about it and came up with a theoretic way that involved theoretical particles that would have quite unusual properties. Soon after, he published his new theory that involved these new fundamental particles, which he called "quarks." By the late 1960s, quarks had been experimentally verified, and over the next decade Gell-Mann's theory became widely accepted.

We now know that matter separates into two families made of intrinsically different component parts. The first group has four levels: atoms, nuclei, hadrons, and quarks. In addition, there is another family, leptons. In simple terms, atoms are made of nuclei (protons and neutrons) and electrons; the parts of the nuclei are the hadrons, and hadrons are themselves composed of quarks. Electrons are members of the lepton family, and they don't decompose. Experiments show leptons to be point particles; they don't have any discernible "size." Furthermore, quarks only appear as component parts of hadrons (protons and neutrons are the most common hadrons). It is believed by many that quarks and leptons are the end of the line — they don't subdivide any further. However, this belief is not universal. What is fair to say is that in our current particle accelerators we can't find any internal structure of either quarks or leptons. Some physicists believe that when we build higher power accelerators, we will discover more levels; some as-yet-undiscovered particles have been tentatively named preons and quinks.

In addition, there are the four fundamental forces: the strong force, the weak force, the electromagnetic force, and gravity. It is believed that at extremely high energy levels these four forces are one: During the earliest part of the Big Bang, these forces separated from each other into our four fundamental forces. The weak force is an interaction that causes radioactivity; the strong force holds quarks together in the nucleus. Gravitational force, which is the easiest for us to comprehend in everyday life, is the most difficult to handle theoretically. Gravity plays almost no role at the atomic level, whereas it is the major player at the cosmological level. The biggest gap in our knowledge is our lack of understanding of gravity; this prevents us from unifying our models of the large and the small in the universe. The shortest time interval is between 10^{-43} and 10^{-44} seconds according to quantum mechanics. Although physics models usually are real-valued and have an indivisible time, it is thought from quantum theory arguments that continuous, indivisible time does not exist as such at this level. We used this argument in an early chapter to argue that no single-processor computer could do two different operations within one of these intervals.

One key difference between computer processing and human thought is a computer's discrete nature versus a human's analog nature. We have always assumed this, and there isn't any experimental reason not to believe it. However, this shortest-time–shortest-length quantum-theoretic issue seems to impose a type of discreteness on humans. This kind of discreteness is not necessarily the same as the type of discreteness found in computers; for example, it doesn't necessarily mean that real-world lengths have to be represented by a rational number.

There are interesting implications here. If there is a discreetness to our time continuum, the integers or rational numbers could be used to model reality instead of the real numbers. As we have seen before, the integers and rationals are the arithmetic of digital computation; therefore, a further implication might be a certain equivalence of computers and humans that we don't believe at this time. Planck's length, 10^{-33} centimeters, is the shortest possible length; however, it is not clear that distances must be integer multiples of this length. If so, it would definitely impart a granularity to the universe; this might also make people discrete in a sense. However, another way of looking at it doesn't lead to this problem: If distances more than Planck's length can be represented by real numbers, but no length can be shorter than Planck's length, then we still need the real numbers to model the real world. And people are still different from digital computers. Our current situation is: (1) We have accurate models of small-and large-scale phenomena (quantum theory, large-scale gravity, and relativity), and (2) there are some unknowns (gravity has several unknown qualities, there are missing particles, many constants need to be calculated from experiment, etc.). The last unknowns will be difficult to resolve — maybe even impossible. At this time, theoreticians believe that there are at least two more levels of models above our current models: GUTs (grand unified theories) and TOEs.

In physics and cosmology, there is a lot of talk about models: the standard model, GUTs, and TOEs. All these models are (or will be) theories that tie together the actions of fundamental particles and fundamental forces with mathematical expressions. Models are a compact expression of our knowledge; when we can't develop a model for some process, then we admit that we can't fully understand it.

The standard model incorporates the quarks, the leptons, antiparticles, and 18 parameters whose values must be derived from experiment, not theory. The grand unified theories would unify three of the four forces (all but gravity). A TOE would include all particles, all forces, and the initial conditions.

Our knowledge of what might lie further down in the particle–force world is limited by the size of our particle accelerators. Accelerators are becoming truly gigantic; the largest current accelerator is at CERN in Europe, and it can generate enough energy to match the temperature in the early universe down until about 10^{-12} seconds after the Big Bang. The now canceled supercollider was to do about a factor of 10 better. However, to verify the theories, we need more energy than that — much more energy. To find the Higgs boson (a very important particle, as it gives other particles the property of mass), it was estimated that we would need an accelerator at least the size of the supercollider. To verify the force unification theories, we would need accelerators that would be light-years in circumference; to verify a TOE might require a galaxy-sized accelerator — hundreds of thousands or millions of light-years in circumference.

Physics may have already run into a limit; the only predicted particle yet undetected is the Higgs boson. Also, there may or may not be a more fundamental level of particles. To go further, to get past these limits, we need to be able to explore the structure of subatomic particles better. In particle physics "better" means "more energy."

The logic behind our problem goes like this: (1) Models represent our understanding; (2) there are unknown parameters, missing particles, and unknown force relationships in our models; (3) our best method for collecting more data is to use high-power particle accelerators; and (4) the accelerator necessary to fill in all unknowns is roughly the size of a galaxy. Conclusion: We can't find the rest of the pieces of the puzzle for the theoreticians to put together.

As impossible as this situation might seem, there may be a way out. There is one plausible alternative: Theoreticians could guess the correct mathematical form of the TOE.

Modeling is not just data collection and then fitting equations with this data and solving for unknown parameters. Insight, intuition, just plain guessing — all these play a role, often a major role. For instance, before Newton, scientists had available orbital data collected by early telescopes and they knew algebra. It is possible to form crude orbital models from strictly algebraic methods (no calculus derivatives). However, a more accurate approach is to use derivatives in the model. Newton's insight, his realization that a new form of mathematical function was necessary, was the key. As many have said, mathematics is unreasonably effective in describing nature. Some completely theoretical math structures have found places in models. Many theoreticians have such faith in the mathematics that they develop mathematical models for years without experimental verification. A case in point is superstrings: Superstring theory still is untested experimentally, and we won't be able to test it for some years to come. Still, intuition tells many researchers that superstrings are right;

a future genius could use intuition or guessing to find the correct form for the fundamental laws of the universe and then verify them by logically or computationally deriving predictions from the model that match observations.

The micro world of particles doesn't seem applicable to the real world nor is it as exciting to read about as the cosmos nor does it cast much light on the computers versus humans issues. Yet, there are final answers here. However, these final answers may be buried too deep for us to ever uncover.

THE LARGE

The other end of the scale is the large, galaxy-sized and above. Although large-scale structure in the universe is an exciting topic by itself, we will only briefly cover it here. Our main goal is to consider the distribution of large-scale structures in the universe since this could disprove the Big Bang theory, which we discuss in the next chapter.

For several years after the Big Bang theory became commonly accepted, the universe was thought to be homogeneous and expanding uniformly. At that time, there wasn't much data; relatively few interstellar objects had been analyzed to determine their red shift. (The amount of red shift in the light from an object corresponds to its velocity and distance away from us. Based on this finding, due originally to Hubble, the red shift now is the basic measure for cosmologists.) To picture the related concepts of Hubble expansion and red shifts, let's consider this example. Think about a sphere 10 feet in radius with three points A, B, and C marked: point A is the center, point B is 5 feet away from the center, and point C is on the edge, 10 feet away from the center. Suppose that the sphere expands to double its size over a time period. After doubling, point A will still be at the center; point B will now be 10 feet from the center; and point C, 20 feet away from the center. Consider how much points B and C have moved relative to A: Point B was initially 5 feet away, now 10, an increase of 5 feet; point C was 10 feet away, now 20, an increase of 10 feet. Therefore, point C moved away from A at twice the velocity that B moved away from A. That is the general rule: *Points further away are moving away faster.* This situation happens in our expanding universe: Stars that are moving away from us faster are further away from us. The point is this: Astronomical distance is difficult to measure; astronomical velocity (relative to us) is fairly easy to measure. Therefore, by measuring the velocity of an interstellar object, we can also get an estimate of the distance of that object.

So how do we measure astronomical velocity? We rely on a physical principle involving waves, both sound waves and light waves. The sound of a train whistle changes depending on whether the train is coming toward you or going away from you. If it is coming toward you, the tone of the whistle is higher than normal; after the train passes, the tone is lower than normal. It's the same with light; starlight is really a summation of light of many different colors (prisms and rainbows split out the colored light that makes up sunlight). If the light source is moving away from you, the spectrum shifts toward the red end of the spectrum (like a train whistle tone lowering). *Red shift* is the technical term: The higher the outgoing velocity, the more pronounced the red shift. The red shift of a visible object can be measured, giving us an estimate of its velocity relative to that of the Earth. This also gives an estimate of the distance by the earlier argument. Hubble was the first to make good, usable measurements of interstellar objects.

Let's consider large-scale structures in the universe, starting with stars and galaxies. Our own galaxy, the Milky Way, contains about 100 billion stars and is about 100,000 light-years in diameter. Stars are separated by 10 light-years in the galaxy, on the average. Galaxies are separated by 10 million light-years in the universe, on the average.[3]

Our own local group of galaxies contains about 30 members, including the Milky Way (the second largest), Andromeda (the largest), the two Magellanic Clouds, and several dwarf galaxies.

There are a few other members too, some of which are hidden by the dense gases and dust in the plane of the Milky Way, which blocks our view of them. This whole group of galaxies and the hundreds of billions of individual stars are all moving together at the rapid rate of about 600 kilometers per second (that is coast to coast in 7 seconds).

Amazingly, the local group movement is not in the expected direction. If there was uniform expansion of the universe, then we would notice a red shift to all other galaxies ranging from a slight red shift (relatively near and not moving away fast) to a pronounced red shift (far distant and moving away quickly). However, very subtle measurements of the cosmic background radiation in 1977 showed that we are actually moving in a different direction, and so is the rest of our local group of galaxies.

The only possible answer was that an enormous object with enormous gravitation pull was literally pulling us toward it, and fast. Astronomers around the world went to work; finally, in 1987 the answer came in: Seven astronomers, David Burstein, Roger Davies, Alan Dressler, Sandra Faber, Donald Llynden-Bell, R. J. Terlevich, and Gary Wegner,[4] had discovered that all nearby galaxies were moving toward a point in space several hundred million light-years away. Later work by Sandra Faber and Alan Dressler identified this *Great Attractor* as a couple of superclusters of galaxies. Other astronomers found more attractors further out; these didn't affect our local group much but did have a large influence on galaxies close to them. The universe seemed full of these large-scale objects whose gravity altered the steady expansion velocities of many galaxies.

The problem was that the Big Bang theory didn't allow for such an occurrence; every model of the universe based on the Big Bang failed to predict such large-scale clustering of matter. It was even worse: Galaxy surveys that identified these superclusters of galaxies, these attractors, also found great voids; these voids were immense volumes of space with few if any galaxies within them. In the 1980s astronomers Margaret Geller and John Huchra had been doing a survey of galaxies that lay in a sector of the sky; when they had enough data, they made up a map of the individual galaxies showing their distribution in space. Neither Geller nor Huchra was expecting anything unusual; at the time, everyone assumed that the distribution should be fairly smooth across a large portion of space, with a few smaller clumpings perhaps.

One stunning intergalactic structure that showed up on their map was a group of galaxies that stretched across 500 million light-years. Easily the largest structure ever seen, it was named the *Great Wall*. This finding galvanized the entire astronomical community. The Geller–Huchra survey had covered only a small fraction of the sky; others rushed off to survey other sectors and see if other large-scale structures were present there. Results were mixed; theorists guessed that structures of all sizes might exist in the universe. However, another type of survey, a *pencil-beam* survey, contested that. The other surveys were broader in width but by necessity had to stop at certain distances because of the amount of galaxies that a large sector of the sky contains. The pencil-beam survey, as its name implies, surveyed only a narrow slice, but it surveyed to a great distance. It concluded that galaxies clump together about every 400 or 500 million light-years but not on larger scales.

These observations are crucial to the validity of the Big Bang models; these models predict a certain smoothness of the universe that will be contradicted if the universe is found to be full of very large scale structures. A final verdict is not yet in, but recent data suggests that the universe is smooth if averaged over large enough sectors of space. We will see more on this in the next chapter.

How large is large? It is so big that you can't personally explore it in the lifetime of the universe — it's that big. How about a grand tour of the universe? There is a little tourist in all of us; this would be the ultimate summer family vacation — a visit to every last star and solar system in the universe, one great way to spend your life. It is not possible; even with all the time in the world (or at least until the world ends), you don't have nearly enough time for this tour. At the speed of light, you could travel 10^{20} light-years in the duration of the universe; that is more than enough to traverse the universe many times (billions of times as a matter of fact). But space is three-dimensional, and to visit each cubic light-year (you could visit one a year if you traveled at the speed of light) in a cube 10,000,000 light-years on a side (hence 10^{21} cubic light-years) would take you more time and distance than you have. A cube this size is a mere speck in a universe that is billions of light-years in breadth.

Chapter 18

The Beginning and the End

*What is the Universe? . . . Is it a cosmic joke,
a giant computer, a work of art by a
Supreme Being, or simply an experiment?*

HEINZ PAGELS
The Cosmic Code[1]

The beginning of the universe and the end of time hold a special fascination for us. These are very distant edges of our reality; we want to know about them just for the sake of knowing. In this chapter, we briefly examine what we believe about the beginning and the end and why we believe it.

Everyone wants to know how it all ends. It's like skipping ahead in a novel to read the ending; people want to know where they are going and how much time they have. At this point, cosmologists are optimistic that they have a good understanding of how the universe began and, furthermore, that with a couple more major discoveries we might know for sure. Maybe this is too optimistic but we have a lot of faith in the cosmologists of the world. As author John Boslough once put it, "cosmologists had become members of an exclusive community that was the perfect priesthood for a secular age."[2] We won't be going into all the theories or details, but suffice it to say that there is a reasonable, logical progression from nothingness to our universe.

THE BEGINNING

The most serious conceptual problem is the idea of creation. Most people are all locked into a type of cause–effect, time-dominated way of thinking. If the universe started with the Big Bang, then they ask two simple questions: What came before the Big Bang, and what caused it? It appears that at some point in meta-time something had to be created out of nothing. Questions like these are not new; they have been argued for centuries. However, it's only been recently that we have developed theories that offer insight. Unfortunately, the theories are very mathematical and probably can't be tested, but they do offer us a logical path from "nothingness" to our present universe.

It is not my intent to develop the theories surrounding the Big Bang, the early moments of the universe, wormholes, baby universes, time travel, and other similar topics. Many others have written about them already. Instead, we will look quickly at some current theories concerning the moment of creation, what evidence we have for them, and, finally, what they say about us, our origin, and how we might end.

Quantum theory also deals with space–time itself. The uncertainty principle shows that at very small sizes, like the Planck distance of 10^{-33} cm, space–time is dominated by randomness. If we could view space–time geometry at that level, we would see a bubbling, churning froth of complete unpredictability and randomness.

We think of "nothing" as an absence of material, but, in reality, "nothing" is made of space–time. Don't mistake the absence of material for the absence of activity or the absence of possibility. Consider the mathematical "nothing," a zero, 0. Now, 0 can be represented in different ways; for example, $0 = -1 + 1$, the sum of a negative number and a positive number. In a sense if we have two things, -1 and $+1$, then we still have "nothing"; we have conserved "nothingness," if you will. Particles and antiparticles are $+1$ and -1 in a sense; put them together and you annihilate both, ending with 0 (of course, you get a lot of energy too). But keep them apart and you have material, two types of material. Quantum theory offers us the possibility that "nothing" can split apart into entities that form material yet still conserve "nothing" in a sense. This is a quantum fluctuation. As physicist and author Heinz Pagels pointed out the sum total of the energy in the universe appears to be close to zero: "If you add up all the energy in the universe it almost adds up to zero."[3] This ability to make something of nothing has been stated in many ways but never more concisely than by theoretician Alan Guth, who once said: "Our universe was the ultimate free lunch."[4]

According to theory, a quantum fluctuation can evolve to a universe by a process named, appropriately enough, *inflation*. Developed by Alan Guth of MIT, inflation theory offers us an explanation of how a microscopic event, a quantum fluctuation, could grow itself into something as large as a universe. Before inflation theory, cosmologists did not have a good idea of how the Big Bang started in the first place; the theory described the process in the early stages when the fireball was expanding but left unanswered what happened right after the beginning. Inflation theory predicts that conditions 10^{-35} seconds after the Big Bang started were such that a type of repelling, antigravitational force pushed matter apart. (Theoreticians don't know what happened in the first 10^{-43} seconds — the Planck era; the inflation era is thought to have taken place between 10^{-35} and 10^{-32} seconds after the Big Bang started.) At this point the universe grew extremely rapidly for a short period of time before settling back down to a slower pace — the Big Bang fireball.

A nice, compact, mathematically logical story — which happens to be unprovable. At this point all theories become mathematical; no experiments can be run to verify them. Since our universe supposedly sprang up out of space–time, the next logical step is to ask, "Could other universes also have been created?" Theory says yes; in fact, there could be an infinite number of other universes — the whole infinite grouping is called the meta-universe.

The meta-universe is thought to be a sea of bubble universes, perhaps connected by a web of wormholes. Individual bubbles are continually being created, inflating, and then (maybe) contracting back into the sea foam of the meta-universe. Each universe leads its own existence in its own set of dimensions, not affecting or being affected by any of the other bubble universes.

It is believed that certain quantum fluctuations can form in space–time and evolve into baby universes that are connected to the parent universe by an umbilical cord called a *wormhole*. Why can't we sense these baby universes? The reason is best stated with the aid of that quantum theory mathematical structure, the Hilbert space. However, there is a simpler description in words: The dimensions of the baby universe are perpendicular to our dimensions, so we can't sense them. For example, suppose that you are in a rowboat in the water at night. You can't see anything except a light on a pier; this pier has a rope tow that is slowly hauling your boat to the shore, so the light always appears to be straight ahead. You can gauge distance to the light by eye, by estimating its apparent size. Now if there is a strong crosscurrent, you will be pushed sideways and not be aware of it. Your forward-motion-measuring method, eyesight, will not be able to measure your lateral movement, since your only reference point is always straight ahead. A crosscurrent pushes you in a dimension perpendicular to your forward direction, and you can't sense it. It is believed that space–time is like this. Dimensions can be created that are perpendicular to our own dimensions, and we would be unaware of them.

Proving the Big Bang hypothesis correct is a tricky matter. Energy levels, matter density, and temperatures that existed during that early time cannot be duplicated here on Earth. Therefore, direct experimental evidence is out. Indirect verification is required; this means comparing results predicted by the Big Bang models with measurements of today's universe. If there is a good match, then this is inferential or indirect verification of the model, therefore supporting the Big Bang hypothesis. Indeed, there are several good matches between Big Bang model predictions and actual measurements.

First is the expanding universe; most interstellar objects are red-shifted, meaning that they are moving away from us, and their relative velocity increases the farther away they are from us — just as predicted.

Second, the background radiation is also very close to the model predictions. The Cosmic Background Explorer (COBE) is a satellite launched in 1989 to record cosmic background radiation from different sectors of the sky. It confirmed that the background radiation was very close to the theoretical prediction by Big Bang models; it found the cosmic background radiation at a temperature of 2.7 degrees Kelvin — as predicted.

Third, Big Bang models can predict the relative abundance of some atoms within the universe. First, the models calculate the predicted density of neutrons and protons; then, with this density estimate, they calculate the amounts of certain elements and isotopes like helium, deuterium, and lithium. Finally, we can measure the relative proportions of these types of matter in the universe and compare the measurements to the theoretically predicted results. Agreement has been very close; theoreticians consider this to be one of the most outstanding successes of Big Bang theory.

Fourth, cosmic models based on inflation predict an overall smoothness to the cosmic background radiation, which has been observed. COBE data has tended to support Big Bang models with inflation. However, as Steven Weinberg pointed out, actually confirming inflation will be difficult: "It is not clear what sort of astronomical observation will ever be able to confirm the idea of inflation."[5] For a few years, there was the worry that observed nonuniformity in the distribution of matter (e.g., the great attractors, the great walls, and the voids discussed in the previous chapter) was too great to ever fit the predictions of a Big Bang model with inflation. Recent analysis now seems to show (in fairness, there are dissenters) that the distribution is uniform enough if you average over a large enough volume of space.

The Big Bang model has been strengthened by developments in the last 10 years. Except for the early and inaccessible Planck era, there is a reasonable logical progression of theory out to today's universe. The key word is "reasonable"; a verification of much of this theory is impossible. Still, the model does seem to predict things that we see in today's cosmos. Meta-universe concepts like a sea of bubble universes and baby universes are still just mathematics in search of data; still, they are some of the most exciting areas of science today.

Stephen Hawking is the most famous theoretician today. Renowned for his early work on black holes, Hawking has continued to be a leading theoretician for almost 30 years. (An incredible record considering that most theoreticians do their best work during their first five or ten years of research. Mathematicians are often past their prime at the age of 30. Theory can be a cruel world.) Hawking is also a great popular science writer; his best-seller *A Brief History of Time* has sold over five million copies. Its lengthy stay on the American best-seller list was unheard of for a book on such a weighty subject.

Stephen William Hawking was born in Oxford, England, 300 years to the day after Galileo's death (January 8, 1942). Perhaps it was a hint of things to come. His father was a medical researcher, his mother a secretary; he also had two sisters and a brother. Theirs was a close-knit family that believed in books and good education, so Hawking was exposed to many a good book and excellent schools. In England, teenagers have to make a choice about the general area they wish to concentrate their studies on; specialization starts much earlier than in America, where both high school and undergraduate study are quite general and single-track specialization does not start until graduate school. By the age of 14, Hawking knew what he wanted was "mathematics, more mathematics and physics." He started at Oxford in 1959 at age 17, graduating with highest honors. Then for graduate study he went on to Cambridge, where he studied under Professor Denis Sciama.[6]

In early 1963 Hawking entered a hospital for a series of tests; he had been having some unexplained muscle control difficulties. The diagnosis came back as amyotrophic lateral sclerosis, Lou Gehrig's disease. The prognosis was that nerve cells in his brain and spinal column would slowly disintegrate; he was given two years to live. Eventually, the disease's advance slowed, but it left him in a wheelchair with a need for permanent nursing support. Pictures of him are so widely published that today he is probably the single most recognized figure in science. Professor Hawking's emphasis in recent years has been on wormholes, initial conditions of the universe, and attempting to link relativity theory with quantum theory. As such, he deals with the beginning of the universe extensively; here is the one place where cause-effect seems to break down, here is the one place where God is often mentioned as an explanation. So Hawking often must field questions about what he thinks of God; is there a need for God or not? His answers are among the best known scientific remarks of our age — the man is definitely quotable. He once wondered: "What is it that breathes life into the equations and makes the universe for them to describe? . . . Why does the universe go to all the bother of existing?"[7] He feels that even if a TOE told us how reality worked, it wouldn't tell us the *why* — why does the universe exist at all?

It may remain unknown and unknowable forever; we are left with the age-old enigma: an explanation without a prior cause, an event without a previous event.

THE END

How the universe ends is not so clear; there are two distinct possibilities: Either the universe collapses or it doesn't. Heinz Pagels put it bluntly: "Physicists find there are basically two ends to the universe — fire or ice; we will either be fried or frozen."[8]

Called the Big Crunch, collapse would be caused by the gravitational force exerted by all the mass in the universe pulling itself back together (this is the ending in fire). We can compute how much mass would be necessary to overcome the outward expansion and start the contraction process; it is not that much — about three hydrogen atoms per cubic meter. (Incidentally, this is the amount that we used in the example in Chapter 12 for the amount of matter in the universe.) If there is more matter than this, then the universe should collapse; there can't be much more than this, or the universe would have collapsed by now.

If there is less mass, then the universe should expand forever (this is the ending in ice; the universe would get colder and colder). There is one special subcase of this: If there is a certain critical density of matter, then the universe's future is "flat," which means that the expansion keeps slowing and eventually approaches a zero expansion rate, but the universe never collapses.

So will the universe collapse or not? It depends on how much mass there is; by adding up all the visible mass (mostly stars), we end up short of the necessary total. Now there is evidence supporting missing mass in the galaxies: This is material that we cannot see with telescopes but for which we have solid evidence. Galaxies spin around their centers, which have huge gravitational forces. Individual stars are like earth satellites; their velocity around the center of the galaxy must generate enough centrifugal force to overcome the gravity, or they would be pulled toward the massive galaxy centers. Too much velocity means a surplus of centrifugal force, and the stars would fly off away from the galaxy. Stars further out on the galaxy disk should move more slowly than those close in. Herein lies the problem and our evidence: Doppler velocity studies show that velocity of stars stays fairly constant for quite a way out from the center of the galaxies. The only explanation is that the galaxies are more massive than previously thought — missing mass. One of today's biggest, hottest questions is: What does this missing mass consist of? According to the two main theories, it consists of dark, cold, normal matter or of exotic particles that we can't even see. We can only see about 1% of the critical mass of the universe, which is the percentage of mass due to bright stars and gases. The rest must be inferred by measurement. However, the universe's mass is widely believed to be exactly the critical mass. Nobel Prize winner Steven Weinberg has stated: "Many astronomers and physicists have suspected for decades that the mass density of the universe is precisely at the critical value. The argument is essentially aesthetic."[9]

If the universe is open or flat, then we are in for a different ending. Eventually, the universe will grow colder and colder. Later after about 100 trillion years (6000 times the present age of the universe — by any normal standard, we are in the universe's infancy), the last of the stars will have burned out. Still later, the remaining planets will come loose from their stars, and the stars from their galaxy centers. By 10^{20} years the universe won't be habitable for life as we know it.

FOREVER LIMITED

What if you could live and never die until the end of time, the end of our universe? Suppose that nanomedicine kept you alive indefinitely; now the universe is expected to last about 10 billion times as long as it has currently existed, or 10^{20} years. Think of all the things that you could do before the end. On the other hand, think of all the things that you couldn't do because there wouldn't be enough time. Let's consider upper limits on you. First, you couldn't do the 100! problem of listing all possible routes between 100 U.S. cities; we already showed that there isn't enough time for that. Second, you couldn't even play out every possible game of chess — too many moves, too little time. These are both mental exercises that involve a multitude of combinations — things that we have seen before quickly become computationally intractable. But there are physical limits, too. A third thing that you couldn't do, as we saw in the last chapter, is tour all the stars and solar systems in the universe during the lifetime of the universe — too many stars, too little time.

Anyhow, the universe has a lot of time left, and we should know in a few more decades whether the universe is open or closed. So we should know how it will end. The beginning is a different matter. Even if we develop a TOE, it won't answer the "why" question. Moreover, we may never answer the "why" question; it is likely to be unknowable.

Chapter 19

Reality and Beyond

*Sometimes I think we're alone in the universe,
and sometimes I think that we're not. In
either case, the idea is staggering.*

ARTHUR C. CLARKE[1]

*I see no conflict between science and religion;
they are basically addressing different
questions. Science asks what and how,
while religion asks why.*

JOHN PHILLIPS[2]

1010101010101010101010101010101010101010101

We have considered many issues in this book. We have come
up with some answers, but more questions. As we spoke of at
the start of the book, there are several "Big questions" that we

as people have a need to answer, and if we can't answer them, we have a need to speculate about them. Computer thought, human consciousness, mathematics, logic, and physics all come to bear on many larger philosophical issues. What is free will, can computers replace humans, can computers ever be conscious, how might life have originated, how might the universe have originated, is eternal life possible — these are major issues that the book has touched upon. Here we want to reconsider them and speculate about what might be.

In the chapters on computers, algorithms, AI, logic, and free will, we saw several aspects of thought: the mechanics of computer thought, how "free" thought might be, upper limits on thought, and the question of whether thought is intrinsically human. The chapters on machines and the mind set the basis for our discussion on how difficult or unusual an event the origin of life on Earth might have been, and considered some more recent speculations that our universe is too suspiciously exacting to have sprung up by chance alone — perhaps it is a created universe or a universe that can only exist if conscious beings like us are around to observe it. Also, we speculated about what eternal life might really be like in terms of memories and consciousness.

COMPUTERS

Our computers versus humans question is still unresolved, but it may be solved in the next century. First, humans are different from computers in mental calculation simply because of the computer discrete data versus human analog data issue. As we have seen before, this probably is not an advantage, just a difference. Humans will be better than computers (meaning that they will be capable of doing some mental process that computers can't do) if computers can't ever be conscious (then consciousness is nonalgorithmic, and humans can do it). Finally, humans will be *much better* than computers if quantum theory requires consciousness for observation (assuming that computers can't be conscious) or if we can ever isolate and characterize free will or if religions are right and humans are central to the universe in some way. As we said before, the outcome hinges on the consciousness issue, and another century or so of improvements in human–computer interfaces and virtual reality may answer that question. The free will and religious aspects are probably beyond scientific proof.

We have seen before that digital computers can approximate infinite numbers to any number of digits, but the numbers stored in computer memory can never have entirely infinite precision. Digital computers can simulate randomness with pseudorandom numbers, but the numbers can never be entirely random in a strict mathematical sense. Also, we saw that digital computers are deterministic: The output is completely and irrevocably determined by the input and the program; the output can never vary with exactly the same input and program. We have discussed at length that these properties might differ from those of the real universe and humans. The real universe might be infinitely complex in detail or precision. Entirely random numbers might be possible. And determinism might be entirely wrong; two identical situations might have two or more different outcomes. Humans, as part of the universe, might share the same nondeterministic properties, and thus human thought or consciousness might never be captured within a computer.

We have focused on computers versus humans and their limits plus computer life. Computer limits won't change; Gödel, Halting, and computational limits are true now and forever more. What of the future of computer life? It might turn out that computer simulations of life are possible; this would be virtual reality where the simulated beings are "alive." Deterministic but conscious sentient beings are entirely possible; computer programs that are advanced enough and have advanced enough sensors could be alive, too. This would allow us to be creators of simulated people and places and universes, all existing within a computer. Like the need to procreate, there may be a need within us to see creatures of our own creation and watch them play out roles in virtual universes where they can live, love, reason, struggle, and die. We can see a little of that in ourselves when we play computer games like "King's Quest." Maybe in the far future the creatures that exist within the computer games will be advanced enough to sense their own existence and be conscious beings in their own right. Maybe the computer creations, too, will create virtual computers and create their own virtual-virtual simulations within.

We have seen that there are upper limits on the scope of human thought: Gödel's incompleteness theorem — certain statements are outside the scope of whatever logic system we use — and the Halting theorem — certain algorithms are simply impossible. In a sense these are upper bounds not on the human mind or a computer but on the system of logic; still, it limits reason in a precise, definable way. What is not clear is what conclusion is to be drawn about the nature of the universe. Are there important physical laws that can never be discovered or proven? Or are the unprovable simply abstract mathematical theorems that don't and never will really matter?

LIFE AND CONSCIOUSNESS

The role of humans — thinking, conscious humans — is an enormous enigma today. Quantum theory seems to require human consciousness to bring quantum effects out of the abstract and into the real. There is some disagreement in this area, and the final word has yet to be spoken; however, if humans are needed to observe the quantum and make it real, then there is a dependence of the universe on humans (and other sentient beings) for its existence. This is the anthropic principle, which is deeply mysterious, enigmatic, and perplexing.

The mind, the human mind, is the key here; but as familiar as we are with it, still we can't isolate it from the rest of our environment. We know that part of it is algorithmic or computerlike; we also feel that it is not deterministic in the strict sense since the universe seems to have an underlying random element. But does it have free will? Can it put aside all the environmental influences on it, all its memories and their influences, all influences placed upon its decisions by its internal circuitry, and make a decision that differs from the one it would make under the exact same conditions without free will?

The human mind has limits: Gödel proved it, and the Halting theorem reinforced it. The human mind cannot be predicted exactly: There is an unpredictable random nature to the universe that precludes exact prediction, and the mind consists of matter like everything else and therefore has a random element to its workings. Of course, most randomness in the thought process is not useful. But sometimes this random nature actually helps us: A creative idea is often that one illogical or random thought that is out of logical sequence yet helps us leap from the problem to the solution. Computers don't have that capability, and there is grave doubt that they ever will. The human mind may or may not have a free-will faculty that allows it to escape all environmental and historical influences and make decisions based on other criteria. The human mind probably can be stored indefinitely (at least partially, the memories), allowing some form of eternal existence. Beyond that, science cannot say. A soul — a conglomerate of individual memories, individual personality, free will, ethical reasoning, and God-given special traits that lasts forever — is a faculty that science could never confirm or deny.

Before the human mind came life on Earth; the question of how life originated might cast light on the mystery of the human mind. Although other forms of molecules that "live" might be possible, the form of life on this planet Earth is based on DNA, RNA, amino acids, and the self-replicating machine that they form in combination with each other. This self-replicating machine is incredibly complex. Furthermore, the complexity appears to be essential to the way that it works. The chances of this complex machine forming from conditions on early Earth are difficult to assess. Was life on Earth a freak chance occurrence: so freak that it is statistically likely that we will never find another life form in the entire universe? It's possible. The fact that no other life form has ever been detected could support this. Perhaps life did not originate on Earth but molecules of life came here from elsewhere. Maybe life's molecules came together by chance somewhere else and either traveled here by chance on meteorites or were seeded by some advanced race. Maybe we are someone else's research project. Or is life an ordinary chain of molecular processes that could happen many other times and places? That is possible too. If this hypothesis is true, then we should be able to create some complicated message-passing, self-replicating molecules in the laboratory in the next century. This would go a long way toward proving life on Earth as not that unusual an occurrence.

THE UNIVERSE — WHAT, HOW, AND WHY

A need to explain how the universe could arise from nothing has challenged the best minds for all of history. Especially difficult has been the issue of whether God was necessary to it all. People have seen it different ways, from Friedrich Schiller — "The universe is one of God's thoughts" — to Auguste Comte (1798–1857) — "The universe displays no proof of an all-directing mind." Modern-day scientists and philosophers often refer to the physical laws of the universe when grappling with the issue of God and creation. As physics professor Ulrich J. Becker once said, "the question of the origin is not answered without addressing who arranged for these laws to cooperate so well."[3] Remarking on the problems facing scientists, physicist Geoffrey Chew once put it like this: "Appeal to God may be needed to answer the 'origin' question: 'Why should a quantum universe evolving toward a semiclassical limit be consistent?' "[4]

What is the universe? We have seen that many cosmologists believe that the universe began as a quantum fluctuation — it literally sprung up from nothing: One instant, nothing; the next instant, mass, energy, space, and time. An extension of this is a theory that sees the universe as a large-scale quantum fluctuation or as a single finite bubble universe in an infinite foam of other bubble universes. One fact that supports a quantum fluctuation is that all the known energy in the universe adds up to close to zero.

How did the universe grow and life evolve? The sprung-up-from-nothing scenario envisions a large-scale quantum fluctuation that initiated the Big Bang and created the universe from nothing in the first place. Then order-from-chaos theory allows intelligent sentient creatures (like ourselves) to have developed eventually from the chaos of the primordial soup followed by chemical evolution from basic amino acids to DNA. (In this scenario, we and the universe are original material in a sense.) This is a theory of the creation of the universe by *sheer random chance*; it can be joined to chaos theory, then chemical evolution theory, and then biological evolution theory to show a chain leading from nothingness to humanity.

Currently, the *scientific* explanation of the progression from *nothing* to *life* is: nothing → quantum fluctuation → inflation → Big Bang fireball → universe full of gases → formation of stars and galaxies → supernovas of first-generation stars forming more complex elements → chaotic disorder leading to order via chemical evolution → self-replicating molecules → life. This chain of logic works mathematically; there are mathematical models that represent these phases. From the statistical functions that describe random quantum fluctuations to the calculus differentials and integrals that form Big Bang models to the nonlinear chaos equations of disorder to the discrete mathematics that describes molecules — it all can be described by mathematics. But still, as Hawking said: "What is it that breathes fire into the equations and makes a universe for them to describe?"[5] Mathematics describes, mathematics doesn't create.

For all this theory, we still are left with the same issue that faced the ancient Greeks: We need an explanation that doesn't require some prior cause, a sequence of events that doesn't require a previous event. This is a coherent theory as theories go, but hollow; after all, if we are simply the products of sheer random chance, then what is the purpose of it all? Then, sadly, maybe the final answer is disappointing: Life may be simply a mechanistic physical process — no real free will, all action determined solely by outside influences. One far-out answer to the "Where is everyone in the universe?" question might be that advanced races have discovered this at some point in their development and find no reason to grow (or communicate) further.

The quantum fluctuation–inflation–Big Bang progression gives a mechanism for universe creation; is there any role for a God in this? Yes, actually there is. We have previously considered the far-out possibility of creating a baby universe from within our own. Christian theology (I've only addressed Christian theology, axioms, and examples in this book; being a Protestant, that is the only religion I feel qualified to discuss) has God as the creator of our universe. Although there isn't any meta-universe mentioned in theology, it wouldn't be inconsistent. Still, the question arises whether creation is naturally occurring or was directed by intelligence.

One long-standing argument is about the need for a creator; another way of saying this is: Is it more likely that our universe sprang up from natural causes (not intelligent direction) or was it created by an intelligent being? An argument that is regularly used revolves around a logical argument called *Occam's razor*. Occam's razor says that we should assume (or make axioms about) as little as possible. Occam's razor gets applied to this theological question of a need for a creator like this: Let N be the axioms that describe any final theory (N for natural); let C be the additional axiom that assumes a creator created our universe. Using Occam's razor, we should not assume C to be true since we don't need it to derive our observed facts from our model (which is how we verify models). Everything we observe can be (supposedly) derived from just N, and by Occam's razor there isn't a need for C. Therefore, there is no need for a creator.

Let's assume for a while that these speculative ideas about a meta-universe of bubble universes are true. Now, if baby universes could be created by intelligent beings, then the logic could go that a naturally occurring universe produced an intelligent being that could create other universes. Now the creator-axiom C becomes a logical consequence of the natural axioms N, and the Occam's razor argument doesn't apply to the second-generation or later baby universes. Therefore, the meta-universe and bubble-universe concepts offer the possibility of a cause for the creation of our universe. You could argue that our universe was created but have no idea about the origin of the creator; you can separate the question of how the universe came to exist from the question of how the creator came to exist. Of course, this brings us full circle; this argument has been around for ages. But now there is at least some scientific support (although speculative, mathematical, nonempirical, and highly theoretic).

Baby universes are only conjectures; so it is unresolved whether they can only be formed by naturally occurring quantum fluctuations or could be formed by some physical process directed by intelligent beings. Then a possibility is a type of creator that evolved within this universe (which itself might have been naturally occurring) and then formed or created baby universes by some unknown physical process. Then the parent universe could have been naturally occurring, while the baby universe would be one that was created by intelligence. This baby universe could be our universe. Or back off another step: An evolved type of creator developed in a two-levels-removed predecessor universe and created a universe, and then a being in that created universe created our universe. Clearly, this logic applies any number of times. Madness lies along this path; still the issue is whether the universe was created.

Then again, maybe we are all virtual creatures locked within some giant computer. This could answer some big questions in quantum theory, like why does a wave function collapse instantly? Inside computers is a clock that controls the execution of each program step. Some program steps are done every so many clock ticks, called a *major cycle*, whereas others are done every clock tick, called *minor cycles*. (A clock analogy: A major cycle would be like every hour, a minor cycle like every second.) Maybe all that we are aware of are the major cycles, and the wave functions are being collapsed during the minor cycles. This would make the wave functions' collapse seem instantaneous to us. Maybe the creator works in the minor cycles.

The anthropic view (while not contradictory to some of these other theories) sees the universe as too perfectly tuned to favorable conditions for life and too dependent on consciousness to be an entirely random event. In some variants of the anthropic view, the universe is created by outside intelligence. The key point of this view is that we are in a universe that made our existence possible. We know that even minor variations in the basic physical constants would have led to the development of the universe in a way that would not have allowed human life to develop. Any change in the fundamental constants of physics, such as the mass of the proton or the strength of the strong or weak nuclear forces, would affect larger-scale phenomena such as the tendency of carbon atoms to form stable molecules that form the building blocks of life. One variation is that there have been many Big Bangs, each with different physical laws that did not allow complexity to develop. Therefore, these universes were sterile of life and dead until their Big Crunchs ended them. Our own particular Big Bang was an unusual one where life was possible. *If* there are other universes *or* there have been other Big Bangs with other universes with different conditions, *then* it may be that we live in a special universe that was contrived for us.

Why would any intelligent being create a universe in the first place? Of course, there is no real answer, but we can speculate. We humans often create virtual worlds, called simulations, on our computers; there are simulations of the economy for economic forecasting, simulations of a city's functions for decision-making purposes, simulations of a drug's effect on a body for medical purposes, and so on. However, you might say that we don't create living virtual creatures that are born, grow, live, love, enjoy, suffer, and die within our simulations. But we could not even if we wanted to; our technology is not advanced enough. If we could, then we probably would find a reason. So we can speculate about reasons. Our universe might be computationally more efficient than a digital computer, and we might be part of a simulation on a quest (a universe-scale "King's Quest"). A creator arises and may be looking for solutions to unknowns about his universe and creates our universe (as a simulation) to help him solve it. (This is *exactly* what we use simulations for.) Good versus evil might be because the creator can't allow evil in his universe, but in ours it forces us to deal with it and develop ideas and theories that he might not. There could be other reasons, too; perhaps similar to the reason why we have children — to watch them grow. There are many other possible reasons, too; theologians have been speculating about reasons for thousands of years.

In the beginning of the book, we noted that there are two assumptions that underlie all of our logical limits: finite speed of calculation and no unseen dimensions. If in another place (dimensions outside our own, another universe or meta-universe) infinite-speed calculations are possible, then all of our limits fall. Gödel and Halting limits fall — implicit in the proof of both is a finite sequence of operations. Computationally intractable and 100! operations limits fall — even an extremely large number of calculations is nothing with infinite-speed calculation. Although the Gödel and Halting theorems are true (and always will be), they wouldn't be applicable in a reality with infinite-speed calculations or an infinite number of calculations, since they assume only a finite number of calculations. We know of an infinite-speed medium, the quantum wave function collapse; however, it can't carry computer information since this would violate the theory of relativity. Still reality is quite strange; who knows how strange it might be somewhere else in the meta-universe.

ANSWERS BEYOND THE HAZE

We don't know the answers for sure and we may never know; many questions have answers that may lie beyond our abilities to observe and reason — like a heavy haze hanging at the end of time. But we can speculate.

Computers are in their early childhood; the next century will see them taking over most of the world's decision making. They have limits as we know. Whether they entirely supplant people rests on the consciousness and free will issues.

Quantum theory seems to be approaching a complete model of the quantum particles, with only a couple left to verify empirically — the most important being the Higgs boson. But quantum theory rests on models that might be replaced later with different models that predict the same but are open to different interpretations that might resolve some philosophical issues.

Living for centuries or forever looks more likely than ever. Preservation of DNA by freezing and then restoring memories with nanotechnology into a new identical body seems quite possible in the future, maybe even for people living today.

The free will issue may never be settled; it depends on the definition of free will. If free will is simply nondeterministic will, then the outcome of quantum theory might settle the question in the near future — randomness in the universe would seem to guarantee this definition. If it relates to a soul or mystical force, then it may never be settled. For it could always be argued that there are extrauniversal forces that can act within our universe and upset our universe's own path.

And how did the universe come to be? Is there a God? Where do we go when we die? The haze at the edges of reality blurs out the answers, maybe only for a time, maybe forever.

101

Notes

1010101010101010101010101010101010101010101

Chapter 1 Scientific Thought — a Quick History

1. As quoted in Famous Quotes, Infobases Incorporated, 1992 (software database).

2. Ian Stewart, *Does God Play Dice?* (Cambridge: Blackwell, 1989), p. 24.

Chapter 2 Numbers — Large and Small

1. John Allen Paulos, *Innumeracy* (New York: Vintage, 1990), p. 3.

2. Ibid, 24.

3. John Gribben, *Unveiling the Edge of Time* (New York: Random House, 1994), p. 234.

4. Alan Lightman, *Time for the Stars* (New York: Warner Books, 1994), p. 106.

5. Steven Weinberg, *The First Three Minutes* (New York: Basic Books, 1977), p. 170.

6. Roger Penrose, *The Emperor's New Mind* (New York: Penguin, 1989), p. 340.

Chapter 3 Modeling Reality

1. As quoted in Famous Quotes, Infobases Incorporated, 1992 (software database).

2. Rudy Rucker, *Mind Tools* (Boston: Houghton Mifflin, 1987), p. 285.

3. As quoted by John Boslough in *Masters of Time* (New York: Addison-Wesley, 1992), p. 144.

4. Steven Weinberg, "Life in the Universe," *Scientific American*, October 1994:46.

Chapter 4 Off the Edge to Infinity

1. As quoted in Famous Quotes, Infobases Incorporated, 1992 (software database).

2. As quoted by Susanna Epp, in *Discrete Mathematics with Applications* (Belmont, California: Wadsworth, 1990), p. 457.

3. John Gribben, *Unveiling the Edge of Time* (New York: Random House, 1994), p. 234.

Chapter 5 Jagged Edges — Limited by Chaos

1. As quoted in Famous Quotes, Infobases Incorporated, 1992 (software database).

2. As quoted in Famous Quotes, Infobases Incorporated, 1992 (software database).

3. John Allen Paulos, *Beyond Numeracy* (New York: Vintage, 1992), pp. 33, 37.

4. Ian Stewart, *Does God Play Dice?* (Cambridge: Blackwell, 1989), p. 220.

5. As quoted by Ian Stewart in *Does God Play Dice?* (Cambridge: Blackwell, 1989), p. 141.

6. John L. Casti, *Searching for Certainty* (New York: William Morrow, 1990), p. 203.

7. Richard J. Maturi, *Divining the Dow* (Chicago: Probus, 1993), p. 82.

8. Victor Sperandeo, *Trader Vic II — Principles of Professional Speculation* (New York: Wiley, 1994), pp. 206–207.

Chapter 6   Computers — the Thinking Machines

1. As quoted by Susanna Epp in *Discrete Mathematics with Applications* (Belmont, California: Wadsworth, 1990), p. 580.

2. Stephen Wolfram, "Computer Software in Science and Mathematics," *Scientific American*, September 1984:151.

3. Roger Penrose, *The Emperor's New Mind* (New York: Penguin, 1989), p. 23.

Chapter 7   Computer Thought — the Difficult and the Impossible

1. Roger Penrose, *The Emperor's New Mind* (New York: Penguin, 1989), p. 17.

2. Paul Hoffman, *Archimedes' Revenge* (New York: Ballantine, 1988), p. 78.

3. As quoted by Paul Hoffman in *Archimedes' Revenge* (New York: Ballantine, 1988), p. 160.

Chapter 8   Logic for Computers — Upper Limits on Reasoning

1. John Allen Paulos, *Beyond Numeracy* (New York: Vintage, 1992), p. 95.

2. Rudy Rucker, *Mind Tools* (Boston: Houghton Mifflin, 1987), p. 198.

3. Rudy Rucker, *Infinity and the Mind* (Boston: Birkhauser, 1982), p. 101.

Chapter 9   Real-World Limits — Mathematics, Programming, and Logic

1. As quoted by John Horgan in "Can Science Explain Consciousness?" *Scientific American:* July 1994: 91.

2. John L. Casti, *Searching for Certainty* (New York: William Morrow, 1990), p. 353.

3. Rudy Rucker, *Mind Tools* (Boston: Houghton Mifflin, 1987), p. 287.

Chapter 10   Real-World Limits — Ethics, Law, and Politics

1. As quoted in Famous Quotes, Infobases Incorporated, 1992 (software database).

2. Adam Yarmolinsky in *No Way — the Nature of the Impossible,* edited by Philip J. Davis and David Park (New York: W. H. Freeman, 1987), p. 216.

3. Ibid, 217.

Chapter 11   Artificial Intelligence and Virtual Reality

1. Ernest Davis in *No Way — the Nature of the Impossible,* edited by Philip J. Davis and David Park (New York: W. H. Freeman, 1987), p. 98.

Chapter 12   Computers Imitating Life

1. As quoted by Paul Davies in *Mind of God* (New York: Touchstone, 1992), p. 123.

2. As quoted by David H. Freedman in *Brainmakers* (New York: Touchstone, 1995), p. 156.

3. As quoted by Paul Davies in *Mind of God* (New York: Touchstone, 1992), p. 125.

4. Marvin Minsky, "Will Robots Inherit the Earth?" *Scientific American*, October 1994:109.

5. As quoted by Heinz Pagels in *The Cosmic Code* (New York: Bantam, 1983), p. 187.

6. Julius Rebek, Jr., "Synthetic Self-Replicating Molecules," *Scientific American*, July 1994:49.

7. Ibid, 48.

8. A. G. Cairns-Smith, *Seven Clues to the Origin of Life* (Cambridge: Cambridge University Press, 1985), p. 37.

Chapter 14 Why the Conscious Mind?

1. As quoted in Famous Quotes, Infobases Incorporated, 1992 (software database).

2. David H. Freedman, *Brainmakers* (New York: Touchstone, 1995), p. 97.

3. Marvin Minsky, "Will Robots Inherit the Earth?" *Scientific American*, October 1994:113.

4. "Can Animals Think?" *Time*, March 22, 1993.

Chapter 15 The Random Edge — Quantum Mysteries

1. As quoted by John Horgan in "Quantum Philosophy," *Scientific American*, July 1992:97.

2. As quoted by John Horgan in "Quantum Philosophy," *Scientific American*, July 1992:96.

3. Nick Herbert, *Quantum Reality* (New York: Anchor, 1985), p. 244.

4. *Washington Post*, July 14, 1995.

5. As quoted by John Horgan in "Quantum Philosophy," *Scientific American*, July 1992:101.

6. Steven Weinberg, "Life in the Universe," *Scientific American*, October 1994.

7. Nick Herbert, *Quantum Reality* (New York: Anchor, 1985), p. 158.

8. Ibid, 167.

Chapter 16 Quantum Consciousness and Free Will

1. As quoted by Wilfred Peterson in Famous Quotes, Infobases Incorporated, 1992 (software database).

2. As quoted by Nick Herbert in *Quantum Reality* (New York: Anchor, 1985), pp. 25–26.

3. Roger Penrose, *The Emperor's New Mind* (New York: Penguin, 1989), p. 383.

4. Jeannette Lawrence, *Introduction to Neural Networks* (Nevada City: California Scientific Software Press, 1988), p. 138.

5. Roger Penrose, *The Emperor's New Mind* (New York: Penguin, 1989), p. 400.

6. Marvin Minsky, "Will Robots Inherit the Earth?" *Scientific American*, October 1994:112.

7. John Horgan, "Can Science Explain Consciousness?" *Scientific American*, July 1994:88.

8. As quoted by John Horgan in "Can Science Explain Consciousness?" *Scientific American*, July 1994:88.

9. As quoted by David H. Freedman in *Brainmakers* (New York: Touchstone, 1995), p. 138.

10. David H. Freedman, *Brainmakers* (New York: Touchstone, 1995), p. 138.

Chapter 17 The Large and the Small

1. As quoted by John Boslough in *Masters of Time* (New York: Addison-Wesley, 1992), p. 35.

2. Ibid, 128.

3. Alan Lightman, *Time for the Stars* (New York: Warner Books, 1994), p. 54.

4. Ibid, 86.

Chapter 18 The Beginning and the End

1. Heinz Pagels, *The Cosmic Code* (New York: Bantam, 1983), p. 307.

2. John Boslough, *Masters of Time* (New York: Addison-Wesley, 1992), p. 7.

3. Heinz Pagels, *The Cosmic Code* (New York: Bantam, 1983), p. 283.

4. As quoted by John Boslough in *Masters of Time* (New York: Addison-Wesley, 1992), p. 204.

5. Steven Weinberg, *The First Three Minutes* (New York: Basic Books, 1977), p. 190.

6. Kitty Ferguson, *Stephen Hawking — Quest for a Theory of Everything* (New York: Bantam, 1992), p. 32–34.

7. Stephen Hawking, *A Brief History of Time* (New York: Bantam, 1988), p. 174.

8. Heinz Pagels, *The Cosmic Code* (New York: Bantam, 1983), p. 285.

9. Steven Weinberg, *The First Three Minutes* (New York: Basic Books, 1977), p. 184.

Chapter 19 Reality and Beyond

1. As quoted in Famous Quotes, Infobases Incorporated, 1992 (software database).

2. As quoted in *Cosmos, Bios, Theos* edited by Henry Margenau and Roy Abraham Varghese (La Salle, Illinois: Open Court, 1992), p. 84.

3. As quoted in *Cosmos, Bios, Theos* edited by Henry Margenau and Roy Abraham Varghese (La Salle, Illinois: Open Court, 1992), p. 29.

4. As quoted in *Cosmos, Bios, Theos* edited by Henry Margenau and Roy Abraham Varghese (La Salle, Illinois: Open Court, 1992), p. 33.

5. Stephen Hawking, *A Brief History of Time* (New York: Bantam, 1988), p. 174.

Index